D0127376

Ken Hom's
Hot Wok

Ken Hom's Hot Wok

Over 150 One-pan Wonders

Photographs by
Philip Webb

BBC BOOKS

DEDICATION

For Sue Burke, for her indispensable support, and Michael Levene, who made it all possible.

This book is published to accompany the BBC television series entitled
Ken Hom's Hot Wok which was first broadcast in 1996.
The series was produced by Independent Image Ltd,
Executive Producer Tom Kinninmont
Series Producer Kate Kinninmont

Published by BBC Worldwide Ltd,
Woodlands, 80 Wood Lane,
London W12 0TT

First published 1996
Reprinted 1996 (twelve times)
Reprinted 1997 (three times)
Reprinted 1998 (twice)
This paperback edition first published 1999
© Taurom Incorporated 1996
The moral right of the author has been asserted

ISBN 0 563 37100 5 (hardback edition)
ISBN 0 563 38468 9 (paperback edition)

Styling by Philip Webb
Home Economist Sarah Ramsbottom
Illustrations by Graham Rosewarne
Designed by Mason Linklater

Set in Gill Sans and Perpetua
Printed and bound in Great Britain by Butler & Tanner Ltd, Frome and London
Colour separations by Radstock Reproductions Ltd, Midsomer Norton
Jacket printed by Lawrence Allen Ltd, Weston-super-Mare
Cover printed by Belmont Press Ltd, Northampton

CONTENTS

ACKNOWLEDGEMENTS

The inspiration for this book came from Heather Holden-Brown, Senior Commissioning Editor at BBC Books, who worked hard to persuade me to take on this project, a task which I am most grateful she undertook. I must thank her first.

Next, thanks to all the hardworking editors at BBC Books who made this book a reality: Charlotte Lochhead, for her careful supervision; Wendy Hobson, for her meticulous editing; Doug Young for his constant support throughout the writing of this book.

I am, of course, deeply appreciative of the beautiful photographs which grace this book. For those I must thank Philip Webb and his stylist Sarah Ramsbottom. And thanks as well to Frank Phillips and Bill Mason for their handsome design.

And thanks to my own personal circle of supportive friends who worked as hard as I did on this book. First, as always, to Gordon Wing who assisted me in testing and questioning every recipe. This book would not be complete without his fine-tuning. Second, to Gerry Cavanaugh for his observant editing and research. And finally to Andrew Walton Smith (Drew) for his copy-editing of the manuscript. His editorial comments certainly were an asset to the final manuscript.

And finally, to my literary agents, Carole Blake and Julian Friedmann. I am eternally grateful for their affection, their guidance, and their wise counsel. Thank you both, and one and all.

NOTES ON THE RECIPES

Eggs are size 2.

•

Wash all fresh produce before preparation.

•

Spoon measurements are level.

•

A tablespoon is 15 ml; a teaspoon is 5 ml.

•

Conversions are approximate and have been rounded up or down.
In a few recipes it has been necessary to modify them very slightly.
Follow one set of measurements only; do not mix metric and imperial.

•

The symbol Ⓥ appearing after a recipe title indicates that it is suitable
for vegetarians. Some dairy products have been used in these recipes,
and sometimes it may be necessary to use alternative ingredients, such
as vegetable stock for chicken stock.

INTRODUCTION

The wok has been central to my life as a professional chef and food writer. But it was central to my childhood and youth as well. To grow up Chinese means enjoying wonderful foods prepared in the wok. It also means learning how essential the wok is in the Chinese idiom. Terms such as 'stir-frying the real estate', to engage in land speculation, and 'breaking the wok', to divorce or to break up the home, indicate how deeply the wok and its telling metaphors have penetrated the language. The wok and its applications dominate the Chinese kitchen and it is well embedded in our expressive understanding of all other aspects of life. Only a devoted Jungian psychologist could exhaust the rich contents of its symbolism.

My mother put together three- or four-course meals every night in a tiny kitchen, ill-equipped by modern Western standards. In my eyes, she did this quickly and smoothly. I never heard her complain of any technical problems. Our dinner was on the table within an hour of her coming home from work.

Usually, the dishes were simple: a soup, which we consumed as a beverage; one or two stir-fried dishes, either pork, chicken or seafood with vegetables, a simple vegetable dish; and, of course, rice. The tool at the centre of this culinary creativity was the richly blackened, perfectly seasoned family wok, expertly manipulated by my mother. It was and remains the indispensable tool in the making of such wonderful foods. There were also a few steamers and pots for soup and rice, but the wok was the rightful ruling monarch of the *batterie de cuisine*.

Today, the wok still commands pride of place in my own professional kitchen. And increasingly, it is becoming central in many Western kitchens. My mother never would have predicted such a development among the non-Chinese. But the wok remains what it has always been, an extremely versatile, reliable and easily mastered implement. Its enduring and endearing qualities are such that it needed only to be discovered to be loved and adopted. With today's hectic lifestyle, in which time in the kitchen is limited and yet people are so mindful of health and nutrition, the wok is something of a wonder. With the wok, the harried cook can prepare nutritious, delectable and satisfying meals in a very short time, just as my mother did so many years ago.

Now, the wok did not just come into being. Chinese cuisine has accurately been defined as a 'cookery of scarcity'. In a geographic situation of limited arable land and even more limited forests, providing food and firewood for a population of so many millions was an enormous challenge. Over the centuries, the Chinese learned how to extract from nature the maximum of edible ingredients and to prepare them tastefully with a minimum of cooking oil and fuel. Out of these necessities, stir-fry cookery and the wok were conceived and fashioned.

Archaeological evidence indicates that the wok came into wide use about 2000 years ago and its appearance coincides with the progression of China's Iron Age, which came much later than Europe's. The word 'wok' is Cantonese. In Mandarin or pin yin Chinese, the word used is 'guo'. While cooking in a wok is common throughout the whole of China, it is the Cantonese who are the great travellers among the Chinese and thus it is their pronunciation of the term that has won worldwide acceptance.

Today traditional Chinese kitchens are sparsely furnished. The substantial kitchen stove is usually in the shape of a large rectangle, with two openings above the fire chamber. Large round-bottomed cast-iron woks fit tightly on these openings so that all the heat is transferred to the wok and none is lost so the proper cooking temperatures are quickly attained. Every tool in the kitchen is versatile, every technique extracts the full nutritional value and flavour from ingredients, the foods themselves are prepared so that they cook quickly in a little oil, and don't waste heat. The wok evolved to its perfection in this environment, a warm stove and versatile wok becoming synonymous with heart and home at the centre of Chinese family life.

There are many types of wok on the market today. I highly recommend the one-handled, heavy carbon steel model with a slightly flattened bottom (made for all types of cookery hobs). This wok offers maximum efficiency and effectiveness in creating the authentic textures and flavours, most particularly the smoky flavours characteristic of wok cookery.

Information in other chapters of the book will describe and clarify in more detail the various uses of the wok, with suggestions on how to get the most out of this venerable kitchen tool. I am sure that with good woks your efforts will be rewarded.

All that remains is to wish you good wokery and delicious enjoyment.

WOK TALK

In over 20 years of demonstrating and writing about cooking with the wok, I have been impressed by how people everywhere tend to ask the same questions. Everyone is fascinated by wok cookery but they often feel intimidated. To calm such anxieties and to facilitate the use of this book, I list here the most frequently asked questions about the wok, to dispel any concerns you may have.

1 Must I use a special spatula/turner to cook in the wok?
No. However, there are special spatulas/turners whose shapes are specifically designed to help turn the food more easily in the hot wok.

2 How do I know when the vegetables are cooked?
Pierce the thickest part of the vegetable with the tip of a small, sharp knife. If it goes through easily, the vegetables are cooked. If the knife meets some resistance, it needs a little more cooking.

3 How can you tell if the meat is cooked?
This is tricky and subject to many considerations. Most meats are cooked when they are slightly firm to the touch. But, as with vegetables, some meats take longer than others. Experience and your own preferences will guide you. My own advice: don't overcook any food. And remember, food removed from a very hot wok continues to cook.

4 Is there any vegetable or food I can't cook in the wok, like, for example, soup?
It depends on the type of wok you have. In a carbon steel wok, certain types of acidic fruits like lemons or pineapple will remove some of the wok's seasoning. This is not harmful to the

wok but it does not look attractive. Also, a very strong vinegar sauce may remove the seasoning in a carbon steel wok. Other than these cases, you can cook almost anything in a wok and it is ideal for making soups too. Its wide surface allows the soup to simmer slowly and to be skimmed efficiently.

5 Why do my vegetables come out soggy?
Sometimes vegetables come out soggy when they are thrown in all at once, regardless of the water content. For example, if you add spinach with asparagus, cabbage, etc., all at once, the water from the spinach and cabbage will make the other vegetables soggy. Vary the quantity of cooking water you add according to how much natural water is in the vegetable you are cooking.

If you are using the wok covered, make sure you have a minimum amount of water in the wok when you cook your vegetables, otherwise the vegetables will oversteam and become soggy.

Soggy vegetables may simply be caused by too many types of vegetables being cooked at once. There should be no more than four to five types of vegetable at the most, some crisper, like green beans, others leafier, such as spinach. They should never be added at the same time. Give the tougher, more textured vegetables a head start.

6 How do you season the wok?
Only carbon steel woks need seasoning. The best way to season it is to scrub it clean with cleanser or detergent the first time you get it. Wipe it dry. Heat it over medium heat, and add about 2 tablespoons of vegetable oil (not olive oil). With clean kitchen paper, rub the

oil over the surface of the wok and repeat this rubbing every 5 minutes for about 20 minutes until the kitchen paper comes out clean. You now have a seasoned wok.

7 How do you wash the wok?
In warm water with a soft sponge. Do not scrub it or use soap or detergent. To avoid rust, dry it quickly over heat or wipe it dry with kitchen towels or paper.

8 My wok is rusty, should I throw it out?
No. If it is a good carbon steel wok, simply scrub the rust out with an abrasive cleaner, wipe it clean, and re-season it.

9 Why does my food stick to the wok when I'm cooking in it?
It could mean that your wok has not been seasoned properly or that you are using detergent to clean the wok each time which wipes out the seasoned surface. Or you may not be cooking properly in it, heating the wok first and getting it hot before you add the oil. Most commonly, food sticking means the wok isn't hot enough.

10 How do I clean the wok with soap if the food is stuck in it?
Simply soak it in warm water and wipe it with a soft sponge. This should work unless the food has really been burnt in the wok. In that case, use the professional Chinese chef method. Heat the wok with any oil and burn the food until it flakes off. Rinse it in warm water. Dry it over high heat and re-season the surface of the wok by adding oil to the surface and rubbing it into the surface of the wok. Then, heat it gently for about 25 minutes.

11 What is the difference between carbon steel and non-stick woks?
I am partial to carbon steel woks because I think that they capture the more authentic flavours of wok cooking. This is because the wok is seasoned and can be heated to a very high temperature, the secret of wok cooking. However, I understand the need for convenience and today there are now good carbon steel, non-stick, woks which are effective.

One great difference is that non-stick woks are non-reactive. This means you can use them with a lemon sauce, or with acidic fruits, and you do not have to worry about re-seasoning the wok.

12 Can I use the wok on an electric/ceramic/halogen/induction surface?
A wok can be used on almost any element, as long as it is hot. The best woks to use with those surfaces are the ones with a slightly flattened bottom so that some of the wok surface comes in contact with the fiercest heat.

13 Why shouldn't I use an electric or stainless steel wok?
Unfortunately, electric woks do not maintain the high heat needed for successful wok cookery. The temperature drops as soon as food is added and it takes a while before it can reach a high heat again. Also, electric woks are quite expensive, as are stainless steel woks. And stainless steel woks have hot spots and when heated to very hot, food can burn very easily. They are therefore not appropriate for good wok cooking.

14 When do you put in the sauces?
That, of course, depends on the recipes. However, a general principal to remember is that you stir-fry food to a certain stage and then it begins to get dry. This is usually the time to add the sauces.

15 How do you cook egg noodles or rice noodles without them sticking in the wok?
Egg noodles should be blanched first, drained and then tossed in sesame oil and cooled before being added to the wok. Hot or wet noodles will stick to the wok.

16 *How do you steam foods in the wok?*
Simply add 5 cm (2 in) of hot water to the wok. Then place either a bamboo steamer or a rack on top of the wok. (It must be set so as to allow the cover to fit snugly.) Place the food to be steamed on a heatproof plate, place the plate on the steamer or rack, cover, and steam according to the recipe.

17 *How do you make fried rice?*
First, you must have already cooked some long-grain white rice, and left it to go cold. Make sure the wok is heated to very hot, add the oil and when the oil is smoking, add the rice. Keep stir-frying until the rice is heated through but not to the point of being crispy. Then add whatever ingredients you want to your fried rice.

18 *Why is Chinese cooking so healthy in the wok?*
Because of the small amount of oil that is used and because high heat tends to cook food rapidly, preserving its nutritional value; very few nutrients are lost or destroyed in proper wok cookery. However, it is important to follow the instructions of the recipes, for example, to drain the meat, etc.

19 *Do you have to use a wok for stir-frying?*
A wok is not absolutely necessary for stir-frying. However, you will find that if you do stir-fry in a flat pan, the food doesn't stay in the pan when you stir it, making the procedure messy, awkward and wasteful.

20 *When do you use the lid on a wok?*
The lid or cover is useful when you are steaming, smoking or braising food in the wok. It can also help you to speed up the cooking of vegetables.

21 *How many portions of food can you make in a wok?*
It is best to make a recipe for four in a wok about 30-35 cm (12-14 in) in diameter. If you need to make more, simply cook a second batch. But do not attempt to put a double portion of a recipe into a wok. You will wind up with food that is steamed instead of stir-fried.

22 *When should you turn down the heat on a wok?*
If the oil is smoking too much, turn down the heat. Sometimes, adding a touch of rice wine or water can rapidly cool the wok down. A good way to cool frying oil immediately is to plunge a cold stainless steel spatula into the oil. This heat transfer method will bring down the temperature substantially.

23 *Why doesn't my food cooked in the wok taste the same as food from a Chinese restaurant? What am I doing wrong?*
Chinese restaurants tend to cook their food in very hot woks. If you are not getting the same taste, it could be because you are not getting your wok hot enough. It is also important to get the right ingredients and sauces.

24 *What is wrong with using a cheaper wok?*
Many Chinese shops sell very cheap woks that are thin-gauge steel, which means they will have a hard time maintaining their seasoning. They can also easily burn through, making them rather dangerous. Invest in a better-grade, heavy-gauge wok.

25 *How should I store my wok if I don't use it a lot?*
Store a seasoned carbon steel wok by rubbing the surface with vegetable oil and then covering the wok with a plastic bag. Store it in a dry place. I hope, however, that you will use your wok often!

INGREDIENTS

Techniques can be learned, implements can be obtained or fashioned, but authentic ingredients can sometimes be elusive. Fortunately, events of the past decades have opened up the kitchens of the world to Asia's many products. This is especially true of Chinese ingredients. In the West today, many of the most exotic foods are readily available. The recipes in this book were all tested with easily obtainable ingredients.

The following is a brief guide to authentic ingredients which I have used in this book. One ingredient commonly used throughout Asia and in China which you will not find mentioned here is monosodium glutamate (also known as MSG, Ve tsin, Accent, seasoning or taste powder). This is a white crystalline extract of grains and vegetables widely used to tenderize and enhance the natural flavour of certain food and some people have an adverse reaction to it. I believe that the natural flavours of the freshest and finest ingredients need no enhancing and I therefore never use MSG.

AUBERGINE

These pleasant, purple-skinned vegetables vary in size from the larger plump ones, easy to find in supermarkets, to the small, thin variety which the Chinese prefer for their more delicate flavour. Look for those with smooth, unblemished skin. Do not peel aubergines since the skin preserves texture, taste and shape. Large aubergines should be cut, sprinkled with a little salt and left to sit for 20 minutes before rinsing and blotting dry with kitchen paper. This process extracts bitter juices and excess moisture from the vegetable before it is cooked. This procedure is unnecessary if you are using Chinese aubergines.

BAMBOO SHOOTS

Bamboo shoots are the young edible shoots of some kinds of bamboo. Fresh bamboo shoots are the best, tinned are an acceptable substitute. Pale yellow with a crunchy texture, they come peeled and either whole or thickly sliced.

Rinse them thoroughly before use and transfer any unused shoots to a jar, cover them with fresh water and keep in the fridge. If the water is changed daily, they will keep for up to a week.

BEANCURD

Beancurd is also known as tofu or doufu. It is highly nutritious and rich in protein and has a distinctive texture, but a bland taste. It is made from yellow soya beans, which are soaked, ground, mixed with water and then cooked briefly before being solidified.

Beancurd is usually sold in two forms: cakes, suitable for stir-frying, braising and poaching, and as a thickish junket called silken tofu, used in soups. Tofu may be kept in the fridge for up to five days, provided the water is changed daily.

BEAN SPROUTS

Now widely available, these are the sprouts of the green mung bean, although some Chinese markets also stock yellow soya bean sprouts, which are much larger. Bean sprouts should always be very fresh and crunchy. They will keep for several days when loosely wrapped in kitchen paper inside a plastic bag in the vegetable crisper of a fridge.

BLACK BEANS

These small black soya beans, also known as salted black beans, are preserved by being fermented with salt and spices. They have a distinctive, slightly salty taste and a rich pleasant aroma. Thus prepared, they are a tasty seasoning, especially when used in conjunction with garlic or fresh ginger.

Black beans are inexpensive and can be obtained from Chinese grocers, usually in tins labelled 'Black Beans in Salted Sauce', but you may also see them packed in plastic bags. These should be rinsed before use; I prefer to chop them slightly, too, as it helps to release their pungent flavour. Transfer any unused tinned beans and liquid to a sealed jar and the beans will keep indefinitely if stored in the fridge.

CAUL FAT

Caul fat is the lower stomach of a pig or cow used by cooks to encase stuffings and to keep food moist while cooking. It is highly perishable so buy it in small quantities and use it quickly.

For longer storage, wrap the caul fat carefully and freeze it. To defrost, rinse in cold water to separate the fat without tearing its lacy and fragile webs. You can order caul fat from your local butcher.

CHILLIES

Chillies are the seed pods of the capsicum plant and can be obtained fresh, dried or ground. One must differentiate between the various types because they vary greatly in taste and pungency.

Fresh Chillies
Fresh chillies can be distinguished by their small size and elongated shape. They should look bright with no brown patches or black spots. There are several varieties. Red chillies are generally milder than green ones because they sweeten as they ripen. To prepare fresh chillies, rinse them in cold water and slit them lengthways. Remove and discard the seeds. Rinse under cold running water, and then follow recipe instructions. Wash your hands, knife and chopping board before preparing other foods, and do not touch your eyes.

Dried Red Chillies
Dried red chillies are small, thin and about 1 cm (½ in) long, and used to season oil used in stir-fried dishes, in sauces and in braising. They are normally left whole or cut in half lengthways with the seeds left in and can be left in the dish during cooking, but, as they are extremely hot and spicy, you may choose just to flavour the cooking oil. They can be kept indefinitely in a tightly covered jar.

CHILLI POWDER

Chilli powder or cayenne pepper is made from dried red chillies. It is pungent, aromatic and ranges from hot to very hot. Your own palate will determine how much you use.

CHILLI BEAN SAUCE *(see Sauces and Pastes, p.21)*

CHILLI OIL/CHILLI DIPPING SAUCE

Chilli oil is sometimes used as a dipping condiment as well as a seasoning and varies in strength and flavour. The Thai and Malaysian versions are especially hot; the Taiwanese and Chinese versions are more subtle. Chilli oil is too dramatic to be used as the sole cooking oil, so combine it with other milder oils. I include pepper and black beans in this recipe for additional flavours so that I can also use it as a dipping sauce. Once made, put the chilli oil in a tightly sealed glass jar and store in a cool dark place where it will keep for months.

150 ml (5 fl oz) oil, preferably groundnut
1 tablespoon chopped dried red chillies
2 teaspoons unroasted Szechuan
  peppercorns
2 tablespoons whole black beans

Heat a wok or frying-pan over a high heat and add the oil. Continue to heat until the oil begins to smoke. Remove the wok or pan from the heat and add the chillies and pepper-corns.

Allow the mixture to cool undisturbed and then pour it into a jar. Let the mixture sit for 2 days, and then strain the oil.

CHINESE BROCCOLI

Chinese broccoli is very crunchy, slightly bitter, and has an earthy 'green' taste. It has deep olive-green leaves and is sometimes sprinkled with white flowers.

When selecting it, look for stems that are firm and leaves which look fresh and green. It is prepared in exactly the same way as ordinary broccoli. Where Chinese broccoli is not to be found, substitute ordinary broccoli.

CHINESE CHIVES

The taste of Chinese chives is much stronger and more garlic-like than common chives; their flowers can be used as well as the blades. They have an earthy, onion taste and can be substituted in smaller quantities for common chives.

Rinse and dry the chives, store them in a plastic bag with slightly damp kitchen paper in the fridge and use as soon as possible.

Chinese yellow chives are Chinese chives which have been grown in the dark and are pale yellow in colour with a more subtle flavour. Select the freshest leaves possible. Trim off any discoloured parts. They are highly perishable and will only keep for one or two days.

CHINESE FLOWERING CABBAGE

Chinese flowering cabbage, or choi sum, is part of the wide mustard green cabbage family. This cabbage has green leaves and may have small yellow flowers which are to be eaten along with the leaves and stems.

CHINESE LEAVES (PEKING CABBAGE)

Chinese leaves comes in various sizes from long, compact barrel-shaped ones to short, squat-looking types. They are also tightly packed with firm, pale green (or in some cases slightly yellow), crinkled leaves.

This versatile vegetable is used for soups and added to stir-fried meat dishes. Its sponge-like ability to absorb flavours and its sweet pleasant taste and texture make it a favourite of chefs, who match it with rich foods.

This is a delicious crunchy vegetable with a mild but distinctive taste. Store it as you would ordinary cabbage.

CHINESE WHITE CABBAGE (BOK CHOY)

Although there are many varieties, the most common bok choy is the one with a long, smooth, milky-white stem and large, crinkly, dark green leaves. Bok choy has a light, fresh, slightly mustardy taste and requires little cooking.

When buying bok choy, look for firm crisp stalks and unblemished leaves, the smaller the better. Store it in the vegetable crisper of your fridge.

CHINESE LONG BEANS

These beans are also known as yard-long beans because they can grow to a metre (yard) in length. There are two varieties: the pale green ones and the dark green, thinner ones. Buy beans that are fresh and bright green, with no dark marks. There is no need to string them before cooking. They have a crunchy taste and texture like string beans but cook faster. Store the fresh beans in a plastic bag in the fridge and use within four days.

CHINESE WHITE RADISH (MOOLI)

Also known as Chinese icicle radish or daikon, it is long and white and rather like a carrot in shape but usually much larger. It is a winter radish or root and can withstand long cooking without disintegrating. It thus absorbs the flavours of other foods while retaining its distinctive radish taste and texture. Look for firm, heavy, solid, unblemished ones. They should be slightly translucent inside, solid and not fibrous. Always peel before use. Store mooli in a plastic bag in the vegetable crisper of your fridge where they will keep for over a week.

CINNAMON STICKS OR BARK

Cinnamon sticks are curled, paper-thin pieces of the bark of the cinnamon tree. Chinese cinnamon is thicker, highly aromatic and more pungent than the ordinary variety. Either adds a refreshing taste to braised dishes and it is an important ingredient of five-spice powder. Store cinnamon in a tightly sealed jar. Ground cinnamon is not a satisfactory substitute.

CITRUS PEEL

Dried citrus peel is usually made from tangerines or oranges and used to flavour braised, smoked and stir-fried dishes. Drying the peel concentrates the flavour, but you can use fresh peel if necessary. Chinese dried citrus peel can be found in Cellophane or plastic packets. Soak the required amount of peel in warm water until it softens, then chop or slice it according to the recipe.

CORIANDER (CHINESE PARSLEY OR CILANTRO)

Fresh coriander is one of the relatively few herbs used in Chinese cookery. It looks like flat-leaf parsley but its pungent, musky, citrus-like flavour gives it a distinctive character which is unmistakable. Often used as a garnish, or chopped and mixed into sauces and stuffings, look for deep green, fresh-looking leaves and substitute with parsley if unavailable. Store coriander by washing, draining, wrapping it in kitchen paper and keeping it in the fridge for several days.

CORNFLOUR

In China there are many flours and types of starch, such as water chestnut powder, taro starch and arrowroot. They are primarily used to bind ingredients, to thicken sauces and to make batter. These exotic starches and flours are difficult to obtain, but I have found cornflour works just as well in my recipes. As part of a marinade, it helps to coat the food properly and it gives dishes a velvety texture. It also protects food during deep-frying by helping to seal in the juices, and it can be used as a binder for minced stuffings. Cornflour is blended with cold water until it forms a smooth paste before it is used in sauces. During the cooking process, the cornflour turns clear and shiny.

EGG WHITE

Egg whites are often used in Chinese recipes as ingredients for batters and as coatings that seal in a food's flavour and juices when the food is plunged into warm oil. One egg white from a large egg generally equals about 2 tablespoons. You can easily freeze the egg whites in table-spoon-size cubes in an ice cube tray.

FISH SAUCE

Fish sauce is also known as fish gravy or nam pla and is a thin brown sauce made from fermented, salted fresh fish. It is sold bottled and has a very fishy aroma and salty taste. However, cooking greatly diminishes the 'fishy' flavour, and the sauce simply adds a special richness and quality to dishes. The Thai brands are especially good.

FIVE-SPICE POWDER

Five-spice powder, five-flavoured powder or five-fragrance spice powder is a mixture of star anise, Szechuan peppercorns, fennel, cloves and cinnamon. A good blend is pungent, fragrant, spicy and slightly sweet at the same time. It keeps indefinitely in a well-sealed jar.

FLOURS

Glutinous Rice Flour
Made from glutinous rice it gives a chewy texture to dough and is used in dim sum pastries. However, it is not an acceptable substitute in recipes that call for ordinary rice flour.

Rice Flour
Made from raw rice and used to make fresh rice noodles. Store it as you would wheat flour.

GARLIC

The Chinese use garlic in numerous ways: whole, finely chopped, crushed and pickled. It is used to flavour oils as well as spicy sauces, and it is often paired with other equally pungent ingredients such as spring onions, black beans and fresh ginger. Select fresh garlic which is firm and preferably pinkish in colour. It should be stored in a cool, dry place but not in the fridge.

GINGER

Fresh root ginger is pungent, spicy and fresh-tasting, adding a subtle but distinctive flavour to soups, meats and vegetables. It is also an important seasoning for fish and seafood since it neutralizes fishy smells. Root ginger can range in size and has pale brown, dry skin which is usually peeled away before use. Select fresh ginger which is firm with no signs of shrivelling. It will keep in the fridge, well wrapped in cling film, for up to two weeks. Dried powdered ginger has a quite different flavour and should not be substituted for fresh root ginger.

GINGER JUICE

Ginger juice is made from fresh ginger and is used in marinades to give a subtle ginger taste without the bite of fresh chopped pieces. Cut unpeeled fresh ginger into 2.5-cm (1-in) chunks and drop them into a food processor with the motor running. When finely chopped, squeeze out the juice by hand through a cotton or linen tea towel.

HAM

Chinese ham has a rich, salty flavour and is used primarily as a garnish or seasoning to flavour soups, sauces, stir-fried dishes, noodles and rice. A good substitute is either Parma ham or lean smoked bacon.

LEEKS

Leeks found in China are large and cylindrical and resemble a giant spring onion with a white garlic-like husk. Leeks found in the West are a good substitute with their mild, slightly sweet, onion flavour. To prepare them, cut off and discard the green tops and roots and slice the leek in half lengthways. Wash them well, and store them in a plastic bag in the vegetable crisper of your fridge.

LEMON GRASS (*CYMBOPOGON CITRATUS*)

This South-east Asian original has a subtle lemony fragrance and flavour. Fresh lemon grass is sold in stalks that can be 60 cm (24 in) long – it looks like a very long spring onion. It is fibrous and lemon grass pieces are always removed after the dish is cooked. Some recipes may call for lemon grass to be finely chopped or pounded into a paste, in which case it becomes an integral aspect of the dish. Avoid dried lemon grass, as it is mostly used for herbal tea purposes. Fresh lemon grass can be kept, loosely wrapped, in the bottom part of your fridge for up to one week. Neither fresh lemon nor citronella grass should be used as a substitute for the unique flavours of lemon grass.

LILY BUDS

Also known as tiger lily buds, golden needles, or lily stems, dried lily buds are an ingredient in muxi (mu shu) dishes and hot and sour soups. They provide texture as well as an earthy taste to any dish. Soak the buds in hot water for about 30 minutes or until they are soft. Cut off the hard ends and shred or cut in half according to the recipe directions. They are quite inexpensive and can be found in Chinese markets. Store them in a jar in a dry place.

MALTOSE SUGAR, *see also Sugar*

This type of malt sugar is a liquid syrup that adds a wonderful richness to stews and sauces without a cloying sweetness. It is found only in Chinese markets and may be stored at room temperature. Honey may be used as a substitute.

MANGETOUT

Sometimes known as snow peas, this familiar vegetable combines a tender, crunchy texture and a sweet, fresh flavour. Look for pods that are firm with very small peas, which means they are tender and young. Mangetout will keep for at least a week in the vegetable crisper of the fridge.

MUSHROOMS

Chinese Dried Mushrooms
There are many varieties, black or brown in colour. The very large ones with a lighter colour and a cracked surface are the best. They are usually the most expensive so use them with a light touch. They can be bought in boxes or plastic bags from Chinese grocers. Store them in an airtight jar. To use, soak the mushrooms in a bowl of warm water for about 20 minutes until soft and pliable. Squeeze out the excess water and cut off and discard the wood stems. Only the caps are used. The soaking water can be saved and used in soups and as rice water. Strain the liquid through a fine sieve to discard any sand or residue from the dried mushrooms.

Chinese Tree Fungus
These tiny, black, dried leaves are also known as cloud ears; when soaked, they puff up to look like little clouds. Soak the dried fungus in hot water for 20-30 minutes until soft. Rinse well, cutting away any hard portions. These fungi are valued for their crunchy texture and slightly smoky flavour. You can find them at Chinese markets, usually wrapped in plastic or Cellophane bags. They keep indefinitely in a jar stored in a cool dry place.

Chinese Wood Ear Fungus

These fungi are the larger variety of the Chinese tree fungi described above. Prepare, soak and trim them in the same manner. In soaking, they will swell up to four or five times their size. Sold in Chinese markets, they keep indefinitely when stored in a jar in a cool dry place.

Straw Mushrooms

These are among the tastiest mushrooms found in China. When fresh they have deep brown caps which are moulded around the stem. In the West they are only available in tins. They can be bought in Chinese grocers and in some supermarkets and delicatessens. Drain them and rinse in cold water before use.

NOODLES OR PASTA

Beanthread (Transparent) Noodles

Also called Cellophane noodles, these are made from ground mung beans and not from a grain flour. They are available dried, are very fine and white and are packed in neat, plastic-wrapped bundles. They are never served on their own, instead being added to soups or braised dishes or deep-fried and used as a garnish. They must be soaked in warm water for about five minutes before use. As they are rather long, you might find it easier to cut them into shorter lengths after soaking. If you are frying them, they do not need soaking beforehand, but they do need to be separated. A good technique for separating the strands is to pull them apart in a large paper bag which stops them from flying all over the place.

Egg Noodles and Wheat Noodles

These are made from hard or soft wheat flour and water. If egg has been added, the noodles are usually labelled as egg noodles. Supermarkets and delicatessens also stock both the dried and fresh varieties. Flat noodles are usually used in soups, and rounded noodles are best for stir-frying or pan-frying. The fresh ones freeze nicely if they are well wrapped. Thaw them thoroughly before cooking.

Rice Noodles

These dried noodles are opaque white and come in a variety of shapes. One of the most common examples is rice stick noodles which are flat and about the length of a chopstick. They can also vary in thickness. Use the type called for in each recipe. Rice noodles are very easy to prepare. Simply soak them in warm water for 20 minutes until they are soft. Drain them in a colander or a sieve, and then they are ready to be used in soups or to be stir-fried.

To Cook Wheat and Egg Noodles

**225 g (8 oz) fresh or dried Chinese egg or
   wheat noodles**

If you are using fresh noodles, immerse them in a pan of boiling water and cook them for 3-5 minutes or until you find their texture done to your taste. If you are using dried noodles, either cook them according to the instructions on the package, or cook them in boiling water for 4-5 minutes. Drain and serve.

If you are cooking noodles in advance or before stir-frying them, toss the cooked and drained noodles in 2 teaspoons of sesame oil and put them into a bowl. Cover this with cling film and chill. The cooked noodles will remain usable for about 2 hours.

OILS

Groundnut Oil

This is also known as peanut oil or arachide oil and is the most commonly used oil in Chinese cookery. It has a pleasant, unobtrusive taste and its ability to be heated to a high temperature without burning makes it perfect for stir-frying and deep-frying. Corn oil can be used instead if groundnut oil is unavailable.

Corn Oil
Corn or maize oil has a high heating point although I find it to be rather bland and with a slightly disagreeable smell. It is high in polyunsaturates and is therefore one of the healthier oils.

Other Vegetable Oils
Some of the cheaper vegetable oils available include soya bean, safflower and sunflower oils. They are light in colour and taste, and can also be used in Chinese cooking, but they smoke and burn at lower temperatures than groundnut oil, and therefore care must be taken when cooking with them.

Sesame Oil
This thick, rich golden brown oil made from sesame seeds has a distinctive, nutty flavour and aroma. It is widely used as a seasoning but is not normally used as a cooking oil because it heats rapidly and burns easily. It is often added at the last minute to finish a dish. Sold in bottles, it can be obtained in Chinese grocers and many supermarkets.

OYSTERS, DRIED

Dried oysters are frequently used in finely minced form to enhance dishes. Use them carefully because they can overwhelm a dish with their assertive flavours. Soak them until soft in a bowl of warm water for anywhere between an hour and overnight. If you wish, you may substitute tinned smoked oysters for the dried variety.

PEANUTS

Raw peanuts add flavour and a crunchy texture; they are especially good when marinated or added to stir-fry dishes. The thin red skins need to be removed before you use the nuts. To do this simply immerse them in a pan of boiling water for about 2 minutes. Drain them and let them cool; then the skins will come off easily.

RICE

Long-grain Rice
This is the most popular rice for cooking in China where there are many different varieties. Although the Chinese go through the ritual of washing it in cold water and rinsing it repeatedly, rice purchased at supermarkets doesn't require this step.

Short-grain Rice
Short-grain rice is most frequently found in northern China and is used for making rice porridge, a popular morning meal.

Glutinous Rice
Glutinous rice is also known as sweet rice or sticky rice. It is short, round and pearl-like and has a higher gluten content than other rices. The Chinese use it in stuffings, rice pudding and pastries. It is used for rice dishes, sometimes wrapped in lotus leaves, and served after Chinese banquets. It is also used for making Chinese rice wine and vinegar. Most Chinese markets and supermarkets stock it. Glutinous rice must be soaked for at least two hours (preferably overnight) before cooking. You may cook it in the same way as long-grain rice *(see p. 210)*.

RICE PAPER (BÁNH TRÁNG)

Made from a mixture of rice flour, water and salt, and rolled out by a machine to paper thinness, it is then dried hard and flat on bamboo mats in the sun, giving them their beautiful cross-hatch imprint or pattern. It is available only in dried form and is used extensively for wrapping Vietnamese spring rolls.

You can buy rice paper in many Chinese grocers and supermarkets in packets of 50-100 sheets but avoid yellowish papers, which may be too old. Store them in a dry cool place. After use, wrap the remaining rice papers carefully in the package they came in and put this in another plastic bag and seal well before storing.

SAUCES AND PASTES

Chinese and Asian cookery involves a number of thick, tasty sauces and pastes. They are essential to the authentic taste of Chinese cooking, and it is well worth making the effort to obtain them. Most are sold in bottles or tins by Chinese grocers and some supermarkets. Tinned sauces, once opened, should be transferred to screw-top glass jars and kept in the fridge where they will last indefinitely.

Chilli Bean Sauce
This thick, dark sauce or paste which is made from soya beans, chillies and other seasonings, is very hot and spicy. It is usually available in jars in Chinese grocers. Be sure to seal the jar tightly after use and store in the larder or fridge. Do not confuse it with chilli sauce (see below) which is a hotter, redder, thinner sauce made without beans and used mainly as a dipping sauce for cooked dishes.

Chilli Sauce
Chilli sauce is a bright red, hot sauce which is made from chillies, vinegar, sugar and salt. It is sometimes used for cooking, but is mainly used as a dipping sauce. There are various brands available in Chinese grocers and many supermarkets, and you should experiment with them until you find the one you like best.

If you find your chilli sauce is too strong, dilute it with a little hot water. Do not confuse this sauce with the chilli bean sauce *(see above)* which is a much thicker and darker sauce used for cooking not dipping.

Hoisin Sauce
This is a thick, dark, brownish red sauce which is made from soya beans, vinegar, sugar, spices and other flavourings. It is sweet and spicy. Hoisin sauce is sold in tins and jars (it is sometimes also called barbecue sauce) and is available in Chinese grocers and supermarkets. If refrigerated, it can keep indefinitely.

Oyster Sauce
This thick, brown sauce is made from a concentrate of oysters cooked in soy sauce and brine. Despite its name, oyster sauce does not taste fishy. It has a rich flavour and is used not only in cooking but also as a condiment, diluted with a little oil, for vegetables, poultry and meats. It is usually sold in bottles and can be bought in Chinese grocers and supermarkets. I find it keeps best in the fridge.

Sesame Paste
This rich, thick, creamy brown paste is made from sesame seeds. It is used in both hot and cold dishes. It is sold in jars at Chinese grocers. If you cannot obtain it, use peanut butter which resembles it in texture.

Soy Sauces
Soy sauce is an essential ingredient in Chinese cooking. It is made from a mixture of soya beans, flour and water, which is then fermented naturally and aged for some months. The liquid which is finally distilled is soy sauce. Most soy sauce sold in supermarkets is dark soy. Be sure you buy the correct one as there are two main types.

LIGHT SOY SAUCE is light in colour, but full of flavour, this is the better one to use for cooking. It is saltier than dark soy sauce. It is known in Chinese grocers as Superior Soy.

DARK SOY SAUCE is aged for much longer than light soy sauce, hence its darker, almost black colour. It is slightly thicker and stronger than light soy sauce and is more suitable for stews. I prefer it to light soy as a dipping sauce. It is known in Chinese grocers as Soy Superior Sauce.

Whole Yellow Bean Sauce
This thick, spicy, aromatic sauce is made of yellow beans, flour and salt which are fermented together. It is quite salty, but it adds a distinctive flavour to Chinese sauces. There are two forms: whole beans in a thick sauce and mashed or puréed beans (sold as crushed yellow bean sauce). I prefer the whole bean variety because it is slightly less salty and has a better texture.

SAUSAGES, CHINESE

Chinese sausages look exactly like thin salami and are about 5 cm (6 in) long. They are made from cured duck liver, pork liver or pork meat. They are dark red in colour with white flecks of fat. Their tasty flavour varies according to type, but they are sweet rather than spicy. They must be cooked before they can be eaten and are most commonly used to season chicken and rice dishes. If they are unobtainable from Chinese grocers, ham can be substituted.

SESAME SEEDS

These are dried seeds of the sesame herb. Unhulled, the seeds range from greyish white to black in colour, and hulled seeds are tiny, somewhat flattened, cream-coloured, and pointed at one end. Keep them in a glass jar in a cool dry place; they will last indefinitely.

To Make Toasted Sesame Seeds
Heat a frying-pan over a burner until hot. Add the sesame seeds and stir occasionally. Watch them closely, and when they begin to brown lightly, about 3-5 minutes, stir them again and pour them on to a plate. When thoroughly cool, store in a jar in a cool, dark place.

Alternatively, you could pre-heat the oven to 160°C/325°F/gas 3. Spread the sesame seeds on a baking sheet, and roast them in the oven for about 10-15 minutes until they are nicely toasted and lightly browned. Allow them to cool, then place in a glass jar until you are ready to use them.

SHAOXING RICE WINE

Rice wine is used extensively for cooking and drinking throughout all of China, but I believe the finest of its many varieties to be from Shaoxing in Zhejiang Province in eastern China. It is made from glutinous rice, yeast and spring water. Chefs use it for cooking as well as in marinades and sauces. Now readily available in Chinese markets and in some wine shops in the West, it should be kept tightly corked at room temperature. A good-quality, dry pale sherry can be substituted but cannot equal its rich, mellow taste. Do not confuse this wine with sake, which is the Japanese version of rice wine and quite different. Western grape wines are not an adequate substitute either.

SHALLOTS

Shallots are mild-flavoured members of the onion family. They are small – about the size of pickling onions – with copper-red skins. They have a distinctive onion taste without being as strong or as overpowering as ordinary onions.

Readily available in all supermarkets, they make an excellent substitute for Chinese shallots, which are difficult to find. In China, you will find them fresh or pickled as a snack. Shallots can be expensive but their sweet flavour permeates food and a few go a long way. Keep them in a cool, dry place (not the fridge) and peel, slice or chop them as you would an onion.

SHERRY

It you cannot obtain rice wine, you can use a good-quality, dry, pale sherry instead. Do not use sweet or cream sherries.

SHRIMPS, DRIED

Dried shrimps are used to perk up fried rice or mixed with meat dishes to give an added dimension. They are sold in packages and may be found in Chinese and Asian speciality markets.

Look for the brands with the pinkest colour and avoid greyish ones. Dried shrimps will keep indefinitely when sealed in a glass container and stored in a cool dry place. When cooked, the dried shrimps' strong odour is moderated, and they add a delicate taste to sauces.

SHRIMP PASTE

This ingredient adds an exotic flavour and fragrance to dishes. Made from shrimps which are ground and fermented, it has an odour before cooking much stronger than its actual taste. It is like anchovy paste in texture. It can be found in Chinese markets, usually in glass jars. Refrigerated, it will keep indefinitely.

SILK SQUASH (CHINESE OKRA)

This is a long, thin, cylindrical squash with deep narrow ridges and one tapered end. Choose firm, unblemished, dark green ones and peel the ridges.

If the vegetable is young, you can leave on some of the green; if older, it is best to peel away all the skin. The inside flesh turns soft and tender as it cooks, tasting like a cross between a cucumber and courgette. Absorbent, it readily picks up flavours of the sauce or food it is cooked with.

SPINACH

Western varieties of spinach are quite different from those used in China. Nevertheless, they make satisfactory substitutes for the Chinese variety. Spinach is most commonly stir-fried, so frozen spinach is unsuitable. Chinese water spinach is available in Chinese markets and has hollow stems and delicate, green, pointed leaves; it is also lighter in colour than common spinach and has a milder taste. It should be cooked when it is very fresh, preferably on the day it is bought.

SPRING ROLL SKINS

These are the paper-thin pastry wrappers which are filled with bean sprouts and other vegetables to make spring rolls. They are about 15 cm (6 in) square, are white, and are made from a soft flour and water dough. As they are very thin and probably too tricky to make at home, I suggest you buy them frozen in packets from Chinese grocers. They keep well in the freezer when wrapped in cling film.

STAR ANISE

The star anise is a hard, star-shaped spice and is the seedpod of an attractive bush. It is similar in flavour and fragrance to common anise, but it is more robust and liquorice-like. Star anise is an essential ingredient of five-spice powder and is widely used in braised dishes to which it imparts a rich taste and fragrance. It is sold in plastic packs by Chinese grocers, and should be stored in an airtight jar in a cool, dry place.

SUGAR

Chinese sugar comes in several forms: as rock or yellow lump sugar, as brown sugar slabs, and as maltose or malt sugar *(see p. 18)*. I particularly like to use rock sugar which is rich and has a more subtle flavour than that of the refined granulated sugar. It also gives a good lustre or glaze to braised dishes and sauces. You can buy it in Chinese grocers where it is usually sold in packets. You may need to break the lumps into smaller pieces with a wooden mallet or rolling pin. If you cannot find it, use white sugar or coffee sugar crystals (the amber, chunky kind) instead.

SZECHUAN PEPPERCORNS

Also known as peppers because they look like flower buds opening and are reddish brown with a strong, pungent aroma which distinguishes them from the hotter black peppercorns. They are the dried berries of a shrub which is a member of the citrus family. Their taste is sharp and mildly spicy. They can be ground in a conventional peppermill and are very often roasted before they are ground to bring out their full flavour. They are inexpensive and sold wrapped in Cellophane or plastic bags in Chinese grocers. They will keep indefinitely if stored in a well-sealed container.

To Roast Szechuan Peppercorns
Heat a wok or heavy frying-pan to a medium heat. Add the peppercorns (you can cook about 150 g/5 oz at a time) and stir-fry them for about 5 minutes until they brown slightly and start to smoke. Remove the pan from the heat and let them cool. Grind the peppercorns in a peppermill, clean coffee grinder or with a mortar and pestle. Seal the mixture tightly in a screw-top jar until you need some. Alternatively keep the whole roasted peppercorns in a well-sealed container and grind them when required.

SZECHUAN PRESERVED VEGETABLE

The root of the mustard green, pickled in salt and hot chillies. Sold in tins in Chinese grocers, it gives a pleasantly crunchy texture and spicy taste to dishes. Before using it, rinse in cold water and then slice or chop as required. Any unused vegetable should be transferred to a covered jar and stored in the fridge where it will keep indefinitely.

TEA, CHINESE BLACK

Chinese black tea is a full-bodied, fragrant and smooth tea with a rich aroma and a superb bouquet. There are various kinds, of which Keemun is one of the most well known. Tea is used in smoked dishes or for simmering. You can purchase Chinese black teas in Chinese grocers, delicatessens and in many supermarkets. I prefer to store tea in tins since these keep it in the freshest possible condition.

VINEGAR

Vinegars are widely used in Chinese cooking. Unlike Western vinegars, they are usually made from rice. There are many varieties, ranging in flavour from the spicy and slightly tart to the sweet and pungent. All these vinegars can be bought in Chinese grocers and will keep indefinitely. If you cannot get Chinese vinegars, I suggest you use cider vinegar. Malt vinegar can be used, but its taste is stronger and more acidic.

White Rice Vinegar
White rice vinegar is clear and mild in flavour. It has a faint taste of glutinous rice and is used for sweet and sour dishes.

Black Rice Vinegar
Black rice vinegar is very dark in colour and rich, though mild, in taste. It is used for braised dishes, sauces, and sometimes as a dipping sauce for crab.

Red Rice Vinegar
Red rice vinegar is sweet and spicy in taste and is often used as a dipping sauce for seafood.

WATER CHESTNUTS

Water chestnuts are a sweet root vegetable or bulb about the size of a walnut. They are white and crunchy.

Fresh water chestnuts can sometimes be obtained from Chinese grocers or good supermarkets. They are tastier than tinned ones and will keep, unpeeled, in a paper bag in the fridge for up to two weeks. Peel them before use, and, if you have any left over, put them back in the fridge covered with cold water. Tinned water chestnuts should be rinsed well in cold water before you use them, and any unused ones stored in a jar of cold water. They will keep for several weeks in the fridge if you change the water daily.

WHEAT STARCH

Wheat starch is a flour-like powder left after the protein is removed from wheat flour itself. It is commonly used as a wrapping for dumplings, especially in China. Bought in Chinese markets, wheat starch will keep indefinitely when tightly sealed and kept in a cool dry place.

WONTON SKINS

Wonton skins are made from egg and flour and can be bought fresh or frozen from Chinese grocers. They are thin pastry-like wrappings which can be stuffed with minced meat and fried, steamed or used in soups. They are normally sold in little piles of 8 cm (3¼ in) yellowish squares and will be wrapped in plastic.

Fresh wonton skins will keep for about five days if stored in cling film or a plastic bag in the fridge.

If you are using frozen wonton skins, just peel off the number you require and thaw them thoroughly before you use them.

EQUIPMENT

Traditional Asian and Chinese cooking equipment is not essential for the preparation of Asian food, but there are some tools which will make it very much easier.

WOK

All your enthusiasm for wok cookery and your own skills will come to naught without a good wok! The wok may be used for stir-frying, blanching, deep-frying and steaming foods. Its shape allows for fuel-efficient, quick and even heating and cooking. In the stir-frying technique, the deep sides prevent the food and oils from spilling over; in deep-frying, much less oil is required because of the shaped concentration of the heat and ingredients at the wok's base.

There are two basic wok types: the traditional Cantonese version, with short, rounded handles on either side of the edge or lip of the wok; and the pau or Peking wok, which has one long handle from 30 to 35 cm (12 to 14 in) long. The long-handled wok keeps you more safely distanced from the possibility of splashing yourself with hot oils or water.

You should know that the round-bottomed wok may only be used on gas hobs. Woks are now available with flatter bottoms designed especially for electric hobs, although this shape really defeats the purpose of the traditional design, which is to concentrate intense heat at the centre, it does have the advantage over ordinary frying-pans of having deeper sides.

Choosing a Wok

Choose a large wok – preferably about 30 to 35 cm (12 to 14 in) in diameter, with deep sides. It is easier, and safer, to cook a small batch of food in a large wok than a large quantity in a small one. Be aware that some modernized woks are too shallow or too flat-bottomed and thus no better than a frying-pan. A heavier wok, preferably made of carbon steel, is superior to the lighter stainless steel or aluminium types, which cannot take very high heat and tend to blacken as well as scorch the food. There are now on the market, good non-stick carbon steel woks that maintain the heat without sticking. However, these woks need special care to prevent scratching. In recent years, the non-stick technology has improved vastly, so that now they can be safely recommended. They are especially useful when cooking foods that have a high acid level such as lemons.

Wok Stand

This is a metal ring or frame designed to keep a conventionally shaped wok steady on the hob, and it is essential if you want to use your wok for steaming, deep-frying or braising. Stands come in two designs. One is a solid metal ring punched with about six ventilation holes. The other is like a circular thin wire frame. If you have a gas cooker, use only the latter type as the more solid design does not allow for sufficient ventilation and may lead to a build-up of gas which could put the flame out completely.

Wok Lid

This light and inexpensive, domed cover, usually made from aluminium, is used for steaming. The lid normally comes with the wok, but if not, it may be purchased at a Chinese or Asian market, or you may use any domed pan lid that fits snugly.

SPATULA

A long-handled metal spatula shaped rather like a small shovel is ideal for scooping and tossing food in a wok. Alternatively any good long-handled spoon can be used.

RACK

When steaming foods in your wok, you will need a wooden or metal rack or trivet to raise the food to be cooked above the water level. Wok sets usually include a rack, but if not, Asian and Chinese grocers sell them separately. Department stores and hardware shops also sell wooden and metal stands which can serve the same purpose. Any rack, improvized or not, that keeps the food above the water so that it is steamed and not boiled will suffice.

BAMBOO BRUSH

This bundle of stiff, split bamboo is used for cleaning a wok without scrubbing off the seasoned surface. It is an attractive, inexpensive implement but not essential. A soft washing-up brush will do just as well.

STEAMERS

Steaming is the best method for preparing many foods of delicate taste and texture, such as fish and vegetables. Bamboo steamers come in several sizes, of which the 25-cm (10-in) one is the most suitable for home use. A tight-fitting bamboo lid prevents the steam escaping; several steamers, stacked one above the other, may be utilized at once. Of course, any kind of wide metal steamer may be used if you prefer. Before using a bamboo steamer for the first time, wash it and then steam it empty for about 5 minutes.

SAND OR CLAY POTS

For braised dishes, soups and rice cooking, the Chinese rely upon these lightweight clay pots, the design of which allows for the infusion of aromas and tastes into food. Their unglazed exteriors have a sandy texture, hence their other name. Clay pots are available in many sizes, with matching lids, and, being quite fragile, they are often encased in a wire frame. They are to be used directly on the hob, but never put an empty sand pot on to a heated element or place a hot sand pot on a cold surface: the shock will crack it. Clay pots should always have at least some liquid in them, and when filled with food, they can take very high heat. If you use an electric stove, employ a heat diffusing pad to insulate the pot from direct contact with the hot coils. Note that, because of the release of hot steam when you lift the lid, always lift the lid *away* from you.

WOK COOKING TECHNIQUES

The wok's versatile concave sides make it an ideal tool for multiple uses. This chapter covers the main techniques used with the wok, although you will find the wok is just as useful for cooking any type of food. For simple omelettes, a well-seasoned wok is ideal. Even bacon and eggs can be made in the wok. In other words, use your wok and you will find what an essential tool it can become in your kitchen.

The preparation of foods and ingredients before cooking is more important, and time-consuming, in wok cookery than in any other type of cookery. However, once the groundwork has been done the rest is comparatively quick and easy, and the results are always rewarding.

Because the wok must be hot when you cook, it presupposes that all the ingredients have been properly prepared for the cooking process. This means that meats and vegetables have been cut into appropriate shapes and sizes to cook quickly and evenly while retaining their natural tastes and textures. As an important by-product, such preparation enhances the visual appeal of whatever is being served.

Several different cooking techniques may be used in the preparation of a single dish. There is nothing mysterious about such techniques and mastery of them comes quickly in almost every case. When you plan your meals, be sure to select dishes that involve a range of techniques. Limit yourself to one stir-fry dish per meal until you have become used to the techniques that this crucial style of cooking employs.

STIR-FRYING

Success with stir-frying depends upon having all the required ingredients prepared, measured out and immediately at hand, and on having a good source of fierce heat. Its advantage is that, properly executed, stir-fried foods can be cooked in minutes in very little oil so they retain their natural flavours and textures. It is very important that stir-fried foods not be overcooked or made greasy. Using a wok is definitely an advantage when stir-frying as its shape not only conducts the heat well but its high sides enable you to toss the ingredients rapidly, keeping them constantly moving while cooking.

Having prepared all the ingredients for stir-frying, the steps are as follows:

Heat the wok or frying-pan until it is very hot before adding the oil. Add the oil and, using a metal spatula or long-handled spoon, distribute it evenly over the surface. When flavouring oil, you will need to work very quickly so that the ingredients will not burn and become bitter. Toss them quickly in the oil for a few seconds. In some recipes these flavourings will then be removed and discarded before cooking proceeds.

Then add the ingredients as described in the recipe and proceed to stir-fry by tossing them over the surface of the wok or pan with the metal spatula or long-handled spoon. If you are stir-frying meat, let each side rest for just a few seconds before continuing to stir. Keep moving the food from the centre of the wok to the sides. Stir-frying is a noisy business and is usually accompanied by quite a lot of splattering because of the high temperature at which the food must be cooked, hence my preference for the long-handled wok.

Some stir-fried dishes are thickened with a mixture of cornflour and cold water. To avoid getting a lumpy sauce, be sure to blend the mixture thoroughly, and remove the wok or pan from the heat for a minute before you add the cornflour mixture. The sauce can then be returned to the heat and thickened.

BLANCHING

Putting food into a wok filled with hot water or into moderately hot oil for a few minutes will cook it briefly but not entirely. It is a sort of softening-up process to prepare the food for final cooking. Chicken is often blanched in oil or water after being velveted (that is, coated in egg white and cornflour). Meat is sometimes blanched to rid it of unwanted gristle and fat and in order to ensure a clean taste and appearance. Blanching in water is common with hard vegetables such as broccoli or carrots. The vegetable is plunged into boiling water for several minutes, then drained and plunged into cold water to arrest the cooking process. In such cases, blanching usually precedes stir-frying, which finishes the cooking. You must always avoid overcooking your foods at the blanching stage.

POACHING

This is a method of simmering food gently in the wok until it is partially cooked. Poached food is then put into soup or combined with a sauce and the cooking process continued. Delicately flavoured and textured foods such as eggs and chicken are often simmered.

DEEP-FRYING

This is one of the most important techniques in Chinese cooking. The trick is to regulate the heat so that the surface of the food is sealed and doesn't become greasy but does not brown so fast that the food is uncooked inside. Some points to bear in mind when deep-frying are as follows.

Wait for the oil to get hot enough before adding the food to be fried. The oil should give off a haze and almost produce little wisps of smoke when it is the right temperature, but you can test it by dropping in a small piece of food. If it bubbles all over then the oil is sufficiently hot. Adjust the heat as necessary to prevent the oil from actually smoking or overheating.

To prevent splattering, use kitchen paper to dry the food thoroughly before cooking. If the food is first steeped in a marinade, remove it with a slotted spoon and let it drain before putting it into the oil. If you are using a batter, make sure all the excess batter drips off before adding the food to the hot oil.

SHALLOW-FRYING

This wok technique is similar to sautéing in a frying pan and is just as effective. It involves more oil than stir-frying but less than for deep-frying. Food is fried first on one side and then on the other. Sometimes the excess oil is then drained off and a sauce added to complete the dish.

SLOW-SIMMERING AND STEEPING

These processes are similar. In slow-simmering, food is immersed in liquid which is brought almost to the boil and then the temperature is reduced so that it simmers, cooking the food to the desired degree. This is the technique used for making stock.

In steeping, food is similarly immersed in liquid (usually stock) and simmered for a time. The heat is then turned off and the remaining heat of the liquid finishes off the cooking process.

BRAISING AND RED-BRAISING

This wok technique is most often applied to tougher cuts of meat and certain vegetables. The food is usually browned and then put into stock which has been flavoured with seasonings and spices. The stock is brought to the boil, the heat reduced and the food simmered gently until it is cooked. Red-braising is simply the technique by which food is braised in a dark liquid such as soy sauce. This gives food a reddish-brown colour, hence the name. This type of braising sauce can be saved and frozen for re-use. It can be re-used many times and becomes rich in flavour.

STEAMING

Steamed foods are cooked by a gentle moist heat which must circulate freely in order to cook the food. It is an excellent method of bringing out subtle flavours and so is particularly appropriate for fish. Bamboo steamers can be used over water in a wok to steam food, but you could use any one of several utensils.

Put about 5 cm (2 in) of water into a wok, then put a metal or wooden rack into the wok. Bring the water to a simmer, and put the food to be steamed on a heatproof plate. Lower the plate on to the rack and cover the wok tightly with a wok lid. Check the water level from time to time and replenish it with hot water as necessary. The water should never make direct contact with the food.

If you do not have a metal or wooden rack you could use a small empty tin can to support the plate of food. Remember that the food needs to remain above the water level and must not get wet. The water should be at least 2.5 cm (1 in) below the edge of the heat-proof plate (see note on Steamers p.27).

TWICE-COOKING

As the name implies, this is a two-step process involving two quite different techniques, such as simmering and stir-frying. It is used to change the texture of food, to infuse it with flavour, and to render foods which are difficult to cook into a more manageable state. It is especially useful for removing fat from meat before final cooking.

RE-HEATING FOODS

Steaming in the wok is one of the best methods of re-heating food since it warms it without cooking it further and without drying it out. To re-heat soups and braised dishes, bring the liquid slowly to a simmer but do not boil. Remove it from the heat as soon as it is hot to prevent overcooking.

SMOKING

The wok is also useful for smoking foods. Simply line the inside of the wok with kitchen foil. Add the smoking ingredients (in Chinese cooking, it is usually black tea leaves, sugar and spices). Place your marinated food on an oiled rack. Slowly heat the ingredients and when it begins to burn and smoke, cover the wok tightly. Turn the heat to low and slowly smoke according to the instructions in the recipe.

APPETIZERS

The wok is an ideal cooking utensil for preparing appetizers because they can almost always be prepared as one's guests gather around the dining room and kitchen. Food for thought is generated as the food for the palate is being prepared.

Many of the appetizers in this chapter, such as Thai Crispy Prawn-coconut Treats *or* Parchment Paper Fish, *should be prepared and served immediately for the best effect. Hot from the wok, the appetizers stimulate the appetite and offer a perfect start to a festive evening. Other appetizers like* Savoury Stuffed Orange Slices *are deliciously unusual: the stuffing is made in the wok and then paired with fresh orange slices for a refreshing starter.*

VIETNAMESE-STYLE SPRING ROLLS

I have long been an admirer and consumer of Vietnamese spring rolls. Their crackling rice paper skin with their savoury filling, all eaten in a leaf of fresh lettuce with either mint or basil, dipped in sauce, is an ideal appetizer. Here I have taken the classic Vietnamese spring roll recipe and have modified it to my own taste. I think you will find it as tasty and fun to eat.

Although they can be made in advance, it is best to deep-fry them at the last minute. They are terrific treats to go with drinks or make a lovely first course for a dinner party when served with the Dipping Sauce (see p. 33).

The rice paper wrappers can be found at Chinese or South-east Asian grocers. They are dry and must be gently soaked before using them. Handle them with care as they are quite fragile. When deep-frying them, do not crowd them in the pan as they tend to stick. If they stick don't separate them as you may risk breaking them.

MAKES ABOUT 25 SMALL SPRING ROLLS

FOR THE FILLING

25 g (1 oz) beanthread (transparent)
   noodles
15 g (½ oz) Chinese dried wood ears
1 tablespoon groundnut oil
1 small onion, finely chopped
2 tablespoons coarsely chopped garlic
2 tablespoons finely chopped spring onions
2 tablespoons finely chopped shallots
225 g (8 oz) minced pork
1½ teaspoons salt
½ teaspoon freshly ground black pepper
175 g (4 oz) cooked fresh crabmeat

5 tablespoons plain flour
5 tablespoons water
1 packet rice paper wrappers
450 ml (15 fl oz) oil, preferably groundnut
8 oz (225 g) iceberg lettuce
Assorted sprigs of fresh basil, mint or
   coriander, or a combination of all three

Soak the noodles in a large bowl of warm water for 15 minutes. When they are soft, drain them and discard the water. Cut them into 7.5-cm (3-in) lengths using scissors or a knife. Soak the wood ears in warm water for about 20 minutes until soft. Rinse well in cold water and squeeze the excess liquid from the wood ears. Remove any hard stems and shred the caps finely.

Heat a wok or large frying-pan over high heat until it is hot. Add the oil, and when it is very hot and slightly smoking, add the onion, garlic, spring onions and shallots and stir-fry for 3 minutes. Add the pork, salt and pepper and continue to stir-fry for 5 minutes. Drain the pork in a colander and allow it to cool.

When the pork is cool, combine it in a large bowl with the beanthread noodles, wood ears and cooked crabmeat. In a small bowl, mix the flour and water together into a paste.

When you are ready to make the spring rolls, fill a large bowl with warm water. Dip one of the rice paper rounds in the water and let it soften. Remove and drain it on a linen tea towel. Put about 2 tablespoons of the filling on each softened rice paper wrapper. Fold in each side and then roll it up tightly. Seal the ends with a little of the flour paste mixture. You should have a roll about 7.5 cm (3 in) long, a little like a small sausage. Repeat the procedure until you have used up all the filling.

Heat the oil in a deep-fat fryer or a large wok until it is hot. Deep-fry the spring rolls, a few at a time, until they are golden brown. They have a tendency to stick to each other at the beginning of the frying, so only fry a few at a time. Do not attempt to break them apart should they stick together. You can do this after they have been removed from the oil. Drain them on kitchen paper.

Serve at once with lettuce leaves, herb sprigs, and dipping sauce.

DIPPING SAUCE

This sauce can be made well in advance.

SERVES 4

4 tablespoons Thai fish sauce
1 teaspoon dried chilli powder or flakes
1 tablespoon finely chopped garlic
1 tablespoon lime juice
4 tablespoons water
1 tablespoon sugar

Combine all the ingredients together in a blender, mixing them thoroughly. Let the mixture sit for at least 10 minutes before using.

THAI CRISPY PRAWN-COCONUT TREATS

O n my frequent visits to Bangkok, I often cook at the famous Oriental Hotel kitchen. Whenever I get the chance, I observe the excellent chefs in the Thai food section of the kitchen. I have discovered that there are many similarities between Chinese and Thai cuisine, but the addition of certain Thai ingredients adds another depth or dimension to Chinese food.

Here is a simple Thai appetizer which would be quite Chinese but for the added twist of coconut and curry paste. These touches turn the dish into a wonderful party treat or a splendid opener for any dinner.

The filling can be made in advance, but the actual stuffing should be done at the last moment, otherwise the pasta will become soggy. These treats should not be frozen.

SERVES 4

FOR THE FILLING

350 g (12 oz) raw prawns, peeled and coarsely minced

100 g (4 oz) minced pork

1 teaspoon salt

½ teaspoon freshly ground black pepper

4 tablespoons finely chopped spring onions

3 tablespoons desiccated coconut

2 teaspoons light soy sauce

2 tablespoons oyster sauce

1½ tablespoons finely chopped orange zest

1 teaspoon Madras curry paste

1 teaspoon sugar

250 g (9 oz) wonton skins

600 ml (1 pint) groundnut or vegetable oil for deep-frying

Put the prawns and pork in a large bowl, add the salt and pepper and mix well, either by kneading with your hand or by stirring with a wooden spoon. Then add the rest of the filling ingredients and stir them well into the prawn and pork mixture. Wrap the bowl with cling film and chill it for at least 20 minutes.

When you are ready to stuff the parcels, put 1 tablespoon of the filling in the centre of the first wonton skin. Dampen the edges with a little water and bring up the sides of the skin around the filling. Pinch the edges together at the top so that the wonton is sealed; it should look like a small, filled bag.

Heat a wok or large frying-pan over high heat until it is hot. Add the oil, and when it is very hot and slightly smoking, add a handful of wontons and deep-fry for 3 minutes until golden and crispy. If the oil gets too hot, turn down the heat slightly. Drain the wontons well on kitchen paper. Continue to fry the wontons until they are all cooked.

CRISPY THAI-STYLE WONTONS

Here is my interpretation of the familiar crispy wontons, but with a touch of various typically Thai flavours. The wontons are easily prepared and their crisp, dry texture goes down well as an appetizer or with drinks. Wonton skins can be bought fresh or frozen from Chinese grocers. (Be sure to thaw them thoroughly if they are frozen.)

SERVES 4-6

FOR THE FILLING

350 g (12 oz) cooked fresh crabmeat

100 g (4 oz) minced pork

1 tablespoon finely chopped garlic

2 teaspoons salt

¼ teaspoon freshly ground black pepper

2 teaspoons Madras curry powder

1½ tablespoons finely chopped fresh
   coriander

3 tablespoons finely chopped spring onions

2 teaspoons Shaoxing rice wine or dry
   sherry

1 teaspoon sugar

1 teaspoon sesame oil

FOR THE SWEET AND SOUR DIPPING SAUCE

150 ml (5 fl oz) water

2 tablespoons sugar

3 tablespoons Chinese white rice vinegar or
   cider vinegar

3 tablespoons tomato purée or tomato
   ketchup

1 teaspoon salt

½ teaspoon freshly ground white pepper

1 teaspoon cornflour mixed with 2
   teaspoons water

250 g (9 oz) wonton skins

600 ml (1 pint) groundnut or vegetable oil
   for deep-frying

Put the crabmeat and pork in a large bowl. Add the garlic, salt and pepper and mix well, either by kneading with your hand or by stirring with a wooden spoon. Add rest of the filling ingredients and stir them well into the crabmeat and pork mixture. Cover the bowl with cling film and chill it for at least 20 minutes.

In a small pan, combine all the ingredients for the sweet and sour sauce, except the cornflour mixture. Bring the ingredients to the boil, stir in the cornflour mixture and cook for 1 minute. Allow to cool.

When you are ready to stuff the wontons, put 1 tablespoon of the filling in the centre of the first wonton skin. Dampen the edges with a little water and bring up the sides of the skin around the filling. Pinch the edges together at the top so that the wonton is sealed. It should look like a small, filled bag.

Heat a wok or large frying-pan over high heat until it is hot. Add the oil, and when it is very hot and slightly smoking, add a handful of wontons and deep-fry for 3 minutes until golden and crispy. If the oil gets too hot, turn down the heat slightly. Drain them well on kitchen paper. Continue to fry the wontons until they are all cooked. Serve immediately with the sweet and sour sauce.

CRISPY PRAWN AND HAM BALLS

The magic of the wok makes this delightful treat easy to prepare and to serve. It performs admirably as a delicious starter, but it can as easily be served by itself or with a salad as a light lunch. Inspired by the prawn appetizers served in dim sum speciality restaurants, I have added here a touch of ham and lemon zest for an East-West variation. For maximum enjoyment, these easy-to-make treats should be cooked at the last minute and served immediately.

If you use fresh water chestnuts, you will need about 225 g (8 oz) unpeeled weight.

SERVES 4-6

FOR THE PRAWN MIXTURE

350 g (12 oz) raw prawns
100 g (4 oz) tinned water chestnuts, coarsely
   chopped
100 g (4 oz) Parma ham, finely chopped
2 teaspoons finely chopped lemon zest
1 teaspoon salt
½ teaspoon freshly ground white pepper
1 egg white
1 teaspoon sesame oil
2 tablespoons spring onions, white part
   only, finely chopped
2 teaspoons cornflour
1 teaspoon sugar

Cornflour, for dusting
600 ml (1 pint) groundnut oil

Peel the prawns and, if you are using large, uncooked ones, remove the fine digestive cord. Wash the prawns and pat them dry with kitchen paper. Using a cleaver or sharp knife, chop the prawns coarsely and then mince them finely into a paste. Put the paste into a bowl and mix in the rest of the ingredients for the prawn mixture. Or, alternatively, you could do this in a food processor. This step can be done hours in advance, but you should then wrap the paste well in cling film and put it into the fridge until you need it.

Using your hands, form the mixture into 4-cm (1½-in) balls about the size of a golf ball. Continue until you have used up all the paste. Dust the balls in cornflour, shaking off any excess.

Heat the oil in a deep-fat fryer or wok to a moderate heat. Deep-fry several prawn balls at a time for about 3–5 minutes or until they are golden. Repeat the process until they are all cooked. Remove with a slotted spoon, drain on kitchen paper and serve at once.

TASTY STIR-FRIED BROAD BEANS

Stir-fried broad beans are an unusual and exotic food to Western eyes. As such, they can make delicious starter to go with drinks (on cocktail sticks) or they can be served as a simple vegetarian first course. They are, of course, most delicious when they are as fresh as can be, but they are also quite acceptable in frozen form. Here they are simply stir-fried in the wok, the various seasonings giving the beans a richness of taste.

SERVES 4

900 g (2 lb) fresh broad beans (unshelled) or
   350 g (12 oz) frozen broad beans
1 tablespoon groundnut oil
1 teaspoon salt
¼ teaspoon freshly ground black pepper
1 teaspoon sugar
2 teaspoons water or *Vegetable Stock (see p.60)*
1 tablespoon Shaoxing rice wine or dry sherry
1 teaspoon seasame oil

If you are using fresh broad beans, shell them and blanch them for 2 minutes in boiling salted water. Drain them thoroughly and refresh them in cold water. When cool, slip off the skins. If you are using the frozen beans, simply thaw them.

Heat a wok or large frying-pan over high heat until it is hot. Add the oil and, when it is very hot and slightly smoking, add the salt, pepper and broad beans. Stir-fry for 1 minute. Then add the sugar, water or stock, and Shaoxing rice wine or dry sherry and continue to stir-fry over high heat for 2 minutes. Finally, stir in the sesame oil, give the mixture two turns and serve at once.

Alternatively, you can allow the dish to cool and serve it at room temperature.

PARCHMENT PAPER FISH

This delightful appetizer is as delicious as it is cleverly contrived: a thin slice of fish is sandwiched between delicate, flavourful ingredients, then wrapped in greaseproof paper and finally deep-fried. As the package cooks, the mixture steams and the flavours marry, the happy result being a uniquely tasty starter.

In the preparation, the package must be wrapped carefully so the oil does not seep in. Although this recipe takes a little more work than others, the outcome is well worth the effort.

SERVES 8 AS A STARTER

250 g (9 oz) firm white boneless fish fillet,
    such as cod, sea bass or halibut, skinned

FOR THE MARINADE

1 tablespoon Shaoxing rice wine or dry
    sherry
1 teaspoon sesame oil
½ teaspoon salt
¼ teaspoon freshly ground black pepper

3 tablespoons finely chopped spring onions
3 tablespoons finely shredded fresh root
    ginger
25 g (1 oz) Parma ham, finely chopped
1.2 litres (2 pints) groundnut oil

Cut the fish into 4-cm x 5-mm (1½ x ¼-in) pieces and combine it with the Shaoxing rice wine or dry sherry, sesame oil, salt and pepper in a glass bowl. Let it marinate in the fridge for at least 1 hour.

Cut 30 pieces of greaseproof paper, each 15 cm (6 in) square. Place one square of greaseproof with a corner towards you and fold the tip in slightly. Put in the centre of the square the following: a piece of fish, a bit of spring onion, 2 shreds of ginger and a bit of ham. Bring the first corner over the ingredients, then fold in the two sides. Now fold the entire package in half, leaving a flap at the furthest corner from you. Finally tuck this flap in to secure the package. Repeat until all the packages have been filled.

Heat a wok over high heat until it is hot, then add the oil. When the oil is hot and slightly smoking, add about 10 packages and deep-fry for about 3 minutes. Remove them with a slotted spoon and drain well. Deep-fry the rest of the packages in batches in the same manner. When they are completely finished, arrange them on a platter and let each of your guests unwrap their own packages.

SAVOURY STUFFED ORANGE SLICES

I like to begin a dinner party with something elegant and unusual that delights the eye and gets the conversation started. At the same time, I want something that is fairly easy to make which will allow me to spend time with my guests. These orange slices certainly fulfil that need. They are light and refreshing with a unique bite. You can assemble them at least an hour before serving.

SERVES 4-6

100 g (4 oz) minced pork
2 teaspoons light soy sauce
1 teaspoon Shaoxing rice wine or dry sherry
½ teaspoon sesame oil
4 large oranges
1 tablespoon groundnut oil
25 g (1 oz) sugar
50 g (2 oz) peanuts, roasted and crushed
½ teaspoon salt
A pinch of freshly ground black pepper
Fresh coriander leaves

Combine the pork with the soy sauce, Shaoxing rice wine or dry sherry and sesame oil.

Peel the oranges and, with a small sharp knife, slice them horizontally into 5-mm ($\frac{1}{4}$-in) thick pieces.

Heat a wok or large frying-pan over high heat until it is hot. Add the oil and, when it is very hot and slightly smoking, add the pork and stir-fry for 4 minutes or until it is cooked through. Drain any fat off the pork, then return it to the wok. Add the sugar and continue to stir-fry for 3 minutes or until the mixture begins to dry out. Then add the peanuts and continue to stir-fry for another 2 minutes. Transfer the pork mixture to a bowl, season with salt and pepper, mix well and allow the mixture to cool.

When the mixture has cooled, place a coriander leaf on each orange slice. Fill each slice with 2 teaspoons of the pork, then fold it over. Continue to fill them until you have used up all the mixture. Arrange on a serving dish.

SWEETCORN PORK FRITTERS WITH CORIANDER

Here is an engaging starter, an enticingly delicious mixture of corn and pork fried to a crispy morsel. You may partially fry them beforehand and then later plunge them into hot oil again just before serving. The pork adds richness and deep flavour to the fritters. This treat works nicely with Sweet and Sour Dipping Sauce *(see p.35).*

SERVES 4-6

450 g (1 lb) fresh sweetcorn on a cob, or 1 x 275-g/10-oz tin sweetcorn, drained

175 g (6 oz) minced pork

1 tablespoon finely chopped fresh coriander

2 tablespoons finely chopped spring onions

2 tablespoons finely chopped garlic

1 tablespoon Shaoxing rice wine or dry sherry

1 tablespoon Thai fish sauce

1 teaspoon salt

½ teaspoon freshly ground white pepper

1 teaspoon sugar

1 tablespoon plain flour

1 teaspoon baking powder

2 eggs, beaten

600 ml (1 pint) groundnut oil, for frying

FOR THE GARNISH

2 tablespoons finely chopped fresh coriander

Clean the corn and remove the kernels with a sharp knife or cleaver. You should end up with about 275 g (10 oz). If you are using tinned corn, drain it, empty the contents into a bowl and set it aside. In a blender or food processor, combine half of the corn with the pork and the rest of the ingredients, except the oil, and purée. Pour this mixture into a bowl and mix in the rest of the corn.

Heat a wok or large frying-pan over high heat until it is hot. Add the oil, and when it is very hot and slightly smoking, spoon a ladle full of mixture into the wok. Continue to spoon ladle-sized fritters into the wok until it is full. Turn the heat to low and cook until they are brown. Turn the fritters over and fry on the other side. Remove them with a slotted spoon and drain on kitchen paper. Continue to fry until all the mixture has been used. Arrange the fritters on a warm platter, garnish with the coriander and serve at once.

CRISPY BEGGAR'S PURSES

T*he sweet and sour sauce can be made a day in advance, chilled and brought to room temperature before serving. Wrappers are now widely available, making this treat even easier to prepare. There are two types of wrappers. The Cantonese-style uses a smooth noodle-type dough and results in a heavier wrapper, while the Shanghai-style, which I prefer, is more like rice paper, translucent and lighter.*

SERVES 6-8

1 packet spring roll skins, preferably the
    Shanghai-type
25 g (1 oz) cloud ear fungus or Chinese
    black mushrooms
100 g (4 oz) beanthread (transparent) noodles
350 g (12 oz) raw prawns, peeled and
    coarsely minced
100 g (4 oz) minced pork
2 teaspoons salt
1 teaspoon freshly ground black pepper
4 tablespoons finely chopped spring onions
3 tablespoons finely chopped garlic
2 tablespoons finely chopped fresh coriander
2 teaspoons Shaoxing rice wine or dry sherry
1 teaspoon sugar
2 teaspoons sesame oil
1 egg white, lightly beaten

FOR THE SWEET AND SOUR DIPPING SAUCE

150 ml (5 fl oz) water
2 tablespoons sugar
3 tablespoons Chinese white rice vinegar or
    cider vinegar
3 tablespoons tomato purée or tomato ketchup
1 teaspoon salt
½ teaspoon freshly ground white pepper
1 teaspoon cornflour mixed with 2
    teaspoons water
2 teaspoons chilli flakes or powder

8 spring onions, green parts only, blanched
    or microwaved on full power for 15 seconds
600 ml (1 pint) groundnut or vegetable oil
    for deep-frying

If frozen, thaw the spring roll skins thoroughly. Soak the fungus or mushrooms in warm water for 20 minutes. If using the fungus, finely shred, cutting off and discarding any hard ends. If using the Chinese mushrooms, squeeze out the excess liquid. Remove and discard the stems and finely chop the caps. Soak the noodles in a large bowl of warm water for 15 minutes. When soft, drain and discard the water. Cut into 7.5-cm (3-in) lengths.

Put the prawns and pork in a large bowl, add salt and pepper and mix well. Then add the rest of the ingredients, noodles and fungus or mushrooms and stir them well into the prawn and pork mixture. Wrap the bowl with cling film and chill it for at least 20 minutes.

Place all the ingredients for the sweet and sour sauce, except the cornflour mixture and chilli in a pan. Bring to the boil, stir in the cornflour mixture and cook for 1 minute. Stir in the chilli flakes. Allow to cool and set aside.

When you are ready to stuff the wontons, put 2 tablespoons of the filling in the centre of each spring roll skin. Dampen the edges with a little water and bring up the sides of the skin around the filling. Pinch edges together at the top so the dumpling looks like a small, filled bag. Tie with a spring onion. Continue, to use up all the filling.

Heat a wok over high heat. Add the oil and, when it is moderately hot, add a handful of dumplings and deep-fry for 3 minutes until golden and crispy. If the oil get too hot, turn it down slightly. Drain on kitchen paper and fry the remaining dumplings. Serve immediately with the sweet and sour sauce.

VEGETARIAN CRISPY BEGGAR'S PURSES

I was invited to cook at John Cleese's final cast party for his film Fierce Creatures. *He requested a vegetarian treat, so I adapted my* Crispy Beggar's Purses *into something fiery and fierce, but without any creatures!*

SERVES 6-8

1 packet spring roll skins, preferably
  Shanghai-type

25 g (1 oz) cloud ear fungus or Chinese
  black mushrooms

100 g (4 oz) beanthread (transparent) noodles

100 g (4 oz) carrots, coarsely grated

100 g (4 oz) mangetout, finely shredded

100 g (4 oz) celery, coarsely chopped

50 g (2 oz) fresh red chillies, seeded and
  finely shredded

2 teaspoons salt

1 teaspoon freshly ground black pepper

4 tablespoons spring onions, finely chopped

1 tablespoon fresh ginger, finely chopped

1 tablespoon garlic, finely chopped

3 tablespoons fresh coriander, finely chopped

1 teaspoon Shaoxing rice wine or dry sherry

1 teaspoon sugar

1 teaspoon sesame oil

8 spring onions, green parts only, blanched

SWEET AND SOUR DIPPING SAUCE

150 ml (5 fl oz) water

2 tablespoons sugar

3 tablespoons Chinese white rice vinegar or
  cider vinegar

3 tablespoons tomato purée or tomato ketchup

1 teaspoon salt

½ teaspoon freshly ground white pepper

1 teaspoon cornflour with 2 teaspoons water

1 teaspoon chilli flakes or powder

½ teaspoon chilli oil

600 ml (1 pint) groundnut or vegetable oil,
  for deep-frying

If frozen, thaw the spring roll skins throughly. Soak the fungus or mushrooms in warm water for 20 minutes. If using the fungus, finely shred, cutting off and discarding any hard ends. If using the Chinese mushrooms, squeeze out the excess liquid. Remove and discard the stems and finely chop the caps. Soak the noodles in a large bowl of warm water for 15 minutes. When soft, drain and discard the water. Cut into 7.5-cm (3-in) lengths.

In a large bowl, combine the carrots, mangetout, celery and chillies, add the salt and pepper and mix well. Add the rest of the ingredients, noodles and fungus or mushrooms (except the spring onions) and stir them to mix well. Wrap the bowl with clingfilm and chill for at least 20 minutes.

Place all the ingredients for the sweet and sour sauce, except the cornflour mixture, chilli and chilli oil in a pan. Bring to the boil, stir in the cornflour mixture and cook for 1 minute. Stir in the chilli flakes and oil. Cool and set aside.

When you are ready to stuff the wontons, put 2 tablespoons of the filling in the centre of each spring roll skin. Bring up the sides of the skin around the filling. Pinch the edges together at the top so the dumpling looks like a small filled bag. Tie with a spring onion. Continue until you have used up all the filling.

Heat a wok or large frying-pan over high heat. Add the oil and when it is moderately hot, add a handful of dumplings and deep-fry for 3 minutes, until golden and crispy. If the oil gets too hot turn it down slightly. Drain them well on kitchen paper. Continue to fry the dumplings until you have finished with all of them. Serve them immediately with the sweet and sour sauce.

CRACKLING RICE CRISPS WITH DIPPING SAUCE

I was delighted to discover how the Thais use fried bits of dried rice as a starter. They simply fry the dried rice in the wok until it is toasty and crackling and then serve it like crisps along with a savoury dip. This is a simple dish to make and is an ideal treat when entertaining because the rice cake can be made days ahead. However, it should be fried at the last minute.

SERVES 4-6

FOR THE RICE CAKE

225 g (8 oz) long-grain white rice
600 ml (1 pint) water
2 teaspoons groundnut oil
1.2 litres (2 pints) groundnut oil

FOR THE DIPPING SAUCE

1½ tablespoons groundnut oil
6 tablespoons finely sliced shallots
3 tablespoons coarsely chopped garlic
1 tablespoon chilli bean sauce
1 teaspoon dried chilli powder or flakes
2 teaspoons sugar
3 tablespoons lime juice
2 tablespoons Thai fish sauce
2 tablespoons coconut milk
1 tablespoon finely chopped fresh coriander

NOTE

The oil used for deep-frying the rice cake can be saved and re-used once it has cooled. Filter it through coffee filter papers before storing it.

Wash the rice and put it in a 23-cm (9-in) wide, heavy pan with the water. Bring to the boil then turn the heat down as low as possible, cover the pan and let the rice cook for about 45 minutes. The rice should form a heavy crust on the bottom. Remove all the loose rice, leaving the heavy crust. The loose rice can be used for making any of the fried rice dishes in the Rice, Noodles and Pasta chapter (see p.185).

Drizzle the 2 teaspoons of oil evenly over the top of the crust and let it cook over a very low heat for 5 minutes. The crust should lift off easily at this point. If it is still sticky, add another teaspoon of oil and continue to cook until it comes loose. Place crust on a plate and set aside. Once cooked, it can be left at room temperature for several days. Don't cover it, or moisture will form and make the cake mouldy. Let the rice cake dry out before using.

Heat a wok over high heat until hot. Add the oil and, when it's very hot and slightly smoking, add the shallots and garlic. Stir-fry for 30 seconds. Turn the heat down and stir-fry until golden brown. Combine the garlic and shallots with the rest of the sauce ingredients and purée in a blender. Set aside.

Just before serving, heat a wok over high heat until it's hot. Add the 1.2 litres (2 pints) of oil and, when very hot and slightly smoking, drop in a small piece of the dried rice cake to test the heat. It should bubble and immediately come to the top. Now deep-fry pieces of rice cake for about 1-2 minutes until they puff up and brown slightly. Remove immediately with a slotted spoon and drain on kitchen paper. Quickly transfer the pieces of hot rice cake to a platter and serve immediately with the dipping sauce.

SOUPS

Soups are easily made in the wok. Heat is distributed evenly throughout the wok while its large, open surface allows for quick skimming. Some of the soup recipes call for a brisk stir-frying of the ingredients beforehand. This will give the ensemble a wonderful, smoky flavour that adds depth to the soup. The Spicy Soup with Spring Onions, *for example, benefits greatly when the ingredients are stir-fried first.*

Other hearty soups, like the Succulent Meatball Noodle Soup, *demonstrate the ability of the wok to make a delicious, wholesome one-dish meal. The wok's rapid heating capability helps ease the pressures of today's lifestyle, when time is at such a premium.*

With the proper stocks at hand, the wok is clearly an asset in the final preparation of this refreshing food. Everybody enjoys a good soup.

SPICY SOUP WITH SPRING ONIONS

The chefs at the Hyatt Regency in Adelaide, Australia, developed this inspired soup as a daily special. I found it simple but classic in its clarity and subtle taste. They combined modest ingredients – vegetables, seasonings, stock – into a most satisfying treat.

The vegetables are first stir-fried in the wok. This imparts a lovely smoky flavour to the dish. chicken or vegetable stock is then added and, as with any soup, a good stock is essential to its final flavour. The Chinese leaves bring a gentle sweetness.

To make a more substantial one-dish meal of this soup, just add cooked rice or wheat noodles or serve it with rice. The soup can thus be a perfect opener for any meal, or it may be a meal in itself. Use vegetable stock for a vegetarian version.

SERVES 4

225 g (8 oz) Chinese leaves (Peking cabbage)

100 g (4 oz) button mushrooms

1 tablespoon groundnut oil

1 teaspoooon salt

¼ teaspoon freshly ground black pepper

1 tablespoon light soy sauce

1.2 litres (2 pints) *Chicken Stock (see p.56)* or *Vegetable Stock (see p.60)*

2 fresh red or green chillies, seeded and finely shredded

4 whole spring onions, finely shredded

5 sprigs of fresh coriander

Cut the Chinese leaves into fine shreds. Finely slice the mushrooms.

Heat a wok or large frying-pan over high heat until it is hot. Add the oil and, when it is very hot and slightly smoking, add the Chinese leaves and stir-fry for 1 minute. Then add the mushrooms, salt, pepper and soy sauce and continue to stir-fry for 2 minutes. Add the stock, turn the heat to low, cover and cook for 10 minutes or until the cabbage is very tender.

Stir in the chillies and spring onions and continue to simmer for 2 minutes. Turn off the heat and stir in the coriander sprigs.

Ladle into a large soup tureen and serve immediately.

REFRESHING CUCUMBER SOUP

In the West, cucumber is most often eaten raw or in salads. In Chinese cuisine, however, cucumbers enjoy higher status. Chinese chefs strive to maintain the cool crispness and varied green colours of this prosaic food. We love to eat it stir-fried, braised, pickled and even stuffed.

When cucumber is used in soup, as in this recipe, it keeps its refreshing cool crunch, which makes a nice contrast to the hot soup. The versatility of the wok is such that it can be used even to make this soup. Once the stock is made, the rest is quickly assembled and on the table in a matter of minutes. It is a sparkling starter for any meal and quite economical as well. The beef in this version of the soup adds richness. If you prefer a delicious vegetarian alternative, however, simply omit the beef and use vegetable stock.

SERVES 4

450 g (1 lb) cucumbers

2 teaspoons salt

100 g (4 oz) lean minced beef

1 teaspoon light soy sauce

1 teaspoon Shaoxing rice wine or dry
  sherry

½ teaspoon sesame oil

1 teaspoon cornflour

¼ teaspoon freshly ground black pepper

1.2 litres (2 pints) *Chicken Stock (see p.56)* or
  Vegetable Stock (see p.60)

2 tablespoons light soy sauce

1 whole spring onion, finely shredded

1 teaspoon sugar

1 teaspoon sesame oil

Cut the unpeeled cucumbers into 2.5-cm (1-in) slices, sprinkle with salt and put them into a colander to drain for 20 minutes. Squeeze the cucumber slices in a linen tea towel to remove any excess moisture and liquid. Blot them dry with kitchen paper.

Combine the beef with the soy sauce, Shaoxing rice wine or dry sherry, sesame oil, cornflour and black pepper.

Heat the stock in a wok, add the beef and stir to break up any lumps. Simmer for 3 minutes. Then stir in the soy sauce, spring onion, sugar and sesame oil. Turn off the heat and stir in the cucumber slices and allow them to sit in the hot stock for 2 minutes.

Ladle into a large soup tureen and serve immediately.

CHINESE-STYLE FISH SOUP

Chinese fish soups are simple affairs that rely on using the freshest possible fish, quickly cooked in a way that enhances its taste.

Easily made in the wok, this soup is also versatile: you can supplement the fish and the broth with a wide variety of complementary ingredients and seasonings. Adding left-overs can turn this soup into a substantial one-dish meal. I add a bit of chilli oil and a touch of vinegar to give the soup real zest.

SERVES 2-4

450 g (1 lb) fresh, firm white fish fillets, such as cod, sea bass or halibut

1 egg white

2 teaspoons salt

1 teaspoon freshly ground white pepper

1 teaspoon sesame oil

2 teaspoons cornflour

1.2 litres (2 pints) *Chicken Stock (see p.56),* *Vegetable Stock (see p.60)* or fish stock

2 tablespoons light soy sauce

2 teaspoons Shaoxing rice wine or dry sherry

2 teaspoons finely shredded fresh root ginger

2 tablespoons finely chopped spring onions

1 teaspoon chilli oil

2 teaspoons black or red rice vinegar

FOR THE GARNISH

1 tablespoon finely chopped fresh coriander

Remove the skin from the fish fillets and then cut them into small pieces, about 2.5cm (1 in) square. Combine the fish, egg white, salt, pepper, sesame oil and cornflour and mix well. Refrigerate this for at least 20 minutes.

Pour the stock into a wok and bring it to a simmer. Add the soy sauce, Shaoxing rice wine or dry sherry, ginger and spring onions and simmer for 30 seconds. Then add the fish and stir gently for 1 minute. As soon as the fish turns white, immediately turn off the heat. Add the chilli oil and vinegar. Ladle the soup into individual bowls or a soup tureen, garnish with the fresh coriander and serve immediately.

VIETNAMESE-STYLE NOODLE SOUP

When I travel, good food is always foremost on my agenda. As Napoleon said, 'An army marches on its stomach'.

When I can't spare the time for a whole meal, I look for Asian-style fast food. I am very rarely disappointed when I find a good Vietnamese restaurant and order home-style noodle dishes flavoured with lemon grass, ginger and garlic.

Here is tasty soup with my own embellishments. It is a delicious, quick and easy, one-dish meal that is ideal for today's hectic and hurried lifestyle. This fragrant dish is at once pleasing and nutritious. The rice noodles give the soup a delicate and light touch. If they are unavailable, dried egg noodles may be substituted. Feel free to add your own touches. Once the broth is made, the rest is assembled very quickly.

SERVES 2-4

50 g (2 oz) thin rice noodles

225 g (8 oz) Chinese leaves (Peking cabbage)

100 g (4 oz) boneless, skinless chicken breasts

1 stalk fresh lemon grass

1 tablespoon groundnut oil

2 garlic cloves, lightly crushed

2 thin slices of fresh root ginger

1 fresh red or green chilli, seeded and finely shredded

1 teaspooon salt

¼ teaspoon freshly ground black pepper

1 tablespoon light soy sauce

1.2 litres (2 pints) *Chicken Stock (see p.56)* or *Vegetable Stock (see p.60)*

4 whole spring onions, finely shredded

FOR THE SAUCE

4 tablespoons Thai fish sauce

1 teaspoon dried chilli powder or flakes

1 tablespoon finely chopped garlic

1 tablespoon lime juice

4 tablespoons water

1 tablespoon sugar

FOR THE GARNISH

Handful of fresh sprigs of coriander

Soak the rice noodles in a bowl of warm water for 25 minutes then drain them in a colander or sieve. (If you are using dried egg noodles, cook them for 3-5 minutes in boiling water, plunge them in cold water, drain them thoroughly and toss them in groundnut oil.) Set them aside.

Combine all the sauce ingredients in a blender, mixing them thoroughly. Let the mixture sit at least 10 minutes before using.

Cut the Chinese leaves into fine shreds, finely slicing them widthways. Then, finely shred the chicken. Peel the lemon grass stalk to reveal the tender, whitish centre and crush it with the flat of a knife. Then cut it into 7.5-cm (3-in) pieces.

Heat a wok or large frying-pan over high heat until it is hot. Add the oil and, when it is very hot and slightly smoking, add the Chinese leaves and stir-fry for 1 minute. Then add the lemon grass, garlic, ginger, chilli, salt, pepper and soy sauce and continue to stir-fry for 2 minutes. Add the stock, turn the heat to low, cover and cook for 5 minutes. Add the noodles and continue to cook for another 5 minutes or until the leaves are very tender.

Stir in the spring onions and chicken and continue to simmer for 2 minutes. Turn off the heat and stir in the coriander. Stir in the sauce, ladle into a large soup tureen and serve immediately.

SUCCULENT MEATBALL NOODLE SOUP

This is a substantial one-dish meal my mother would serve on the cold winter nights of my childhood in Chicago.

Once the meatballs are made, the rest is easily assembled. You can, of course, add any vegetable in season to supplement the soup. This is characteristic Chinese family cooking: simple, but solid, nutritious and tasty.

SERVES 4

50 g (2 oz) beanthread (transparent) noodles

FOR THE MEATBALLS

275 g (10 oz) fresh water chestnuts or
   175 g (6 oz) tinned water chestnuts
225 g (8 oz) minced pork
½ egg white
2 tablespoons cold water
1 tablespoon light soy sauce
2 teaspoons dark soy sauce
1 tablespoon Shaoxing rice wine or dry
   sherry
2 teaspoons sesame oil
2 teaspoons sugar
1 teaspoon salt
¼ teaspoon freshly ground black pepper
1 teaspoon cornflour
1.2 litres (2 pints) *Chicken Stock (see p.56)* or
   Vegetable Stock (see p.60)
1½ tablespoons light soy sauce
2 teaspoons sesame oil

Soak the noodles in warm water for 15 minutes. Drain well.

If you are using fresh water chestnuts, peel them and coarsely chop them. If you are using tinned ones, rinse them well and coarsely chop them. Mix the pork with the egg white and cold water by hand. The mixture should be light and fluffy. Do not use a blender as it would make the mixture too dense. Then add the water chestnuts, soy sauces, Shaoxing rice wine or dry sherry, sesame oil, sugar, salt, pepper and cornflour and mix thoroughly. Divide the mixture into 12 equal parts and roll each part into a meatball.

Heat a wok until it is hot. Add the stock, turn the heat down to a simmer, add the meatballs and stir slowly. Simmer gently for about 5 minutes, then add the noodles and soy sauce and continue to cook for another 5 minutes. Now add the sesame oil and give the soup several good stirs. Ladle the soup into a tureen and serve at once.

CREAMY CORN AND CRAB SOUP

*T*his *is a popular East-West dish that has found its way on to Chinese restaurant menus all over the world. I suspect that it was invented by Chinese-American Cantonese cooks, who then transported it back to Hong Kong and southern China. It eventually went to the United Kingdom, as well as Australia where it continues to be a standard item on many menus. Rather than use tinned creamed corn, I prefer to make it with fresh corn and to get the creaminess from the starch of the corn. It is a bit thinner than the version you find in Chinese restaurants, but I think, better-tasting. Use the best, freshest crabmeat you can find for this rather lusty dish.*

SERVES 4

450 g (1 lb) fresh sweetcorn on a cob, or 1 x 275-g (10-oz) tin plain sweetcorn

1.2 litres (2 pints) *Chicken Stock (see p. 56)*

2 tablespoons finely chopped spring onions

1 teaspoon finely chopped fresh root ginger

1 tablespoon Shaoxing rice wine or dry sherry

1 tablespoon light soy sauce

1 teaspoon salt

¼ teaspoon freshly ground white pepper

1 teaspoon sugar

2 teaspoons cornflour blended with 2 teaspoons water

225 g (8 oz) fresh crabmeat

1 egg

1 teaspoon sesame oil

½ teaspoon salt

FOR THE GARNISH

2 tablespoons finely chopped fresh coriander

Clean the corn and remove the kernels with a sharp knife or cleaver. You should end up with about 275 g (10 oz). If you are using tinned corn, empty the contents into a bowl and set it aside.

In a blender, combine half of the chicken stock with the corn and purée. Pour this mixture into the wok with the remaining stock and bring the soup to a simmer. Simmer for 10 minutes, uncovered, then add the spring onions, ginger, Shaoxing rice wine or dry sherry, soy sauce, salt, pepper and sugar. Now add the cornflour mixture. Bring it back to the boil, then lower the heat and simmer for another 5 minutes. Add the crabmeat to the soup and stir slowly to mix well.

In a small bowl, combine the egg with the sesame oil and salt. Slowly pour the egg, salt and sesame oil mixture in a steady stream into the wok, stirring all the time, pulling the strands slowly as they cook. Ladle the soup into a tureen, garnish with coriander and serve.

WINTER MELON SOUP

*W*inter melon, despite the name, grows in tropical climates and is harvested in the summer. The unripe melons are green in colour, but the mature melons develop a blotchy white skin that appears to be a light dusting of snow, hence the name 'winter melon'. Moreover, the melon keeps well in cold storage (as in a potato cellar) and is most often eaten in the winter months, other melons having long since been consumed.

Winter melon can grow to weigh as much as 50 kg (110 lb). These giants are usually reserved for elaborate banquets, at which they are carved and served whole as an organic tureen filled with broth and other ingredients. Such huge tureens are called 'winter melon ponds'. The melon is steamed whole and the soup is scooped out with some of the tender flesh of the melon. It has a subtle soft taste that complements the seasonings in the broth.

The version I remember the most is that made by my mother. Chinese grocers will cut the melons into variously sized pieces and my mother would buy a small piece and simply simmer it in broth and toss in whatever appropriate meats or ingredients she had left in the fridge. Her family-style winter melon soup was just as delicious as any 'winter melon pond' soup.

If you are unable to obtain winter melon, you can easily substitute courgettes. This is a delicious substantial soup that is almost a meal in itself. It also re-heats well.

SERVES 4-6

450 g (1 lb) Chinese winter melon or
   courgettes
50 g (2 oz) Chinese dried mushrooms
175 g (6 oz) boneless, skinless chicken
   breasts
2 teaspoons egg white, beaten
1 teaspoon cornflour
¼ teaspoon salt
1.2 litres (2 pints) *Chicken Stock (see p.56)* or
   Vegetable Stock (see p.60)
100 g (4 oz) frozen peas
175 g (6 oz) Parma ham, finely shredded
2 tablespoons finely chopped spring onions
1 teaspoon finely chopped fresh root ginger
2 teaspoons light soy sauce

Peel off the hard skin of the winter melon and scoop out all the soft, pulpy interior together with any seeds. Cut the winter melon or courgettes into 2.5-cm (1-in) pieces. Bring a large pan of salted water to the boil, blanch the melon or courgettes for 5 minutes and drain.

Soak the mushrooms in warm water for 20 minutes. Then drain them and squeeze out the excess liquid. Remove and discard the stems and cut the caps into 2.5-cm (1-in) pieces.

Cut the chicken into 2.5-cm (1-in) pieces. Combine them with the egg white, cornflour and salt and mix well. Chill for 20 minutes.

Bring a medium-sized pan of water to a boil then remove it from the heat and immediately add the chicken pieces, stirring vigorously to keep them from sticking. When the chicken turns white (about 2 minutes), quickly drain it.

Bring the stock to a simmer in a wok, add the blanched winter melon or courgettes and mushrooms and simmer for 15 minutes or until the melon or courgettes are soft. Then add the peas, ham, spring onions, ginger, soy sauce and chicken. Simmer for another 5 minutes, then serve at once.

CHICKEN STOCK

Chicken stock is an all-purpose base for soups and sauces. Its chief ingredient is inexpensive, it is light and delicious and it marries well with other foods, enhancing and sustaining them. Small wonder, then that from the Imperial kitchens to the most humble food stalls, good stock is a basic ingredient. The usual Chinese chicken stock is precisely that: the essence of chicken, with complements of ginger and spring onions often added. Combined with the condiments that give Chinese food its distinctive flavour, good stock captures the essential taste of China.

Many of the most famous recipes in the Chinese repertoire require stock. There are two basic types. One is a clear stock made from chicken bones and meat; the other is a richer stock that uses ham and pork bones as well. Different recipes call for one or other of these stocks but both types make a solid base for soups and sauces.

During the Qing dynasty, the last Imperial dynasty (1644-1911), Chinese cuisine reached its peak of classic perfection. One of the most highly prized dishes featured in the Imperial banquets was a bowl of clear soup, a consommé of chicken stock, much appreciated for its subtle, light, flavourful elegance.

This serves as a reminder that stock can also be used as a clear soup. I find that the richer stocks made with ham or pork bones are heavier and not quite suited to my tastes. The following simple recipe for stock therefore reflects what I believe works best for any Chinese dish.

There are commercially prepared tinned or cubed (dried) stocks but many of them are of inferior quality, being either too salty or containing additives and colourings that adversely affect your health as well as the natural taste of good foods. Stock does take time to prepare but it is easy to make your own — and when home-made, it is the best. I prefer to make large quantities of it at a time and freeze it. Once you have a supply of stock available you will be able to prepare any number of soups or sauces very quickly. Here are several important points to keep in mind when making stock:

- good stock requires meat to give it richness and flavour, so it is necessary to use at least some chicken meat, if not a whole bird
- the stock should never boil — if it does, it will be undesirably cloudy and the fat will be incorporated into the liquid; flavours and digestibility come with a clear stock
- use a tall, heavy-based pan so the liquid covers all the solids and evaporation is slow
- simmer slowly and skim the stock regularly — be patient and you will reap the rewards each time you prepare a Chinese dish
- strain the finished stock well through several layers of muslin or a fine mesh sieve.
- let the stock cool completely, chill and remove any fat before freezing it.

The classic Chinese method for ensuring a clear stock is to blanch the meat and bones before simmering. I find this unnecessary. My method of careful skimming achieves the same result with far less work.

Remember to save all your uncooked chicken bones and carcasses for stock. They can be frozen until you are ready to make it. You can halve the quantities given in the recipes if it makes too much for your needs.

MAKES ABOUT 3.4 LITRES (6 PINTS)

2 kg (4½ lb) uncooked chicken bones, such
   as backs, feet, wings, etc.
750 g (1½ lb) chicken pieces, such as wings,
   thighs, drumsticks, etc.
4 litres (7 pints) cold water
6 slices fresh root ginger
9 spring onions
6 whole garlic cloves, unpeeled
2 teaspoons salt
1 teaspoon whole black peppercorns

Put the chicken bones and chicken pieces into a very large pan. (The bones can be put in either frozen or defrosted.) Cover them with the cold water and bring it to a simmer. Meanwhile cut the ginger into diagonal slices, 5 x 1 cm (2 x ½ in). Remove the green tops of the spring onions. Lightly crush the garlic cloves, leaving the skins on.

Using a large, flat spoon, skim off the scum as it rises from the bones. Watch the heat as the stock should never boil. Keep skimming until the stock looks clear. This can take from 20-40 minutes. Do not stir or disturb the stock.

Now turn the heat down to a low simmer. Add the ginger, spring onions, garlic cloves, salt and peppercorns. Simmer the stock on a very low heat for 2-4 hours, skimming any fat off the top at least twice during this time. The stock should be rich and full-bodied which is why it needs to be simmered for such a long time. This way the stock (and any dishes you make with it) will have plenty of flavour.

Strain the stock through several layers of dampened muslin or through a very fine meshed sieve, then let it cool thoroughly. Remove any fat which has risen to the top. It is now ready to be used or transferred to containers and frozen for future use.

DOUBLE-STEAMED CHINESE CABBAGE SOUP

Yet another wok-friendly soup, the unusual technique for making this soup is not difficult to master. Double-steaming is a process in which rich ingredients are steamed for hours in a covered casserole filled with soup. This diffuses and marries all the flavours of the different ingredients. It is a technique often used for making the classic Shark's Fin and Bird's Nest Soups.

The result is a distinctive consommé, clear and rich but also light. Here the delicate sweet flavour of the cabbage plays gently with the subtle taste of the ham. This elegant soup is a refreshing starter for any dinner party. It can be made in advance and frozen, as it re-heats well.

SERVES 4

450 g (1 lb) **Chinese leaves (Peking cabbage)**
25 g (1 oz) **Chinese dried mushrooms**
50 g (2 oz) **Parma ham or lean smoked bacon**
4 slices **fresh root ginger**
1.2 litres (2 pints) *Chicken Stock (see p.56)*
4 whole **spring onions**
2 tablespoons **Shaoxing rice wine or dry sherry**
½ teaspoon **salt**
¼ teaspoon **freshly ground white pepper**
2 teaspoons **sesame oil**

Using a sharp, heavy knife or cleaver, cut the Chinese leaves in half lengthways, then into 5-cm (2-in) segments. Soak the mushrooms in warm water for 20 minutes. Drain them and squeeze out the excess liquid. Remove and discard the stems and finely shred the caps into thin strips. Cut the Parma ham or bacon into very fine shreds and cut the ginger into slices 5 cm x 5 mm (2 x ¼ in).

Next set up a steamer or put a rack into a wok or deep pan and fill it with 5 cm (2 in) of water. Bring the water to the boil.

Meanwhile, bring the stock to the boil in another large pan and then pour it into a heat-proof glass or china casserole. Add the Chinese leaves, ham, ginger, spring onions, Shaoxing rice wine or dry sherry, salt, pepper and sesame oil to the casserole and cover it with a lid or foil. Put the casserole on the rack and cover the wok or deep pan tightly with a lid or foil. You now have a casserole within a steamer, hence the term 'double-steaming'. Turn the heat down and steam gently for 1½ hours. Replenish the hot water from time to time. An alternative method is simply to simmer the soup very slowly in a conventional pan, but the resulting taste will be quite different.

When the soup is cooked, place the contents into a large soup tureen. The soup can be served immediately or cooled and stored in the fridge or freezer to be re-heated when required.

VEGETABLE STOCK

Vegetable stock can be tasty and light. Stir-frying vegetables in the wok with oil before simmering helps to impart a wonderful smoky flavour to the stock. Use the recipe as it is or, by all means, experiment and suit your own taste. You can cut the quantities in half if the recipe makes too much for your needs.

MAKES ABOUT 4.5 LITRES (8 PINTS)

25 g (1 oz) Chinese dried mushrooms
900 g (2 lb) carrots
900 g (2 lb) Chinese leaves (Peking cabbage)
4 celery sticks
900 g (2 lb) onions
4 leeks
225 g (8 oz) shallots
2 tablespoons groundnut oil
6 spring onions
6 slices fresh root ginger
8 garlic cloves, crushed
1 tablespoon whole black peppercorns
1 tablespoon whole Szechuan peppercorns
4 bay leaves
2 tablespoons salt
2 tablespoons Shoaxing rice wine or dry
  sherry
4.5 litres (8 pints) water
3 tablespoons light soy sauce

Soak the dried mushrooms in warm water for 20 minutes, drain them, squeeze out any excess liquid and coarsely chop the caps and stems. Strain and reserve the mushroom liquid. Coarsely chop the carrots, Chinese leaves, celery and onions. Wash, cut and discard the green part of the leeks and coarsely chop the white portion. Peel the shallots but leave them whole.

Heat a large pan or wok over a moderate heat. Add the oil, spring onions, ginger, garlic and shallots and stir-fry for 1 minute. Then add the carrots, celery, leeks and onions and continue to cook for 5 minutes. Put all the vegetables and the rest of the ingredients into a very large pan. Cover them with the reserved mushroom liquid and cold water and bring it to a simmer. Using a large, flat spoon, skim off the foam as it rises to the top, this will take about 5 minutes. Bring the stock to a boil. Now turn the heat down to a moderate simmer and cook for about 2 hours.

Strain the stock through a large colander and then through a very fine-meshed sieve, and then let it cool thoroughly. It is now ready to be used or transferred to containers and frozen for future use.

SIZZLING RICE SOUP

There are few ingredients which complement and enhance the natural flavour of a good home-made rich chicken stock better than a crispy rice crust. When this simple dish comes to the dining table and the hot toasty crust meets the liquid soup, it all sizzles and steams dramatically. You need first to make the rice cake as directed for Crackling Rice Crisps with Dipping Sauce on p. 45. Do not use 'easy-cook' rice for this dish because it does not have enough starch to form a crust; use long-grain white rice. If you use vegetable stock, you can turn this soup into a spectacular vegetarian treat.

SERVES 4-6

1 quantity rice cake *(see p.45)*
1.2 litres (2 pints) groundnut oil

FOR THE SOUP

25 g (1 oz) Chinese dried black mushrooms
225 g (8 oz) firm beancurd
1.2 litres (2 pints) *Chicken Stock (see p.56)* or
　Vegetable Stock (see p.60)
100 g (4 oz) frozen peas
3 tablespoons finely shredded spring onions
1½ tablespoons light soy sauce
½ teaspoon salt
¼ teaspoon freshly ground white pepper

FOR THE GARNISH

1 tablespoon finely chopped spring onions,
　green tops only
2 teaspoons sesame oil

After making the rice cake (as directed on p. 45), soak the mushrooms in warm water for 20 minutes. Then drain them and squeeze out the excess liquid. Remove and discard the stems and finely shred the caps into thin strips. Rinse the beancurd well in cold water and blot dry with kitchen paper. Cut the beancurd into 1-cm (½-in) pieces.

Bring the stock to a simmer in a large pan, add the mushrooms and beancurd and simmer gently for 10 minutes. Then add the peas, spring onions, soy sauce, salt and pepper. Allow to simmer for another 5 minutes. Stir in the garnishing spring onions and sesame oil and ladle the soup into a large tureen.

Now you are ready to fry the rice cake. Heat a wok or deep-fryer until it is hot. Add the 1.2 litres (2 pints) of oil and, when it is very hot and slightly smoking, drop in a small piece of the dried rice cake to test the heat. It should bubble all over and immediately come up to the surface. Now deep-fry the pieces of rice cake for about 1-2 minutes until they puff up and brown slightly. Remove them immediately with a slotted spoon and drain on a plate lined with kitchen paper. Then quickly transfer the pieces of hot rice cakes to a warm platter and drop the cakes into the soup. They should sizzle dramatically. Once you are skilled at preparing this dish, you can attempt to perform this trick at the dinner table. (The oil used for deep-frying the rice cake can be saved and re-used once it has cooled. Filter it through coffee filter papers before storing it.)

HEARTY MEATBALL VEGETABLE SOUP

I have always loved those hearty soups which are a meal in themselves. Combined with Chinese flowering cabbage and beanthread noodles, the meatballs make this a rich and savoury soup that is perfect for a cool autumn or rainy evening. It is easy to make, once you have the stock.

   The soup can be cooled and re-heated. You can, of course, use any vegetables instead of the Chinese flowering cabbage. This soup is delicious with Chinese leaves, spinach, even cabbage. Serve it with a good bread or with rice if you have some.

SERVES 4

350 g (12 oz) Chinese greens, such as Chinese flowering cabbage or bok choy
50 g (2 oz) beanthread (transparent) noodles
1.2 litres (2 pints) *Chicken Stock (see p.56) or Vegetable Stock (see p.60)*
1 tablespoon light soy sauce
2 teaspoons Shaoxing rice wine or dry sherry
½ teaspoon salt
2 teaspoons sesame oil

FOR THE MEATBALL MIXTURE

350 g (12 oz) minced beef
1 egg white
3 tablespoons very cold water
1 teaspoon salt
1½ tablespoons light soy sauce
1 teaspoon freshly ground black pepper
1 tablespoon sesame oil
1 teaspoon finely chopped fresh ginger
3 tablespoons finely chopped fresh coriander
3 tablespoons finely chopped spring onions
1 teaspoon cornflour
2 teaspoons sugar

Cut the Chinese greens into 5-cm (2-in) pieces. Peel the stalks and cut them at a slight diagonal into 5-cm (2-in) pieces. Soak the noodles in a large bowl of warm water for 15 minutes. When soft, drain and discard the water. Cut into 7.5-cm (3-in) lengths using scissors or a knife.

Whizz the beef in a food processor for a few seconds. Slowly add the egg white and cold water and mix them for a few more seconds until they are fully incorporated into the meat. Then add the rest of the meatball ingredients and mix for about 1 minute until the meat mixture has become a light paste. Using your hands, form the mixture into about twelve 4-cm (1½-in) balls about the size of a golf ball.

Bring a large pan of water to the boil, gently drop in the meatballs and simmer for 5 minutes or until the meatballs float to the top. Remove them immediately with a slotted spoon and drain well.

In a large pan, bring the stock to a simmer, then add the beanthread noodles, soy sauce, Shaoxing rice wine or dry sherry and salt. Add the Chinese greens and simmer gently for 5 minutes. Return the meatballs to the simmering stock and cook for another 5 minutes. Add the sesame oil and give the soup several good stirs. Ladle into a soup tureen or individual bowls and serve at once.

FISH AND SHELLFISH

The wok's versatility is highlighted by the ways in which it can be used to cook fish and shellfish. The wok's range is demonstrated as it is used in a simple stir-fried dish, such as Stir-fried Fish with Black Bean Sauce, *and in the more complex preparations of* Deep-fried Salt and Pepper Oysters. *The wok can be most gentle, as it cooks the delicate* Steamed Scallops *with warm hot vapours, or as it infuses* Singaporean-style Curry Crab *with exotic spices and savoury flavours.*

But the wok can also be dramatically assertive, as in deep-frying techniques, where the wok's excellence is unbeatable. Its depth allows for proper deep-frying without using a great deal of oil. The wide surface allows for easy removal of deep-fried foods, and it is simple to adjust the heat if the wok gets too hot. In fact, you will find the wok indispensable when preparing fish and shellfish.

The recipes here are derived from the cuisines of China and South-east Asia, with a few 'East meets West' touches of my own.

LILLIAN'S BEIJING-STYLE SWEET AND SOUR FISH

illian Robyn was born in Beijing and grew up in Taipei, Taiwan. She later married an American and moved to California — a wonderful marriage of East and West. Her Chinese cultural heritage remains a vibrant part of her life, and she is an expert in Chinese cuisine.

I enjoyed this particular dish one evening in her home and I immediately set out to duplicate it. Well, not quite; her recipe calls for raw garlic and I have altered it ever so slightly by browning the garlic.

SERVES 2-4

450 g (1 lb) fresh, firm fish fillets, such as
  cod, halibut or sea bass
1 teaspoon salt
¼ teaspoon freshly ground black pepper
Potato flour or cornflour, for dusting
150 ml (5 fl oz) plus 1 tablespoon
  groundnut oil
2 tablespoons thinly sliced garlic

FOR THE SWEET AND SOUR SAUCE

3 tablespoons Chinese black vinegar or
  cider vinegar
2 tablespoons sugar
1 tablespoon light soy sauce

FOR THE GARNISH

3 tablespoons finely shredded spring onions

Pat the fish fillets dry using kitchen paper, then cut them into 5-cm (2-in) pieces. In a medium-sized bowl, combine the fish with the salt and pepper, mixing well. Coat the fish well with potato or cornflour, shaking off any excess.

To make the sauce, combine the vinegar, sugar and soy sauce in a small bowl.

Heat the wok or large frying-pan over a high heat until it is hot. Add the 150 ml (5 fl oz) of oil and, when it is very hot and slightly smoking, lower the heat and pan-fry the fish for 2 minutes or until it is browned. Turn it over and brown the other side for 2 minutes. Remove and drain on kitchen paper. You may have to do this in two batches. Place on a warm platter.

Drain all the oil from the wok, wipe clean and re-heat. When it is hot again, add the 1 tablespoon of oil and the garlic. Stir-fry for 45 seconds or until it is brown. Remove and scatter this over the fish. Now pour the vinegar mixture over the fish, garnish with the spring onions and serve at once.

AROMATIC FIVE-SPICE TROUT

Fresh trout makes an elegant centrepiece for lunch or dinner. With its clean and delicate taste and texture, it is a foundation course in any meal, a light and wholesome treat.

All that it needs is a touch of seasoning to complement its own unique flavour. Here I have dusted it with aromatic five-spice powder, the subtle flavours of which enhance the special qualities of trout.

This is an easy dish to put together; it browns quickly and perfectly in the wok.

SERVES 4

4 small trout, cleaned
2 tablespoons potato flour or cornflour
1 teaspoon salt
1 teaspoon five-spice powder
3 tablespoons groundnut oil
1 tablespoon finely chopped garlic
2 teaspoons finely chopped fresh root ginger
3 tablespoons finely chopped spring onions
1 lemon, quartered

FOR THE GARNISH

Fresh sprigs of coriander

Blot the trout dry inside and out with kitchen paper. Combine the potato flour or cornflour with the salt and five-spice powder. Dust the trout on the outside thoroughly with this mixture.

Heat a wok or large frying-pan over a high heat until it is hot. Add 2 tablespoons of the oil and, when it is very hot and slightly smoking, turn the heat down to medium and pan-fry the trout. You may have to do this in two batches, depending on the size of your wok or pan. When the fish is brown and crispy, turn it over and pan-fry the other side for about 4 minutes. When the fish is cooked, transfer it to a warm platter.

Re-heat the wok with the remaining oil. When it is hot, add the garlic, ginger and spring onions and stir-fry for 2 minutes. Pour this mixture on top of the trout, arrange the lemon wedges on the platter and garnish with coriander. Serve at once.

SPICY FISH CURRY

I have eaten this wonderful fish curry many times in Singapore and Malaysia. In those countries, surrounded as they are by water, fresh fish is a standard staple in every home and on every menu. This recipe is a simplified version of the original. Most fish have a delicate taste and texture and one must be careful in applying any seasoning or spice. I have found Madras curry paste a great convenience; it works almost as well as the time-consuming hand-made curry paste. Added to a firm white fish fillet, it makes a fragrant, savoury, delectable treat that goes perfectly with plain rice.

SERVES 2-4

450 g (1 lb) fresh boneless, skinless, firm
   white fish fillets, such as cod, halibut or
   sea bass
1 egg white
1 teaspoon salt
½ teaspoon freshly ground black pepper
2 teaspoons cornflour
600 ml (1 pint) groundnut oil or
   1 litre (1¾ pints) water
175 g (6 oz) onions, coarsely chopped
1½ tablespoons finely chopped fresh root
   ginger
1 tablespoon finely chopped garlic
3 tablespoons Madras curry paste
1 tablespoon light soy sauce
1 teaspoon salt
1 teaspoon sugar
150 ml (5 fl oz) tinned coconut milk

FOR THE GARNISH

2 tablespoons finely chopped spring onions

Cut the fish into 5-cm (2-in) pieces and then combine them with the egg white, salt, pepper and cornflour in a medium-sized bowl. Mix well and chill for 20 minutes.

Heat a wok until it is very hot, then add the oil. When the oil is very hot, remove the wok from the heat and immediately add the fish pieces, stirring vigorously to prevent them from sticking. When the fish pieces turn white (about 2 minutes), quickly drain the fish and all the oil in a stainless steel colander set in a bowl. Reserve 2 tablespoons of the oil and discard the rest.

If you choose to use water instead of oil, bring it to the boil in a pan. Remove the pan from the heat and immediately add the fish pieces, stirring vigorously to keep them from sticking. When the fish pieces turn white (about 2 minutes), quickly drain the fish in a stainless steel colander.

Re-heat the wok, add 2 tablespoons of the reserved oil (if you used the water method, add 2 tablespoons of fresh oil), and when it is hot, add the onions, ginger and garlic and stir-fry for 3 minutes. Then add the curry paste, soy sauce, salt, sugar and coconut milk. Bring the mixture to a simmer and cook for 5 minutes. Add the fish pieces and heat for 3 minutes. Garnish with the spring onions and serve at once.

SINGAPORE-STYLE OYSTER OMELETTE

first tasted this treat, not in Singapore but in London, England. A close friend of mine, Jenny Lo, took me to dinner at the Singapore Garden restaurant, near Swiss Cottage in north-west London. The experience was a revelation to me. Jenny hails from Malaysia, so she knows where Singapore-style cooking at its best is to be had in England.

This recipe is derived from the standard Singapore fish hawker's version. With such an origin, you can expect a flavourful, satisfying and easy-to-make dish — and so it is. Oysters are mild, eggs are mild, so they need a little spice and seasonings; the ones in the Singapore Garden's recipe work perfectly. The use of sweet potato flour gives the omelette a delightful, slightly chewy texture and a quite unusual flavour. The flour may be obtained at a Chinese grocers.

Serve this omelette as a main course or as an entrée for a special meal.

SERVES 4

1 dozen small oysters, shelled

100 g (4 oz) sweet potato flour

450 ml (15 fl oz) water

2 teaspoons salt

2 teaspoons Shaoxing rice wine or dry
   sherry

4 eggs, beaten

2 tablespoons groundnut oil

3 tablespoons finely chopped garlic

3 tablespoons finely chopped spring onions

1½ tablespoons chilli bean sauce

Drain the oysters in a colander and then pat them dry with kitchen paper.

Make a batter by mixing the sweet potato flour with the water, salt and Shaoxing rice wine or dry sherry. Now combine it with the eggs.

Heat a wok or large frying-pan over high heat until it is hot. Add the oil and, when it is very hot and slightly smoking, pour in the egg mixture and stir quickly for 30 seconds. Then add the garlic, spring onions and chilli bean sauce and stir-fry for 1 minute. Now add the oysters and continue cooking until the egg has set. Reduce the heat and cook for another 3 minutes. Serve at once.

FRAGRANT PRAWN CURRY

This is a delightful stir-fry dish. I enjoyed it for the first time in Singapore some time ago. The aromatic lemon grass gives it a unique fragrance. Prawns have a distinct but delicate taste and the clean, mildly citrus touch of the lemon grass is a perfect counterpart. The quick cooking style of the wok ensures that the two main ingredients are at their best.

Use fresh lemon grass whenever possible — in a dish like this it is worth a detour to obtain it. If your search is fruitless, you may substitute 2 tablespoons of lemon zest.

SERVES 2-4

450 g (1 lb) raw prawns
½ teaspoon salt
1 stalk fresh lemon grass
1 fresh red or green chilli
2 tablespoons groundnut oil
100 g (4 oz) onions, coarsely chopped
2 tablespoons finely chopped garlic
2 teaspoons finely chopped fresh root
  ginger
2 teaspoons Madras curry paste
1 teaspoon chilli bean sauce
1 teaspoon sugar
2 tablespoons water
1 tablespoon Shaoxing rice wine or dry
  sherry
2 teaspoons light soy sauce
¼ teaspoon freshly ground black pepper

FOR THE GARNISH

Fresh sprigs of coriander

Peel the prawns and discard the shells. Using a small sharp knife, remove the fine digestive cord. Wash the prawns in cold water with the salt, rinse well and pat them dry with kitchen paper.

Remove the outer layer of the lemon grass until you get to the tender, whitish core. Chop the lemon grass core finely. Split the chilli in half and carefully remove and discard the seeds. Chop the chilli finely and combine it with the lemon grass.

Heat a wok or large frying-pan over high heat until it is hot. Add the oil and, when it is very hot and slightly smoking, add the onions, garlic, ginger, lemon grass and chilli and stir-fry for 1 minute. Then add the prawns and continue to stir-fry for 1 minute. Now add the rest of the ingredients and continue to stir-fry for 4 minutes or until the prawns are firm and cooked. Turn the mixture on to a warm serving platter, garnish with the coriander and serve at once.

PRAWN AND PORK STIR-FRY

The Chinese combine foods in an unusual way, sometimes mixing seafood with meats, especially pork. The result is delicious, savoury and quite tasty. Here minced pork is used to extend the more expensive prawns.

The best prawns to use are the uncooked variety. Although they often come frozen, a rinse in cold water with a tablespoon of salt is a technique used by Chinese cooks to refresh them. This recipe is equally good with fresh scallops.

SERVES 4

225 g (8 oz) raw prawns

1 egg white

2 teaspoons cornflour

1 teaspoon salt

1 teaspoon sesame oil

¼ teaspoon freshly ground white pepper

450 ml (15 fl oz) groundnut oil or water

1 tablespoon groundnut oil

2 tablespoons coarsely chopped black beans

1½ tablespoons finely chopped fresh root ginger

2 teaspoons finely chopped garlic

450 g (1 lb) minced pork

1 tablespoon dark soy sauce

2 teaspoons light soy sauce

1 tablespoon Shaoxing rice wine or dry sherry

½ teaspoon salt

¼ teaspoon freshly ground white pepper

½ teaspoon sugar

2 teaspoons sesame oil

FOR THE GARNISH

2 tablespoons finely chopped spring onions

Peel the prawns and, if you are using large uncooked ones, cut them to remove the fine digestive cord. Wash them and pat them dry with kitchen paper. Combine the prawns with the egg white, cornflour, salt, sesame oil and pepper. Mix well and leave in the fridge for 20 minutes.

Heat a wok until it is very hot, then add the oil. When the oil is very hot, remove the wok from the heat and immediately add the prawns, stirring vigorously to keep them from sticking. When the prawns turn white (about 2 minutes), quickly drain them, discarding the oil.

If you choose to use water instead of oil, bring it to the boil in a pan. Remove the pan from the heat and immediately add the prawns, stirring vigorously to keep them from sticking. When the prawns turn white (about 2 minutes), quickly drain them.

Re-heat the wok or large frying-pan over high heat until it is hot. Add the 1 tablespoon of oil and, when it is very hot and slightly smoking, add the black beans, ginger and garlic and stir-fry for 10 seconds. Add the pork and continue to stir-fry for 5 minutes. Drain the pork of any excess oil and return the pork to the wok. Then add the prawns to the wok, together with the soy sauces, Shaoxing rice wine or dry sherry, salt, pepper and sugar. Stir-fry the mixture for 1 minute. Stir in the sesame oil. Turn on to a warm platter, garnish with spring onions and serve at once.

DEEP-FRIED SALT AND PEPPER OYSTERS

A popular Hong Kong-style of cooking seafood is to deep-fry it quickly in hot oil, then drain and stir-fry again in a spicy salt and pepper mixture. I have found this style especially delicious when used for oysters. Here they are dipped and then fried in a crispy batter. The soft, briny oysters make a wonderful contrast to the batter and the spices. This dish makes a delicious opener for any dinner party or can be served as a simple appetizer with drinks.

SERVES 4

450 g (1 lb) oysters, shelled
450 ml (15 fl oz) groundnut oil
1 tablespoon finely chopped garlic
1 teaspoon salt
½ teaspoon ground, roasted Szechuan
   peppercorns
½ teaspoon five-spice powder
½ teaspoon freshly ground black pepper

FOR THE BATTER

65 g (2½ oz) potato flour or cornflour
25 g (1 oz) plain flour
1 teaspoon baking powder
1 teaspoon bicarbonate of soda
A pinch of salt and pepper
2 teaspoons sesame oil
150 ml (5 fl oz) water

FOR THE GARNISH

2 tablespoons finely chopped spring onions
1 lemon, cut into wedges

Drain the oysters in a colander and pat them dry with kitchen paper.

Prepare the batter by mixing the potato flour or cornflour, plain flour, baking powder, bicarbonate of soda, salt, pepper, sesame oil and water together in a small bowl until smooth. Let the mixture stand for about 20 minutes.

Heat a wok or large frying-pan over a high heat until it is hot. Add the oil and, when it is very hot and slightly smoking, turn the heat down to medium. Dip some of the oysters into the batter and deep-fry them until they are golden brown. This should take just a few minutes. Drain them on kitchen paper and repeat the process until you have cooked all the oysters.

Drain off all but 1 tablespoon of the oil. Re-heat the wok until it is hot, add the garlic, salt, Szechuan peppercorns, five-spice powder and black pepper and stir-fry for 10 seconds. Then return the oysters to the wok and stir-fry for 1 minute or until the oysters are coated with this mixture. Transfer to a warm platter. Garnish with the spring onions and lemon wedges and serve at once.

STIR-FRIED FISH WITH BLACK BEAN SAUCE

M*y mother loved making this dish because it was quick, easy and delicious. The pungency of the black beans, garlic and ginger turn an ordinary fish into a gourmet's delight. When served with vegetables and rice, it becomes the type of light, wholesome, satisfying meal that is the hallmark of the best Chinese home cooking.*

SERVES 4

450 g (1 lb) fresh, firm white fish fillets, such as cod, halibut or sea bass

2 teaspoons salt

3 tablespoons groundnut oil

1½ tablespoons coarsely chopped black beans

1 tablespoon finely chopped garlic

2 teaspoons finely chopped fresh root ginger

3 tablespoons finely chopped spring onions

1 tablespoon light soy sauce

1 teaspoon dark soy sauce

1 tablespoon Shaoxing rice wine or dry sherry

1 teaspoon sugar

1 tablespoon water

2 teaspoons sesame oil

FOR THE GARNISH

3 tablespoons finely shredded spring onions

Cut the fish fillets into strips 2.5-cm (1-in) wide and sprinkle the salt evenly over them. Let them stand for 20 minutes.

Heat a wok or large frying-pan over high heat until it is hot. Add the oil and, when it is very hot and slightly smoking, turn the heat down to medium and add the fish strips. Stir-fry these gently for about 2 minutes or until they are brown on both sides, taking care not to break them up. Remove them with a slotted spoon and drain on kitchen paper. Drain off all but 1½ tablespoons of the oil.

Re-heat the wok. When it is hot, add the black beans, garlic, ginger and spring onions and stir-fry for 30 seconds. Then add the soy sauces, Shaoxing rice wine or dry sherry, sugar and water and bring to a simmer. Return the fish to the wok and gently finish cooking in the sauce for about 1 minute. Then add the sesame oil and give the mixture a good stir. Using a slotted spoon, arrange the fish on a warm serving platter, garnish with the spring onions and serve at once.

SAVOURY CLAMS AND PORK IN LETTUCE CUPS

This recipe is typical of Chinese dishes, where cooks often stir-fry seafood combined with a small amount of minced pork. The result is a rich savoury mixture that is extremely tasty. Only the freshest, preferably live, clams should be used.

Here the mixture is served with fresh lettuce leaves, which provide a crisp contrast to the soft clam and pork mix. Each guest puts a portion of the clam and pork mixture into a hollow lettuce leaf and then eats it with their fingers.

This dish makes an unusual, delicious first course.

SERVES 4

225 g (8 oz) minced pork
1 teaspoon light soy sauce
1 teaspoon plus 2 tablespoons Shaoxing rice wine or dry sherry
1 teaspoon sesame oil
1 teaspoon cornflour
150 ml (5 fl oz) water
1 kg (2¼ lb) fresh live clams, well scrubbed
225 g (8 oz) iceberg lettuce
1½ tablespoons groundnut oil
1 tablespoon finely chopped fresh root ginger
1 tablespoon coarsely chopped garlic
2 tablespoons finely chopped shallots
3 tablespoons finely chopped spring onions
1 tablespoon oyster sauce
½ teaspoon freshly ground white pepper
1 teaspoon sugar

Put the minced pork into a bowl together with the soy sauce, the teaspoon of Shaoxing rice wine or dry sherry, sesame oil and cornflour and mix well. Leave to marinate for about 20 minutes.

Bring the water to the boil in a large pan and add the clams. Remove them as soon as they begin to open. Finish opening them by hand and remove them from their shells. Discard the shells. Set the clam meat aside.

Separate and wash the lettuce leaves and set them aside, wiping off any excess water.

Heat a wok or large frying-pan over high heat until it is hot. Add the oil and, when it is very hot and slightly smoking, add the ginger, garlic and shallots and stir-fry for 20 seconds. Then add the pork and continue to stir-fry for 3 minutes. Then add the spring onions, the 2 tablespoons of Shaoxing rice wine or dry sherry, the oyster sauce, pepper and sugar and continue to stir-fry for 2 minutes. Finally return the clam meat to the wok and stir-fry for 1 minute to re-heat. Turn on to a warm serving platter. Arrange the lettuce on a separate platter and serve at once.

STIR-FRIED PRAWNS WITH WATER CHESTNUTS

This was a favourite of our customers in the restaurant I worked in when I was young. It is easy to see why. Rich, tasty prawns are paired with crispy water chestnuts and sweet green peas. It really is a most appealing dish, light and delectable.

This recipe makes a good starter for any dinner party, or a delicious main course for a light meal, where it would go nicely with plain rice and a vegetable dish.

SERVES 4

450 g (1 lb) raw prawns

1 egg white

2 teaspoons cornflour

1 teaspoon salt

1 teaspoon sesame oil

½ teaspoon freshly ground white pepper

225 g (8 oz) fresh or tinned (drained weight) water chestnuts

175 g (6 oz) frozen small garden peas or petit pois

450 ml (15 fl oz) groundnut oil or water

1 tablespoon groundnut oil

1½ tablespoons finely chopped fresh root ginger

1 tablespoon finely chopped garlic

½ small onion, thinly sliced

1 tablespoon Shaoxing rice wine or dry sherry

1 teaspoon salt

½ teaspoon freshly ground white pepper

½ teaspoon sugar

2 teaspoons sesame oil

FOR THE GARNISH

2 tablespoons finely chopped spring onions

Peel the prawns and, if you are using large uncooked ones, cut them to remove the fine digestive cord. Wash them and pat them dry with kitchen paper. Combine the prawns with the egg white, cornflour, salt, sesame oil and pepper. Mix well and leave to sit in the fridge for 20 minutes. Peel the water chestnuts if fresh, or rinse if tinned, and slice. Put the peas in a small bowl and let them thaw.

Heat a wok until it is very hot and then add the oil. When the oil is very hot, remove the wok from the heat and immediately add the prawns, stirring vigorously to keep them from sticking. When the prawns turn white (about 2 minutes), quickly drain them.

If you choose to use water instead of oil, bring it to a boil in a pan. Remove the pan from the heat and immediately add the prawns, stirring vigorously to keep them from sticking. When the prawns turn white (about 2 minutes), quickly drain them.

Re-heat the wok or large frying-pan over high heat until it is hot. Add the 1 tablespoon of oil and, when it is very hot and slightly smoking, add the ginger and garlic and stir-fry for 10 seconds. Add the onion and continue to stir-fry for 2 minutes. Then return the prawns to the wok, together with the water chestnuts, peas, Shaoxing rice wine or dry sherry, salt, pepper and sugar. Stir-fry the mixture for 3 minutes. Stir in the sesame oil. Turn on to a platter, garnish with spring onions and serve at once.

STIR-FRIED SCALLOPS WITH MANGETOUT

The delicate scallop is a perfect seafood to prepare in the wok. It requires little cooking to bring out its naturally sweet taste, and the hot wok heats it flawlessly; just enough to cook it without overcooking.

Here I have combined scallops with mangetout, a delectable and toothsome vegetable that complements the scallop's sweetness.

An easy dish to make, this can easily be a wonderful first course to any meal or a special treat as a main course with rice and another vegetable dish.

SERVES 4

2 tablespoons groundnut oil

1 tablespoon finely chopped fresh root
   ginger

3 tablespoons finely shredded spring onions

450 g (1 lb) scallops, including the corals

2 tablespoons Shaoxing rice wine or dry
   sherry

2 teaspoons light soy sauce

1 teaspoon sugar

½ teaspoon salt

½ teaspoon freshly ground white pepper

225 g (8 oz) mangetout, trimmed

2 tablespoons water

2 teaspoons sesame oil

Heat a wok or large frying-pan over a high heat until it is hot. Add 1 tablespoon of oil and, when it is very hot and slightly smoking, add the ginger and spring onions and stir-fry for 10 seconds. Immediately add the scallops and stir-fry them for 1 minute. Then add 1 tablespoon of Shaoxing rice wine or dry sherry, the soy sauce, sugar, salt and pepper. Continue to stir-fry for 2 minutes. Remove the scallops to a bowl together with the sauce and set aside.

Wipe the wok clean and re-heat over a high heat. When it is hot and slightly smoking, add the remaining oil and the mangetout and stir-fry for 10 seconds. Immediately add the remaining Shaoxing rice wine or dry sherry and the water and stir-fry for 2 minutes. Return the scallops to the wok and continue to stir-fry for an additional 2 minutes. Now add the sesame oil and stir-fry for another minute. Serve at once.

SINGAPOREAN-STYLE CURRY CRAB

*S*ingapore is an Asian city rich in many different cultures. One of the joys of visiting such a fascinating city is to sample its diverse foods. The blending of disparate traditions can be seen in the street hawkers' stalls. A dish I often love to eat is Singapore's Curry Crab, which is a mixture of Chinese and Indian influences. Although the authentic recipe has ingredients which may be difficult to obtain outside Singapore, I have adapted the idea and made my own mixture with delicious results. The spices are a wonderful contrast to the sweet crabmeat. Serve it with plain rice and another vegetable dish for a complete meal. Remember, it is important to buy the freshest crab available, preferably live.

It is perfectly good manners to eat the crab with your fingers, but I suggest that you have a large bowl of water decorated with lemon slices on the table so that your guests can rinse their fingers.

SERVES 4

1.4 kg (3 lb) live or freshly cooked crab on the shell
2 stalks fresh lemon grass
2 tablespoons groundnut oil
8 garlic cloves, thinly sliced
2 tablespoons finely shredded fresh root ginger
4 tablespoons thinly sliced small onions or shallots
3 tablespoons finely shredded spring onions
3 tablespoons Madras curry paste
400 ml (15 fl oz) tinned coconut milk
1 teaspoon salt
2 teaspoons sugar

To cook a live crab, bring a large pan of water to the boil, drop in the crab and boil until there is no movement; this will take about 2 minutes. Remove the crab and drain thoroughly.

Remove the tail-flap, push the body with legs still attached away from the shell (A) and remove the stomach sac and feathery gills from the crab (B). Using a heavy knife or cleaver, cut the crab, shell included, into large pieces.

Cut the lemon grass into 5-cm (2-in) segments. With the flat side of a large knife or cleaver, smash the lemon grass pieces to release their aromatic oils.

Heat a wok or large frying-pan over high

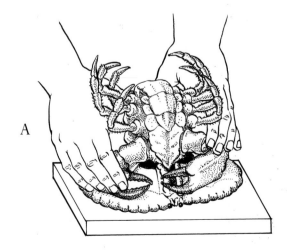

A

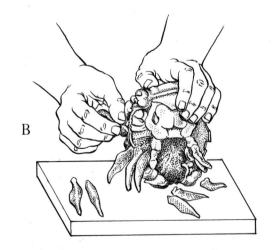

B

heat until it is hot. Add the oil and, when it is very hot and slightly smoking, add the lemon grass pieces, garlic, ginger and onions or shallots and stir-fry for 1 minute. Add the spring onions and crab pieces and stir-fry for 2 minutes. Now add the remaining ingredients and continue to stir-fry the mixture over a high heat for about 2 minutes. Turn the heat to low, cover and simmer for 10 minutes. Turn the curry on to a large, warm serving platter and serve.

STEAMED SCALLOPS WITH CHILLI AND GINGER

Fresh scallops are sweet and rich. Perhaps the best way to preserve their qualities is the Chinese technique of steaming. Using hot, wet vapours, this method brings out the succulent texture of scallops without overcooking them. Their briny seafood taste is emphasized, and the bonus is that they are very simple to prepare and take literally minutes to cook. This dish is ideal for a quick and easy, as well as a healthy, meal and I think it makes an ideal opener for any dinner party.

SERVES 4

450 g (1 lb) fresh scallops, including the
  corals
2 fresh red chillies, seeded and chopped
2 teaspoons finely chopped fresh root
  ginger
1 tablespoon Shaoxing rice wine or dry
  sherry
1 tablespoon light soy sauce
¼ teaspoon salt
¼ teaspoon freshly ground black pepper
3 tablespoons finely chopped spring onions

Place the scallops evenly on a heatproof platter. Then evenly distribute the chillies, ginger, Shaoxing rice wine or dry sherry, soy sauce, salt, pepper and spring onions on top.

Next set up a steamer or put a rack into a wok or deep pan and fill it with 5 cm (2 in) of water. Bring the water to the boil over a high heat. Carefully lower the platter of scallops into the steamer or on to the rack. Turn the heat to low and cover the wok or pan tightly. Steam gently for 5 minutes. Remove and serve at once.

SHAOXING RICE WINE PRAWNS

Shaoxing or yellow wine is a fragrant, mellow, rich wine that gives seafood a special taste and aromatic flavour. River prawns in Eastern China are sometimes cooked in Shaoxing rice wine in a simple recipe that produces a delicious treat.

This dish makes a good opener for any meal.

SERVES 4

450 g (1 lb) raw prawns
1 tablespoon groundnut oil
2 teaspoons finely chopped garlic
2 teaspoons finely chopped fresh root
  ginger
2 tablespoons finely chopped spring onions
1 fresh red or green chilli, seeded and finely
  shredded
150 ml (5 fl oz) Shaoxing rice wine or dry
  sherry
1 teaspoon salt
½ teaspoon freshly ground white pepper

FOR THE GARNISH

2 tablespoons finely chopped spring onions
1 tablespoon finely chopped fresh
  coriander

Peel the prawns and, if you are using large uncooked ones, cut them to remove the fine digestive cord. Wash them and pat them dry with kitchen paper.

Heat a wok or large frying-pan over a high heat until it is hot. Add the oil and, when it is very hot and slightly smoking, add the garlic, ginger, spring onions and chilli and stir-fry for 10 seconds. Then add the prawns and continue to stir-fry for 1 minute. Then add the Shaoxing rice wine or dry sherry, salt and pepper, turn the heat down, cover and cook for 3 minutes. Place on a warm platter and garnish with spring onions and coriander and serve at once.

GINGER SCALLOPS WITH CHINESE GREENS

Almost any type of seafood tastes terrific when it has been quickly stir-fried in a hot wok. The intense heat and the little oil used gives seafood a slightly smoky flavour akin to grilled foods. In this recipe, scallops are combined with ginger, a classic Chinese pairing, and then mixed with fresh Chinese greens, in this case, bok choy or Chinese flowering greens. The sweet, rich taste of the scallops is balanced by the sharp, zesty flavour of ginger. The result is a healthy, tasty dish that is easy to make. Serve it as a first course in a multicourse meal or simply as a main course with rice and another vegetable dish for a satisfying meal.

SERVES 4

750 g (1¾ lb) Chinese greens, such as
   Chinese flowering cabbage or bok choy
2 tablespoons groundnut oil
1½ tablespoons finely chopped fresh root
   ginger
1 tablespoon finely chopped garlic
2 tablespoons finely chopped spring onions
450 g (1 lb) scallops, including the corals
1 tablespoon Shaoxing rice wine or dry
   sherry
2 teaspoons light soy sauce
1 teaspoon sugar
½ teaspoon salt
½ teaspoon freshly ground white pepper
2 tablespoons thinly sliced garlic
2 teaspoons sesame oil

Cut the Chinese greens into 7.5-cm (3-in) pieces.

Heat a wok or large frying-pan over a high heat until it is hot. Add 1 tablespoon of oil and, when it is very hot and slightly smoking, add the ginger, garlic and spring onions and stir-fry for 10 seconds. Immediately add the scallops and stir-fry them for 1 minute. Then add the Shaoxing rice wine or dry sherry, soy sauce, sugar, salt and pepper and continue to stir-fry for 2 minutes. Remove the scallops from the wok with any sauce and set aside.

Wipe the wok clean and re-heat over a high heat. Add the remaining oil and, when it is very hot and slightly smoking, add the sliced garlic and stir-fry for 10 seconds. Then add the Chinese greens and stir-fry for 3 minutes or until the greens have wilted a little. Return the scallops to the wok and continue to stir-fry for an additional 3 minutes. Now add the sesame oil and stir-fry for a further minute. Serve at once.

STIR-FRIED SQUID WITH PEAS

The Chinese love squid quickly stir-fried in a hot wok as then it is just cooked and beautifully tender. This is a subtle offering from the sea and combines well with the green peas. Once the squid is prepared, the rest of the cooking is easy. Serve it as a first course or as a main course with rice and vegetables.

SERVES 4

450 g (1 lb) squid, fresh or frozen

175 g (6 oz) fresh or frozen petit pois

1½ tablespoons groundnut oil

2 tablespoons thinly sliced garlic

2 teaspoons finely chopped fresh root ginger

75 ml (3 fl oz) *Chicken Stock (see p.56)*

1 tablespoon Shaoxing rice wine or dry sherry

2 tablespoons oyster sauce

2 teaspoons light soy sauce

2 teaspoons cornflour blended with 1 tablespoon water

2 teaspoons sesame oil

The edible parts of the squid are the tentacles and the body. If it has not been cleaned by your fishmonger, you can do it yourself by washing off the purple outer skin and pulling the head and tentacles away from the body (A). Using a small sharp knife, split the body in half and remove the transparent bony section (B). Wash the halves thoroughly under cold running water. Cut the tentacles from the head, cutting just above the eye (C). (You may also have to remove the polyp or beak from the base of the ring of tentacles.) If you are using frozen squid, make sure it is properly thawed before cooking it. Cut the squid meat into 4-cm (1½-in) strips.

If you are using fresh peas, bring a large pan of salted water to the boil, add the peas and blanch them for 3 minutes, then drain and set aside. If you are using frozen peas, simply thaw them and set them aside.

A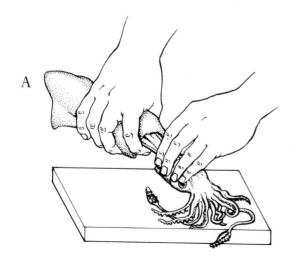

B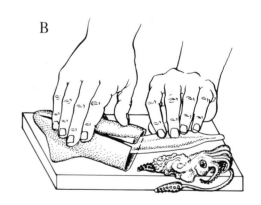

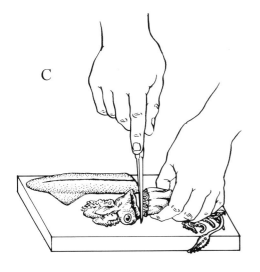

C

Heat a wok or large frying-pan over a high heat until it is hot. Add the oil and, when it is very hot and slightly smoking, add the garlic and ginger and stir-fry for 15 seconds. Then add the squid and stir-fry for 1 minute. Add the rest of the ingredients, except the cornflour mixture and sesame oil, and continue to stir-fry for 3 minutes. Add the cornflour mixture and bring the mixture to a simmer. Give it a quick stir, then add the sesame oil and mix well. Cook for 30 seconds more. Serve at once.

FRIED FISH WITH THAI DIPPING SAUCE

Thailand's long coastline naturally means that fish have played a major role in its cuisine. Indeed, Thai cookery has made a supreme art of transforming the most common seafood and fish into glorious foods.

Here, fish is simply pan-fried in the wok until golden brown and crispy. It is then served in a zesty sauce that can be made hours ahead. I find this dish goes very well with rice.

SERVES 2

2 x 225-g (8-oz) or 1 x 450-g (1-lb) whole flat
   white fish, such as Dover sole or plaice
1 teaspoon salt
½ teaspoon freshly ground black pepper
Potato flour, cornflour or plain flour, for
   dusting
300 ml (10 fl oz) groundnut oil

FOR THE DIPPING SAUCE

2 fresh red chillies, seeded and finely
   shredded
3 tablespoons finely sliced shallots
2 teaspoons lime juice
2 tablespoons Thai fish sauce

Dry the fish well. Evenly salt and pepper each side of the fish. Dust the fish well with potato flour, cornflour or flour, shaking off any excess.

Make the dipping sauce by combining the chillies, shallots, lime juice and fish sauce in a small bowl.

Heat a wok or large frying-pan over a high heat until it is hot. Add the oil and, when it is very hot and slightly smoking, turn the heat down to moderate. Add the fish and slowly brown. Turn the fish over and cook and brown the other side. Remove the fish and drain on kitchen paper. Place the fish on a warm platter and serve at once with the dipping sauce.

MUSSELS IN COCONUT CURRY SAUCE

Mussels are an ideal quick and easy food and they tend to be quite economical. Once they have been scrubbed clean in cold water to remove all sand, they cook very rapidly, announcing that they are ready by opening their shells. Make sure they are firmly sealed before cooking; throw away any that do not close up when poked. Any that do not open during cooking should also be discarded.

Mussels are very much a seafood, redolent of salty tides. They are therefore prime candidates for a robust and distinctive sauce. It is an ideal dish to serve with plain steamed rice.

This simple dish can easily be increased for larger gatherings. I prefer to use smaller mussels, so if you have a choice, try them.

SERVES 4-6

1½ tablespoons groundnut oil

3 tablespoons coarsely chopped garlic

2 tablespoons finely chopped fresh root ginger

2 tablespoons coarsely chopped spring onions

1.5 kg (3 lb) fresh mussels, well scrubbed

2 tablespoons Madras curry powder or paste

2 tablespoons Thai fish sauce

1 teaspoon sugar

400 ml (15 fl oz) tinned coconut milk

3 tablespoons water

Heat a wok or large frying-pan over a high heat until it is hot. Add the oil and, when it is very hot and slightly smoking, add the garlic, ginger and spring onions and stir-fry for 20 seconds, then add the mussels and stir-fry for 1 minute. Add the curry powder or paste, fish sauce, sugar, coconut milk and water, cover and continue to cook for 5 minutes or until all the mussels have opened. Discard any that do not open. Give the mixture a final stir and serve at once.

FISH WITH RAINBOW VEGETABLES

*F*resh fish takes on added dimensions when served with colourful vegetables, as in this 'rainbow' effect.

Once the fish has been velveted, it takes literally minutes to complete the preparations. You may substitute other vegetables, but the basic principle is the same – velvet the fish to keep it moist and silky. The rest of the dish is quickly assembled in the wok and an elegant meal of fresh fish with colourful vegetables is the result. Serve this with a rice dish and another vegetable dish for a wholesome, complete and tasty meal.

SERVES 2-4

50 g (2 oz) Chinese dried mushrooms
450 g (1 lb) fresh firm white fish, such as sea
   bass, halibut or cod
1 egg white
2 teaspoons cornflour
1 teaspoon salt
½ teaspoon freshly ground white pepper
100 g (4 oz) mangetout
100 g (4 oz) carrots
600 ml (1 pint) groundnut oil or water
1 tablespoon groundnut oil
1 tablespoon coarsely chopped garlic
1 tablespoon finely shredded fresh root
   ginger
1 tablespoon Shaoxing rice wine or dry
   sherry
1 tablespoon dark soy sauce
2 teaspoons light soy sauce
1 teaspoon salt
1 tablespoon chilli bean sauce
2 teaspoons rock sugar or plain sugar
6 tablespoons water

Soak the mushrooms in warm water for 20 minutes, then drain them and squeeze out the excess liquid. Remove and discard the stems and finely shred the caps into thin strips.

Cut the fish into 5-cm (2-in) pieces and combine them with the egg white, cornflour, salt and pepper in a medium-sized bowl. Mix well and chill for 20 minutes.

Trim the mangetout and leave whole. Cut the carrots on the diagonal into 3-mm (⅛-in) thick slices. Blanch the carrots for 3 minutes in a large pan of boiling salted water. Drain, refresh in cold water and set aside.

Heat a wok until it is very hot and then add the oil. When the oil is very hot, remove the wok from the heat and immediately add the fish, stirring vigorously to keep the pieces from sticking. When the fish pieces turn white (about 2 minutes), quickly drain them.

If you choose to use water instead of oil, bring it to a boil in a pan. Remove the pan from the heat and immediately add the fish pieces, stirring vigorously to keep them from sticking. When the fish pieces turn white (about 2 minutes), quickly drain them.

Wipe the wok clean and re-heat over a high heat. When it is hot, add the 1 tablespoon of oil, the garlic and ginger and stir-fry for 20 seconds. Then add the mushrooms, mangetout and carrots and stir-fry for about 2 minutes. Then add the rest of the ingredients. Now add the fish pieces and heat through. Stir several times and serve at once.

THAI-STYLE PRAWNS WITH LEMON GRASS

This is a dish inspired by one of my many visits to Bangkok where I frequently conduct food promotions for the Oriental Hotel. Working with their superb Thai chefs, I was able to learn the essentials of their rich and aromatic cuisine. One of my favourites consists of prawns and lemon grass, a very popular standard for their luncheon buffet.

Their version is made in a quite unusual brass wok. Your usual wok will do nicely, however. Note that, rather than being stir-fried, the prawns are simmered, and in coconut milk at that. The delicate taste of the prawns benefits from such tender care. The result is a hearty, satisfying main dish, redolent of chillies and garlic. It goes well with plain rice.

SERVES 4

450 g (1 lb) raw prawns

FOR THE SAUCE

2 stalks lemon grass
400 ml (14 fl oz) tinned coconut milk
2 tablespoons seeded and chopped fresh red chilli
1 tablespoon coarsely chopped fresh coriander
3 tablespoons coarsely chopped garlic
2 tablespoons coarsely chopped shallots
3 tablespoons water
2 tablespoons Thai fish sauce
1 tablespoon sugar
2 teaspoons shrimp paste

FOR THE GARNISH

A handful of fresh basil leaves

Peel the prawns and discard the shells. Using a small sharp knife, remove the fine digestive cord. Wash the prawns and pat them dry with kitchen paper.

Peel the lemon grass stalks to reveal the tender, whitish centre and crush with flat of a knife. Cut it into 7.5-cm (3-in) pieces.

Reserve 1 tablespoon of coconut milk and set aside. Bring the rest of the coconut milk to a simmer in the wok. Add the lemon grass stalks and simmer for 10 minutes.

Combine the chilli, coriander, garlic and shallots in a blender or food processor with the reserved coconut milk and 3 tablespoons of water and mix well. Add this paste to the simmering coconut milk together with the fish sauce, sugar and shrimp paste. Continue simmering for 2 minutes. Now add the prawns and continue to simmer for 3 minutes or until the prawns are cooked. Toss in the basil leaves and give the mixture several good turns. Serve at once.

PAN-FRIED SALMON WITH TOMATOES

The wok is not only good for stir-frying but also for pan-frying. Not pancakes, perhaps, but it makes short work of pan-fried fish and, in this case, provides a quick and easy, as well as healthy, meal.

This colourful and savoury dish will go well with plain rice.

SERVES 2-4

450 g (1 lb) boneless salmon fillet, skinned
   and quartered
1 teaspoon salt
¼ teaspoon freshly ground white pepper
450 g (1 lb) fresh or tinned tomatoes
2 tablespoons plain flour, for dusting
3 tablespoons groundnut oil
2 tablespoons thinly sliced garlic
2 tablespoons finely chopped shallots
2 tablespoons finely chopped spring onions
1 tablespoon finely chopped fresh root
   ginger
1½ tablespoons Shaoxing rice wine or dry
   sherry
1 tablespoon light soy sauce
2 teaspoons sugar

FOR THE GARNISH

2 tablespoons finely chopped spring onions
Small handful of fresh coriander leaves

Sprinkle the salmon pieces evenly with salt and pepper.

If you are using fresh tomatoes, drop them into boiling water for 10 seconds, remove, skin, seed and cut them into 2.5-cm (1-in) cubes. If you are using tinned tomatoes, chop them into small chunks.

Dust the salmon with the flour, shaking off any excess.

Heat a wok or large frying-pan over a high heat until it is hot. Add the oil and, when it is moderately hot, add the salmon pieces and pan-fry them for 3 minutes. Turn them over and brown the other side. Remove and drain on kitchen paper, then arrange on a warm platter. Pour off all but 1 tablespoon of the oil, add the garlic, shallots, spring onions and ginger and stir-fry for 1 minute. Then add the tomatoes, Shaoxing rice wine or dry sherry, soy sauce and sugar and simmer for 5 minutes. Pour this over the fish, garnish with the spring onions and coriander and serve at once.

Pan-fried Salmon with Tomatoes

STIR-FRIED PRAWNS WITH FRESH ASPARAGUS

*A*sparagus is a relatively recent addition to the Chinese culinary repertoire. It immediately became extremely popular in Hong Kong, and its use has spread to other Asian cookery influenced by the New Hong Kong cuisine.

In any event, its popularity is well earned because this vegetable in season is colourful, crunchy and with a pleasing taste all its own. Moreover, it works well with almost all types of food. Here I have combined it with prawns. The unique tastes of these two wonderful foods is complemented by their contrasting textures – the soft prawns and the snap of the asparagus.

Once the prawns have been velveted, the whole dish is put together very quickly in the versatile wok.

SERVES 4

450 g (1 lb) asparagus

450 g (1 lb) raw prawns

1 egg white

2 teaspoons cornflour

1 teaspoon salt

1 teaspoon sesame oil

½ teaspoon freshly ground white pepper

450 ml (15 fl oz) groundnut oil or water

1½ tablespoons groundnut oil

1½ tablespoons finely chopped fresh root ginger

3 tablespoons water

1 tablespoon Shaoxing rice wine or dry sherry

1 tablespoon light soy sauce

1 teaspoon salt

½ teaspoon freshly ground white pepper

2 teaspoons sesame oil

FOR THE GARNISH

2 tablespoons finely chopped spring onions

Slice the asparagus thinly at a slight diagonal, discarding the tough ends. Peel the prawns and, if you are using large uncooked ones, cut them to remove the fine digestive cord. Wash them and pat them dry with kitchen paper.

Combine the prawns with the egg white, cornflour, salt, sesame oil and pepper. Mix well and and let the mixture sit in the fridge for 20 minutes.

Heat a wok until it is very hot and then add the oil. When the oil is very hot, remove the wok from the heat and immediately add the prawns, stirring vigorously to keep them from sticking. When the prawns turn white (about 2 minutes), quickly drain them.

If you choose to use water instead of oil, bring it to a boil in a pan. Remove the pan from the heat and immediately add the prawns, stirring vigorously to keep them from sticking. When the prawns turn white (about 2 minutes), quickly drain them.

Re-heat the wok or large frying-pan over a high heat until it is hot. Add the 1½ tablespoons of oil and, when it is very hot and slightly smoking, add the ginger and stir-fry for 10 seconds. Add the asparagus and 3 tablespoons of water and stir-fry for 3 minutes. Then return the prawns to the wok, together with the Shaoxing rice wine or dry sherry, soy sauce, salt and pepper. Stir-fry the mixture for 1 minute. Stir in the sesame oil and give the mixture 2 turns. Turn on to a platter, garnish with spring onions and serve at once.

COCONUT PRAWNS

The coconut milk should alert you to the Thai origins of this recipe. It is a delicious treat that relies on the prawns marinating long enough to absorb the various aromatic flavours of the marinade. That being accomplished, the results are an extremely tasty platter that can serve as a main course or a wonderful opener. It is easy and quick to cook in the wok and makes lovely, exotic eating.

SERVES 4

450 g (1 lb) raw prawns
Plain flour, for dusting
2 eggs, beaten
900 ml (1½ pints) groundnut oil

FOR THE MARINADE

1 stalk lemon grass
2 tablespoons finely chopped garlic
2 tablespoons finely chopped shallots
1 tablespoon seeded and chopped fresh
   red chilli
1 tablespoon lime juice
1 teaspoon salt
½ teaspoon freshly ground black pepper
400 ml (14 fl oz) tinned coconut milk

Peel the prawns and discard the shells. Using a small sharp knife, remove the fine digestive cord. Wash the prawns and pat them dry with kitchen paper.

Peel the lemon grass stalk to reveal the tender, whitish centre and crush it with the flat of a knife, then finely chop it. In a large bowl, combine the lemon grass, garlic, shallots, chilli, lime juice, salt and pepper with the coconut milk. Mix well and add the prawns. Allow the prawns to marinate for 1 hour.

Lift the prawns from the marinade with a slotted spoon and dust them with flour. Dip them in the beaten egg and dust them again with flour, shaking off any excess.

Heat a wok or large frying-pan over high heat until it is hot. Add the oil and, when it is very hot and slightly smoking, turn the heat to moderate and deep-fry the prawns. You may have to do this in several batches. Remove them when they are pink and crispy. Drain on kitchen paper and serve at once.

MEAT

The wok is a perfect implement to use when preparing meats, especially if they are to be stir-fried. The very hot temperature of the wok seals in all the juices and flavours of the meat, whether it be pork, beef or lamb. The concave sides allow the meat to be stir-fried evenly so that all the meat is sealed rapidly.

Once the meats have been browned and drained of any excess oil, other foods, such as vegetables, may be added, and thus a complete dish is prepared in no time at all.

The wok is also useful for braising dishes such as Braised Korean-style Spareribs *or* Savoury Pork Tomato Sauce. *Ordinary meats are transformed into luscious aromatic platters which tempt the palate.*

In this chapter, many spices are utilized to give meats new tastes and flavours. The combinations are taken from my own personal favourites and from recipes I have gathered in my extensive travels.

HUNAN-STYLE LAMB

L amb is not a standard item on southern Chinese menus. It is much more common in northern and central China. The prejudice against lamb may be discerned in a southern proverb: 'There are seventy-two ways of cooking lamb; most of them result in something quite unpalatable'.

But this is unfair to lamb. As this recipe shows, it lends itself to imaginative uses. Hunan (the birth-province of Mao) is famous for its rather fiery cuisine. Chilli bean and hoisin sauces, as in this recipe, are among the spices most often employed. If you prefer something a bit milder than the hot Hunanese style, simply reduce the amount of chilli bean sauce.

The most tender parts of lamb, such as steaks and chops, are best for this dish. For a complete, well-balanced meal, serve it with rice and a vegetable dish.

SERVES 4

450 g (1 lb) lean lamb steak or fillet, or boned loin chop meat

1 tablespoon groundnut oil

3 tablespoons finely chopped spring onions, white part only

6 garlic cloves, thinly sliced

2 teaspoons finely shredded fresh root ginger

1 tablespoon chilli bean sauce

1½ tablespoons hoisin sauce

1 teaspoon sugar

1 teaspoon sesame oil

FOR THE MARINADE

1 tablespoon Shaoxing rice wine or dry sherry

2 teaspoons dark soy sauce

1 tablespoon light soy sauce

2 teaspoons sesame oil

1½ teaspoons cornflour

Cut the lamb into thin slices and put it into a bowl. Mix in the Shaoxing rice wine or dry sherry, soy sauces, sesame oil and cornflour and leave to marinate for 20 minutes. Then drain off and reserve the marinade.

Heat a wok or large frying-pan until it is hot. Add the oil and, when the oil is very hot and slightly smoking, add the marinated lamb pieces with just a little of the reserved marinade. Stir-fry for 2 minutes. Now add the spring onions, garlic and ginger and continue to stir-fry for another 2 minutes. Add the chilli bean sauce, hoisin sauce and sugar and continue to stir-fry for 2 minutes. Then stir in the sesame oil, turn on to a warm serving platter and serve immediately.

FRAGRANT STIR-FRIED BEEF WITH PEPPERS

My many trips to Thailand have led me to elevate the virtues of lemon grass almost to the status enjoyed by garlic and ginger. It has a subtle but quite distinctive flavour that adds a certain something to the most prosaic recipes.

Fortunately, it has recently become generally available in most metropolitan areas in Western countries and it is well worth searching for.

Here I have adapted the Thai version by pairing the lemon grass with sweet red peppers, which add colour as well as contrasting tastes and texture.

SERVES 4

450 g (1 lb) lean beef steak

FOR THE MARINADE

1 tablespoon light soy sauce
1 tablespoon Shaoxing rice wine or dry sherry
2 teaspoons sesame oil
2 teaspoons cornflour
3 stalks fresh lemon grass
225 g (8 oz) red or green pepper (1 large or about 2 small)
3 tablespoons groundnut oil
2 teaspoons finely chopped fresh root ginger
100 g (4 oz) shallots, thinly sliced
3 garlic cloves, thinly sliced
1 tablespoon light soy sauce
1½ tablespoons Shaoxing rice wine or dry sherry
½ teaspoon salt
½ teaspoon freshly ground black pepper
1½ teaspoons sugar
2 teaspoons sesame oil

Cut the beef into thin slices 5 cm (2 in) long, cutting against the grain. Put the beef into a bowl together with the soy sauce, Shaoxing rice wine or dry sherry, sesame oil and cornflour. Mix well, and then let the mixture marinate for about 20 minutes.

Peel the lemon grass stalks to reveal the tender, whitish centre and cut into 5-cm (2-in) pieces, then crush them with the flat of a cleaver or knife. Cut the peppers into 2.5-cm (1-in) pieces.

Heat a wok or large frying-pan over high heat until it is very hot. Add the oil and, when it is very hot and slightly smoking, remove the beef from the marinade with a slotted spoon. Add it to the pan and stir-fry it for 2 minutes until it browns. Remove it and leave to drain in a colander or sieve. Pour off all but 1 table-spoon of the oil. Re-heat the wok or pan over a high heat and then add the lemon grass, ginger, shallots and garlic slices and stir-fry for 20 seconds. Then add the peppers, soy sauce, Shaoxing rice wine or dry sherry, salt, pepper and sugar and continue to stir-fry for 3 minutes. Then return the beef to the wok and stir-fry for 4 minutes, mixing well. Drizzle in the sesame oil and give the mixture a few stirs. Transfer to a warm platter and serve at once.

CRUNCHY PEANUT BEEF

This savoury recipe combines beef with crunchy peanuts. It is a delicious combination that has a wonderful texture. This dish will go well with noodles, pasta or just plain rice. Serve with a vegetable dish for a complete meal.

SERVES 4

1 tablespoon groundnut oil

1½ tablespoons finely chopped garlic

1 tablespoon finely chopped fresh root ginger

3 tablespoons finely chopped spring onions

450 g (1 lb) minced beef

3 tablespoons whole yellow bean sauce

1½ tablespoons Shaoxing rice wine or dry sherry

1 tablespoon dark soy sauce

1 teaspoon salt

½ teaspoon freshly ground black pepper

2 teaspoons chilli bean sauce

2 teaspoons sugar

3 tablespoons *Chicken Stock (see p.56)* or water

FOR THE GARNISH

50 g (2 oz) roasted peanuts, crushed

3 tablespoons coarsely chopped spring onions

Heat a wok or large frying-pan over a high heat until it is hot. Add the oil and, when it is very hot and slightly smoking, add the garlic, ginger and spring onions and stir-fry for 15 seconds. Add the beef, stir well to break up all the pieces and continue to stir-fry for about 2 minutes or until the beef loses its pink colour. Then add the rest of the main ingredients, stirring all the time. Bring the mixture to the boil, turn the heat down to low and simmer for 5 minutes. Transfer the contents of the wok to a warm, deep-sided platter. Sprinkle on the peanuts and spring onions, mix everything together well and serve at once.

SAVOURY BEEF WITH ASPARAGUS

*A*sparagus is the favourite vegetable of many lovers of good food. It is easy to see why. The cooked stalks combine crunchy and soft textures, subtle and distinct flavours. And in the spring, when it is in season and readily available, it is not overly expensive.

Asparagus is congenial with almost any type of food, but it goes uncommonly well with beef. Both of these main ingredients stand up well against the hearty black beans and garlic seasonings. This is a delicious, quick, wholesome dish.

SERVES 4

450 g (1 lb) lean beef steak
450 g (1 lb) fresh asparagus
3 tablespoons groundnut oil
100 g (4 oz) onions, thinly sliced
2 tablespoons black beans, coarsely chopped
1½ tablespoons finely chopped garlic
2 teaspoons finely chopped fresh root ginger
3 tablespoons *Chicken Stock (see p.56)* or water
1 tablespoon Shaoxing rice wine or dry sherry
1½ teaspoons salt
½ teaspoon freshly ground black pepper
1 teaspoon sugar
2 tablespoons oyster sauce

FOR THE MARINADE

2 teaspoons light soy sauce
2 teaspoons Shaoxing rice wine or dry sherry
2 teaspoons sesame oil
½ teaspoon salt
¼ teaspoon freshly ground black pepper
2 teaspoons cornflour

Put the beef in the freezer for 20 minutes. This will allow the meat to harden slightly for easier cutting. Then cut it into thin slices 4 cm (1½ in) long. Put the beef slices into a bowl and add the soy sauce, Shaoxing rice wine or dry sherry, sesame oil, salt, pepper and cornflour. Mix well and let the slices steep in the marinade for about 15 minutes.

Meanwhile, slice the asparagus on the diagonal into 7.5-cm (3-in) pieces and set aside.

Heat a wok or large frying-pan over a high heat until it is very hot. Add the oil and, when it is very hot and slightly smoking, add the beef from the marinade and stir-fry for about 2 minutes. Remove the meat and drain it in a colander. Pour off all but 1½ tablespoons of the oil and re-heat it over a high heat. When it is very hot, add the onions, black beans, garlic and ginger and stir-fry for 1 minute. Then add the asparagus and stir-fry for 1 minute. Now add the stock or water, Shaoxing rice wine or dry sherry, salt, pepper and sugar. Continue to stir-fry for 3 minutes or until the asparagus is slightly tender. Add more water as necessary. Quickly return the meat to the wok, add the oyster sauce and stir well. Turn the mixture on to a warm platter and serve at once.

STIR-FRIED BEEF WITH CORN

O*ften in Thailand, beef or chicken is combined with toothsome baby corn. This Thai-inspired recipe with my own touches is easy to make and delectable.*

Often this type of sweetcorn is imported from Thailand or grown locally. It has become quite popular and is now easily found in supermarkets. It is easy to cook and, when it is stir-fried in the wok, it has a slightly smoky taste that adds to the enjoyment of this unique vegetable. Although baby corn can be found in tins, it is best fresh.

SERVES 4

450 g (1 lb) lean beef steak

3 tablespoons groundnut oil

1 small onion, thinly sliced

2 tablespoons thinly sliced garlic

2 tablespoons finely chopped spring onions

225 g (8 oz) fresh or tinned baby corn

150 ml (5 fl oz) *Chicken Stock (see p.56)*

1 tablespoon Shaoxing rice wine or dry sherry

3 tablespoons oyster sauce

Handful of fresh basil leaves

FOR THE MARINADE

1 tablespoon light soy sauce

1 teaspoon five-spice powder

2 teaspoons sesame oil

1 tablespoon Shaoxing rice wine or dry sherry

2 teaspoons cornflour

Cut the beef into thin slices 5 cm (2 in) long and 5 mm (¼ in) thick and put them into a bowl. Add the soy sauce, five-spice powder, sesame oil, Shaoxing rice wine or dry sherry and cornflour. Leave the mixture to marinate for 20 minutes.

Heat a wok or large frying-pan until it is very hot. Add the oil and, when it is very hot and slightly smoking, add the beef slices and stir-fry for 3 minutes or until they are lightly browned. Remove them and drain them well. Discard all but 1 tablespoon of the oil.

Re-heat the wok over a high heat until it is hot. Add the onion and garlic and stir-fry for 1 minute. Then add the spring onions and baby corn and continue to stir-fry for 1 minute. Now add the stock and Shaoxing rice wine or dry sherry and continue to cook for 3 minutes or until the corn is tender. Then add the oyster sauce and bring it to a simmer. Return the drained beef slices and toss them thoroughly with the sauce. Add the basil leaves and give the mixture several stirs. Turn the mixture on to a warm serving platter and serve at once.

BRAISED KOREAN-STYLE SPARERIBS

K orean food is one of the least known of all the Asian cuisines. It is a cuisine that uses many of the same ingredients as Chinese cuisine but combines them in different ways. One delicious dish that I have eaten in Korean restaurants is this one with spareribs. I have added my own touches.

As it is a braised dish, it re-heats well. It makes a substantial meal and is perfect for a cool evening. Serve it with rice and another vegetable dish.

SERVES 4

750 g (1¼ lb) meaty pork spareribs
1 tablespoon groundnut oil
5 garlic cloves, crushed
1 tablespoon finely chopped fresh root
    ginger
3 tablespoons finely chopped spring onions
3 tablespoons rock or plain sugar
3 tablespoons Shaoxing rice wine or dry
    sherry
300 ml (10 fl oz) *Chicken Stock (see p. 56)*
2 tablespoons light soy sauce
2 tablespoons sesame paste or peanut butter

Have your butcher separate the spareribs into individual ribs and then into chunks which are about 7.5 cm (3 in) long. Alternatively do this yourself using a heavy, sharp cleaver that can cut through the bones.

Heat a wok or large frying-pan over a high heat until it is hot. Add the oil and, when it is very hot and slightly smoking, add the spareribs and stir-fry for 5 minutes or until they are brown. Remove them with a slotted spoon and discard all the oil and fat. Wipe the wok clean.

Put the rest of the ingredients into the clean wok or frying-pan. Bring the mixture to the boil and then reduce the heat. Add the spareribs, cover and simmer slowly for about 45 minutes, stirring occasionally. If necessary, add a little water to the sauce to prevent the dish from drying out. Skim off any surface fat, turn on to a warm serving platter and serve immediately.

STIR-FRIED GARLIC PORK

G arlic and pork are two very familiar items in Chinese cuisine. Mainly for geographic reasons, pork is the 'red meat' of Chinese cookery. The lack of grazing land and pastures make raising beef on a large scale impossible. Garlic is one of the three main spices (with ginger and soy sauce) in Chinese cuisine. And the two ingredients go so well together, with the garlic nicely enhancing the fine qualities of the pork.

The black beans in this recipe are also important, giving the dish its trademark salty pungency. It is altogether very much a southern Chinese concoction, balancing crisp, clean, distinct flavours. My mother often made this dish and it has always been a favourite of mine. She would vary the taste once in a while by adding a dash of spicy chilli bean sauce.

An easy dish to make in the wok, it goes perfectly with plain rice and any stir-fried vegetable.

SERVES 4

450 g (1 lb) lean pork
2 tablespoons groundnut oil
3 tablespoons finely chopped garlic
3 spring onions, thinly sliced diagonally
2 teaspoons chilli bean sauce
3 tablespoons black beans
1 tablespoon light soy sauce
1 teaspoon Shaoxing rice wine or dry
  sherry
1 teaspoon sugar
1 tablespoon *Chicken Stock (see p.56)* or water
1 tablespoon sesame oil

FOR THE MARINADE

1 tablespoon Shaoxing rice wine or dry
  sherry
1 tablespoon light soy sauce
2 teaspoons sesame oil
1 teaspoon cornflour

Cut the pork into thin slices 5 cm (2 in) long. Put the slices into a small bowl and mix them well with the Shaoxing rice wine or dry sherry, soy sauce, sesame oil and cornflour. Leave to marinate for about 20 minutes.

Heat a wok or large frying-pan until it is hot. Add half the oil and, when it is very hot and almost smoking, lift the pork out of the marinade with a slotted spoon, put it in the wok and quickly stir-fry for about 2-3 minutes. Drain well.

Wipe the wok clean, re-heat it and add the rest of the oil. Then quickly add the garlic, spring onions and chilli bean sauce. A few seconds later add the rest of the ingredients. Bring the mixture to a boil and then return the pork to the wok or pan. Stir-fry the entire mixture for another 5 minutes. Turn it on to a warm platter and serve at once.

SZECHUAN-STYLE PORK

*S*zechuan *is among my favourite food regions of China. I love the lusty flavours of the spices and diversity of its cuisine. Many of the best dishes are the home-cooked ones. These utilize simple ingredients to make a delicious meal.*

Here pork is stir-fried with Szechuan preserved vegetables for a robust, tasty dish that is quite easy to prepare. In the wok, it literally takes minutes. The key to success in this recipe is not to overcook the pork. You can buy the preserved vegetables in Chinese grocers or delicatessens.

SERVES 4

450 g (1 lb) lean, boneless pork

50 g (2 oz) beanthread (transparent) noodles

1½ tablespoons groundnut oil

2 tablespoons coarsely chopped garlic

2 teaspoons finely chopped fresh root ginger

4 tablespoons Szechuan preserved vegetables, rinsed and coarsely chopped

1 tablespoon light soy sauce

1 tablespoon Shaoxing rice wine or dry sherry

1 teaspoon sugar

150 ml (5 fl oz) *Chicken Stock (see p.56)* or water

FOR THE MARINADE

1 tablespoon Shaoxing rice wine or dry sherry

1 tablespoon light soy sauce

2 teaspoons sesame oil

2 teaspoons cornflour

Cut the pork into thin slices 5 cm (2 in) long. Put the sliced pork into a bowl and mix in the Shaoxing rice wine or dry sherry, soy sauce, sesame oil and cornflour. Let the mixture sit for 10-15 minutes so that the pork absorbs the flavours of the marinade.

Soak the noodles in a large bowl of warm water for 15 minutes. When soft, drain and discard the water. Cut into 7.5-cm (3-in) lengths using scissors or a knife.

Heat a wok or frying-pan to a very high heat. Add the oil and, when it is very hot and slightly smoking, add the pork slices and stir-fry them until they are brown. Add the garlic, ginger and Szechuan vegetables. Add the beanthread noodles, soy sauce, Shaoxing rice wine or dry sherry, sugar and stock and continue to stir-fry until the pork is cooked and slightly firm. This should take about 5 minutes. Remove and arrange the pork, noodles and vegetables on a warm serving platter. Pour any juices remaining in the wok over the pork and serve at once.

GINGER TOMATO BEEF

I remember eating this delightful and refreshing dish during a visit to Malaysia. The ginger plant of tropical South-east Asia, with its yellowish-green flowers and strongly aromatic rhizome, is a basic seasoning throughout Asia. The lively and zesty flavour pairs well with tomatoes, they in turn balancing the robust beef. This dish can be served with pasta or rice.

SERVES 4

450 g (1 lb) lean beef steak
1 tablespoon light soy sauce
2 teaspoons Shaoxing rice wine or dry
   sherry
1 teaspoon sesame oil
2 teaspoons cornflour
450 g (1 lb) fresh or tinned tomatoes
3 tablespoons groundnut oil
225 g (8 oz) onions, coarsely chopped
1 tablespoon finely chopped fresh root
   ginger
2 tablespoons coarsely chopped garlic
1 teaspoon salt
½ teaspoon freshly ground black pepper
1 teaspoon sugar
½ teaspoon chilli flakes

FOR THE GARNISH

Handful of fresh sprigs of coriander

Cut the beef into thick 5 mm (¼ in) x 5 cm (2-in) slices and put them into a bowl. Add the light soy sauce, Shaoxing rice wine or dry sherry, sesame oil and cornflour and mix well.

If you are using fresh tomatoes, peel, seed and cut them into 2.5-cm (1-in) cubes. If you are using tinned tomatoes, chop them into small chunks.

Heat a wok or large frying-pan over a high heat until it is hot. Add the oil and, when it is very hot and slightly smoking, add the beef and stir-fry for 2 minutes to brown. Remove the beef with a slotted spoon and drain in a colander. Drain off all but about 1 tablespoon of oil.

Re-heat the wok, add the onions, ginger and garlic and stir-fry for 2 minutes. Then add the tomatoes, salt, pepper, sugar and chilli flakes. Turn the heat to low, cover and simmer for 15 minutes. Return the beef to the wok and heat through. Garnish with the coriander and serve at once.

SPICY ORANGE LAMB

Although Chinese ordinarily do not like lamb, they have not tasted lamb in the West, where it is delicate and more subtle than the stronger-tasting one from China.

Here I have combined the lamb with orange for a lovely contrast to the rich meat. The tartness of the fresh orange peel works well to balance the robust taste of the lamb. It is an easy dish to make and the spicy flavours add to its appeal. Serve it with plain rice and vegetables for a wholesome meal.

SERVES 4

450 g (1 lb) lean boneless lamb chops

3 tablespoons groundnut oil

1½ teaspoons finely chopped fresh root
   ginger

2 tablespoons thinly sliced garlic

1 tablespoon grated orange zest

1 teaspoon roasted Szechuan peppercorns,
   finely ground (optional)

2 tablespoons orange juice

1 tablespoon dark soy sauce

2 teaspoons chilli bean sauce

½ teaspoon salt

½ teaspoon freshly ground black pepper

1 teaspoon sugar

2 teaspoons sesame oil

FOR THE MARINADE

1 tablespoon light soy sauce

2 teaspoons Shaoxing rice wine or dry
   sherry

1 teaspoon sesame oil

2 teaspoons cornflour

Cut the lamb into thin slices 5 cm (2 in) long, cutting against the grain. Put the lamb into a bowl together with the soy sauce, Shaoxing rice wine or dry sherry, sesame oil and cornflour. Mix well and then let the mixture marinate for about 20 minutes.

Heat a wok or large frying-pan over a high heat until it is very hot. Add the oil and, when it is very hot and slightly smoking, remove the lamb from the marinade with a slotted spoon. Add it to the pan and stir-fry it for 2 minutes until it browns. Remove it and leave to drain in a colander or sieve. Pour off all but about 2 teaspoons of the oil.

Re-heat the wok or pan over a high heat and then add the ginger, garlic, orange zest and peppercorns. Stir-fry for 20 seconds. Then return the lamb to the pan, add the rest of the ingredients and stir-fry for 4 minutes, mixing well. Serve the dish at once.

STIR-FRIED VIETNAMESE-STYLE LEMON GRASS BEEF

*B*eef *goes especially well with lemon grass in this Vietnamese-inspired recipe. The delicate citrus flavour is a complement to the hearty beef. The garnish of roasted peanuts adds texture and crunch to this unusually aromatic dish, which you can serve with rice and another vegetable dish to create a complete meal.*

SERVES 4

450 g (1 lb) lean beef steak

3 tablespoons groundnut oil

100 g (4 oz) onions, thinly sliced

2 fresh red or green chillies, seeded and
  coarsely chopped

3 tablespoons coarsely chopped garlic

1 tablespoon Shaoxing rice wine or dry
  sherry

2 teaspoons sugar

FOR THE MARINADE

2 teaspoons Thai fish sauce

2 teaspoons Shaoxing rice wine or dry
  sherry

2 teaspoons sesame oil

½ teaspoon salt

¼ teaspoon freshly ground black pepper

2 teaspoons cornflour

2 stalks fresh lemon grass

FOR THE GARNISH

25 g (1 oz) roasted peanuts, coarsely
  chopped

Handful of fresh sprigs of coriander

Put the beef in the freezer for 20 minutes. This will allow the meat to harden slightly for easier cutting. Then cut it into thin slices 4 cm (1½ in) long. Put the beef slices into a bowl and add the fish sauce, Shaoxing rice wine or dry sherry, sesame oil, salt, pepper and cornflour. Peel the lemon grass stalk to reveal the tender, whitish centre and crush it with the flat of a knife. Then cut it into 7.5-cm (3-in) pieces. Add this to the meat mixture. Mix well and let the slices steep in the marinade for 30 minutes.

Heat a wok or large frying-pan over a high heat until it is very hot. Add the oil and, when it is very hot and slightly smoking, add the beef, marinade and lemon grass and stir-fry for about 2 minutes. Remove the meat and drain it in a colander.

Pour off all but 1½ tablespoons of the oil and re-heat it over a high heat. When it is very hot, add the onions, chillies and garlic and stir-fry for 1 minute. Then add the Shaoxing rice wine or dry sherry and sugar. Continue to stir-fry for 3 minutes. Quickly return the meat to the wok and continue to stir-fry for 2 minutes or until the beef is heated through. Turn the mixture on to a warm platter, garnish with the chopped peanuts and coriander and serve at once.

SAVOURY PORK TOMATO SAUCE

*T*his is a tasty sauce that is delicious over rice, noodles or pasta. It is a variation of the bean sauce used with noodles. Tomatoes, a relatively recent arrival to the Asian food scene, have become very popular and are used in every way possible. No wonder, they are such a wonderful food.

This sauce can be made in advance, even frozen. It is easily re-heated, which makes it ideal for entertaining as well as for a quick family dinner.

SERVES 4

1½ tablespoons groundnut oil

3 tablespoons coarsely chopped garlic

1 tablespoon finely chopped fresh root
 ginger

3 tablespoons finely chopped spring onions

2 small onions, thinly sliced

2 red or green chillies, seeded and finely
 chopped

450 g (1 lb) minced pork

2 teaspoons salt

½ teaspoon freshly ground black pepper

1 tablespoon sugar

450 g (1 lb) fresh tomatoes, cored and
 quartered

300 ml (10 fl oz) *Chicken Stock (see p.56)* or
 water

2½ tablespoons Thai fish sauce

2 tablespoons light soy sauce

FOR THE GARNISH

Handful of fresh sprigs of coriander

Heat a wok or large frying-pan over a high heat until it is hot. Add the oil and, when it is very hot and slightly smoking, add the garlic, ginger, spring onions, onions and chillies and stir-fry for 2 minutes.

Add the pork, stir well to break up all the pieces and continue to stir-fry for about 5 minutes or more until the pork loses its pink colour. Then add the salt, pepper, sugar and tomatoes.

Finally add the stock or water, fish sauce and soy sauce. Bring the mixture to the boil, turn the heat down to low and simmer for 15 minutes. Transfer the sauce to a warm platter, garnish with the coriander and serve at once.

THAI-STYLE MEATBALLS

*W*alking through the streets of Bangkok, one is pleasantly overwhelmed by the exotic fragrances and mouth-watering aromas characteristic of Thai cooking. They emanate from the many small restaurants and street-stall kitchens that line the thoroughfare.

Street vendors sell an assortment of fish cakes, snacks and meatballs, and I first tasted this dish at such a stall. What makes the meatballs so good is the spices blending so nicely into the succulent beef and pork. The egg whites give the meatballs a delicate, light texture.

The meatballs are very easy to prepare and they are excellent party snacks with drinks.

SERVES 4

100 g (4 oz) minced beef

100 g (4 oz) minced pork

2 egg whites

2 tablespoons very cold water

1 teaspoon salt

½ teaspoons freshly ground black pepper

2 tablespoons finely chopped garlic

3 tablespoons finely chopped fresh
   coriander

3 tablespoons finely chopped spring onions

2 teaspoons Thai fish sauce

2 teaspoons sugar

Plain flour, for dusting

400 ml (15 fl oz) groundnut oil

Mix the beef and pork in a food processor for a few seconds. Slowly add the egg whites and cold water and mix them for a few more seconds until they are fully incorporated into the meat. Then add the rest of the ingredients except the flour and oil and mix for about a minute until the meat mixture has become a light paste.

Using your hands, form the mixture into 4-cm (1½-in) balls, about the size of a golf ball. (This recipe makes about 10 balls.) Dust them evenly with the flour, shaking off any excess. The meatballs will be quite fragile and soft.

Heat a wok or large frying-pan over a high heat until it is hot. Add the oil and, when it is very hot and slightly smoking, gently drop in as many meatballs as will fit easily in one layer. Carefully fry them for about 4 minutes until the meatballs are crispy and browned. Adjust the heat as necessary. Take the meatballs out with a slotted spoon and drain on kitchen paper. (You may have to do this in several batches.) Serve them at once.

SZECHUAN-STYLE PORK WITH PEANUTS

This is a pork version of a classic Szechuan Chinese dish that is usually made with chicken. It is quick and easy to make and is quite savoury – as is to be expected from any Szechuan recipe. The pork is quite robust enough to stand up to the various seasonings, while the peanuts add a wonderful textural quality to the dish. Serve it with plain rice and another vegetable dish for a complete meal.

SERVES 4

450 g (1 lb) boneless pork chops
1½ tablespoons groundnut or peanut oil
1 dried red chilli, split lengthways
75 g (3 oz) raw peanuts, shelled *(see p.20)*

FOR THE MARINADE

1 tablespoon light soy sauce
2 teaspoons Shaoxing rice wine or dry sherry
1 teaspoon sesame oil
2 teaspoons cornflour

FOR THE SAUCE

2 tablespoons *Chicken Stock (see p.56)* or water
2 tablespoons Shaoxing rice wine or dry sherry
1 tablespoon dark soy sauce
2 teaspoons sugar
1 tablespoon coarsely chopped garlic
1½ tablespoons finely chopped spring onions
2 teaspoons finely chopped fresh root ginger
1 tablespoon Chinese black rice vinegar or cider vinegar
1 teaspoon salt
1 teaspoon sesame oil

Cut the pork into 2.5-cm (1-in) cubes. Combine the pork with the light soy sauce, Shaoxing rice wine or dry sherry, sesame oil and cornflour.

Heat a wok or large frying-pan over a high heat. Add the oil and, when it is hot, add the chilli and stir-fry for a few seconds. (You may remove it when it turns black or leave it in; leaving it in will make the flavour stronger.) Add the peanuts and stir-fry them for 1 minute. Remove the peanuts from the wok and reserve.

Lift the pork from the marinade with a slotted spoon, add to the wok and stir-fry for 3 minutes or until the pork is lightly browned. Remove the pork and drain in a colander.

Wipe the wok clean and put all the sauce ingredients, except the sesame oil, into the wok. Bring the sauce to a boil and then turn the heat down. Return the pork to the wok and cook for about 2 minutes in the sauce, mixing well all the time. Finally, return the peanuts and add the sesame oil, give the mixture a good stir and serve immediately.

STIR-FRIED CURRY BEEF

*A*lthough curry, as such, is not a Chinese seasoning, it has nevertheless made its way into Chinese cuisine in a rather mild form. The hint of exotic spices adds a special, very subtle flavour to any Chinese dish. Curry works extremely well when beef is matched with vegetables.

This is a substantial dish that easily makes a filling meal for two or three. It may also be served as part of a multicourse Chinese-style menu.

The best type of curry paste or powder to use is the Madras variety. It is favoured by most Chinese cooks.

SERVES 2-4

450 g (1 lb) lean beef steak
3 tablespoons groundnut oil
225 g (8 oz) onions, sliced
2 tablespoons coarsely chopped garlic

FOR THE MARINADE

1 tablespoon light soy sauce
2 teaspoons sesame oil
1 tablespoon Shaoxing rice wine or dry
  sherry
2 teaspoons cornflour

FOR THE CURRY SAUCE

1 tablespoon Shaoxing rice wine or dry
  sherry
1 tablespoon Madras curry paste or powder
1 tablespoon dark soy sauce
1 teaspoon light soy sauce
1 teaspoon sugar
2 tablespoons *Chicken Stock (see p.56)* or
  water

FOR THE GARNISH

1½ tablespoons finely chopped spring
  onions

Cut the beef into thin slices 5 cm (2 in) long and 5 mm (¼ in) thick and put them into a bowl. Add the light soy sauce, sesame oil, Shaoxing rice wine or dry sherry and cornflour. Let the mixture marinate for 20 minutes.

Heat a wok or large frying-pan until it is very hot. Add the oil and, when it is very hot and slightly smoking, add the beef slices and stir-fry for 3 minutes or until they are lightly browned. Remove them and drain them well in a colander set inside a bowl.

Wipe the wok or pan clean and re-heat it over a high heat until it is hot. Add 1 tablespoon of the drained oil, then add the onions and garlic and stir-fry for 1 minute. Add all the curry sauce ingredients and bring the mixture to a simmer and cook for 3 minutes. Return the drained beef slices to the wok or pan and toss them thoroughly with the sauce. Turn the mixture on to a warm serving platter, garnish with the spring onions and serve at once.

VIETNAMESE-STYLE BEEF STEW

This recipe is a Vietnamese version of beef stew that is similar in some ways to the Chinese one. However, the seasonings are slightly different, with the use of aromatic lemon grass.

Be sure to use an inexpensive cut of beef such as brisket or shin. This is a perfect dish for a cold winter's night. Plain steamed rice is an ideal accompaniment to this hearty and very tasty dish. The stew can also be made and allowed to cool, then re-heated later, garnished and served.

SERVES 4-6

4 stalks fresh lemon grass

1.4 kg (3 lb) stewing beef, such as brisket or shin

4 spring onions

2 tablespoons groundnut oil

1 small onion, coarsely chopped

6 slices fresh root ginger

6 garlic cloves, lightly crushed

1 tablespoon crushed red chilli

450 g (1 lb) carrots

FOR THE BRAISING SAUCE

900 ml (1½ pints) *Chicken Stock (see p.56)*

50 g (2 oz) rock sugar or plain sugar

3 tablespoons light soy sauce

2 tablespoons dark soy sauce

3 tablespoons Shaoxing rice wine or dry sherry

4 whole star anise

2 teaspoons five-spice powder

2 tablespoons tomato paste

2 teaspoons salt

1 teaspoon freshly ground black pepper

FOR THE GARNISH

6 tablespoons coarsely chopped fresh basil

Peel the lemon grass stalks to reveal the tender, whitish centre and crush with the flat of a knife. Then cut it into 7.5-cm (3-in) pieces. Cut the meat into 5-cm (2-in) cubes. Slice the spring onions at a slight diagonal into 5-cm (2-in) segments.

Heat a wok or large frying-pan until it is hot. Add the oil and, when it is very hot and slightly smoking, add the beef. Pan-fry until it is brown. This should take about 10 minutes. Pour off all but 1 tablespoon of oil from the pan. Add the spring onions, chopped onion, ginger, garlic and chilli and stir-fry with the beef for about 5 minutes.

Transfer this mixture to a large casserole or pan. Add the braising sauce ingredients. Bring the liquid to the boil, skim off any fat from the surface and turn the heat as low as possible. Cover and braise for 1½ hours.

Meanwhile, peel the carrots and cut them at a slight diagonal into 5-cm (2-in) chunks. Add these to the meat and continue to cook the mixture for another 30 minutes or until the beef is quite tender. Remove the vegetables with a slotted spoon and set aside. Then turn the heat up to high and rapidly reduce the liquid for about 15 minutes. The sauce should thicken slightly. Return the vegetables to the pan and cook for 2 minutes or until they are warmed through. Ladle the stew into a large warm dish. Garnish with the chopped fresh basil and serve immediately.

CALVES' LIVER WITH SPICY BLACK BEAN SAUCE

The sturdy flavour and distinct taste of liver almost demands something as spicy as Chinese black bean sauce. This delightful recipe is an delicious alternative to the usual liver with onions. The dish is easy to make. Liver should never be overcooked; it should remain moist, soft in texture and slightly pink in colour. Thus, the stir-frying time is quite short, which means you can quickly make this dish the centre attraction of a nutritious menu.

SERVES 4

450 g (1lb) fresh calves' liver
Cornflour, for dusting

FOR THE MARINADE

1 tablespoon Shaoxing rice wine or dry
 sherry
2 teaspoons sesame oil
2 teaspoons salt
½ teaspoon freshly ground black pepper

FOR THE SAUCE

4 tablespoons groundnut oil
1½ tablespoons coarsely chopped black
 beans
1 tablespoon finely chopped garlic
2 teaspoons finely chopped fresh root
 ginger
3 tablespoons finely chopped spring onions
1 tablespoon chopped shallots
1 tablespoon light soy sauce
2 teaspoons dark soy sauce
1 tablespoon chilli bean sauce
1 teaspoon sugar
1 tablespoon *Chicken Stock (see p.56)* **or water**
1 tablespoon sesame oil

Cut the calves liver into thin slices 7.5 cm (3 in) long. Mix together the marinade ingredients in a bowl, add the liver slices and coat them thoroughly with marinade. Cover the bowl tightly with cling film and leave to marinate in the fridge for at least 20 minutes. Remove the liver slices from the marinade and dust with cornflour, shaking off any excess.

Heat a wok or large frying-pan over a high heat until it is hot. Add 3 tablespoons of the oil and, when it is very hot and slightly smoking, add the liver and stir-fry for about 2-3 minutes. Drain well in a colander.

Re-heat the wok, adding 1 tablespoon of oil, then add the black beans, garlic, ginger, spring onions and shallots. A few seconds later add the rest of the ingredients. When the sauce comes to the boil, return the liver to the wok or pan and toss it well, coating it with the sauce. Stir-fry for 30 seconds, turn it on to a warm platter and serve at once.

SPICY PORK WITH FRAGRANT BASIL

This is a mouth-watering Thai-inspired dish. The minced pork is quickly stir-fried and tossed with so much fragrant basil that the seasoning almost plays the role of a green vegetable. Thai cookery, it seems, can never use too much basil. And here it is used to such good effect, helping to produce a marvellously aromatic dish that goes extremely well with plain rice. It is easy to make and is therefore ideal for a quick but exotic family meal.

SERVES 4

1½ tablespoons **groundnut oil**

3 tablespoons **coarsely chopped garlic**

3 tablespoons **seeded and finely chopped red chilli**

450 g (1 lb) **minced pork**

2 tablespoons **finely chopped fresh coriander**

2 tablespoons **Thai fish sauce**

1 tablespoon **oyster sauce**

2 teaspoons **sugar**

150 ml (5 fl oz) *Chicken Stock (see p.56)*

A large handful of fresh basil leaves

Heat a wok or large frying-pan over a high heat until it is hot. Add the oil and, when it is very hot and slightly smoking, add the garlic and chilli and stir-fry for 30 seconds. Then add the pork and continue to stir-fry for 3 minutes. Then add the coriander, fish sauce, oyster sauce, sugar and stock. Continue to stir-fry for 3 minutes. Then add the basil and stir-fry for another minute. Turn on to a warm platter and serve at once.

THAI-STYLE CHILLI BEEF

Imitation being the sincerest form of flattery, this recipe is an admitted replica of one of the culinary creations of my good friend, Chalie Amatylakul. He is among the foremost authorities on Thai cookery and has taught me very much about the essentials of this great cuisine.

With the exception of the fresh chillies, it is quite similar to many stir-fried Chinese dishes. It is delightful, aromatic and quick to make. Serve it with rice, as a main course, or with another vegetable dish.

SERVES 4

450 g (1 lb) lean beef steak

1 teaspoon salt

½ teaspoon freshly ground black pepper

1 teaspoon sesame oil

25 g (1 oz) Chinese dried mushrooms

1½ tablespoons groundnut oil

225 g (8 oz) onions, shredded

2 tablespoons coarsely chopped garlic

4 red chillies, seeded and finely shredded

1 tablespoon Shaoxing rice wine or dry sherry

1 tablespoon oyster sauce

1 tablespoon light soy sauce

1 teaspoon sugar

3 tablespoons *Chicken Stock (see p.56)* or water

FOR THE GARNISH

1½ tablespoons finely shredded spring onions

Cut the beef into thin slices 5 cm (2 in) long and 5 mm (¼ in) thick, then finely shred them. In a bowl, combine the beef with the salt, pepper and sesame oil.

Soak the mushrooms in warm water for 20 minutes. Then drain them and squeeze out the excess liquid. Remove and discard the stems and finely shred the caps into thin strips.

Heat a wok or large frying-pan until it is very hot. Add the oil and, when it is very hot and slightly smoking, add the onions and garlic and stir-fry for 3 minutes. Then add the beef and chillies and continue to stir-fry for 2 minutes. Finally, add the Shaoxing rice wine or dry sherry, oyster sauce, soy sauce, sugar and stock or water. Add the mushrooms and continue to stir-fry the mixture for 2 minutes until the beef is thoroughly mixed through. Turn the mixture on to a serving platter, garnish it with the spring onions, and serve at once.

STIR-FRIED CHILLI PORK WITH CASHEWS

Pork, the preferred Chinese 'red meat', is delicious when combined with the taste and texture of nuts — in this case, cashews. A touch of chilli bean sauce is added for zest and you have a quick, savoury dish that can grace the centre of a family table. Serve this with plain rice and another vegetable dish for a wholesome and satisfying meal.

SERVES 4

450 g (1 lb) lean boneless pork chops

1½ tablespoons groundnut or peanut oil

1 teaspoon salt

½ teaspoon freshly ground black pepper

50 g (2 oz) cashew nuts

1 tablespoon Shaoxing rice wine or dry sherry

1 tablespoon light soy sauce

1 tablespoon chilli bean sauce

2 teaspoons sugar

FOR THE MARINADE

1 tablespoon Shaoxing rice wine or dry sherry

2 teaspoons light soy sauce

2 teaspoons sesame oil

1 teaspoon cornflour

FOR THE GARNISH

1 tablespoon finely chopped spring onions

Cut the pork into thin slices 5 cm (2 in) long. Put the sliced pork into a bowl and mix in the Shaoxing rice wine or dry sherry, soy sauce, sesame oil and cornflour. Let the mixture sit for 10-15 minutes so that the pork absorbs the flavours of the marinade.

Heat a wok or frying-pan over a very high heat. Add the oil and, when it is very hot and slightly smoking, add the pork slices, salt and pepper and stir-fry for 2 minutes. Remove them with a slotted spoon. Add the cashew nuts and stir-fry them for 1 minute. Then add the rest of the ingredients. Return the pork to the wok or pan and stir-fry the mixture for another 2 minutes. Garnish with the spring onions and serve at once.

POULTRY

Like meats, poultry is very easy to cook in the wok. The hot wok seals in the juicy flavours of the chicken, then allows it to unite with an array of seasonings and aromatics. Garlic, chilli bean sauce, lemon grass and ginger are some of the many flavours used to turn prosaic poultry into a special treat. Many of these recipes are inspired not only by my Chinese heritage but also by my travels to South-east Asia.

The wok, widely used in that part of Asia, is clearly a key piece of equipment in the kitchen. You will find many of these tasty recipes easy to make and, from Peter Ng's Sesame-ginger Chicken *to* Indonesian-style Coconut Chicken, *the wok transforms the lowly chicken into wonderful savoury dishes.*

PETER NG'S SESAME-GINGER CHICKEN

Peter Ng is a lover of good food and an excellent cook. Of Chinese descent, he was born in Malaysia and now lives in Adelaide, Australia. His cultural inheritance is obvious in his cooking, which combines Malaysian flavours with Chinese techniques.

Peter recalls that this recipe was prepared by his mother as a special treat for his sister when she was pregnant. Ginger is highly regarded by the Chinese who believe its 'warming' (or yang) properties are beneficial to both mother and child. Be that as it may, ginger, chicken thighs and selected spices make a happy marriage as they cook in the wok. The dish is the centrepiece of a marvellous meal when combined with rice and vegetables.

SERVES 4

450 g (1 lb) boneless, skinless chicken thighs

1 tablespoon groundnut oil

2 teaspoons sesame oil

3 tablespoons finely shredded fresh root ginger

2 tablespoons dark soy sauce

2 teaspoons sugar

1 teaspoon salt

½ teaspoon freshly ground black pepper

150 ml (5 fl oz) *Chicken Stock (see p.56)* or water

2 tablespoons Shaoxing rice wine or dry sherry

FOR THE MARINADE

2 teaspoons light soy sauce

1 teaspoon dark soy sauce

1 tablespoon Shaoxing rice wine or dry sherry

½ teaspoon salt

½ teaspoon freshly ground black pepper

1 teaspoon sesame oil

2 teaspoons cornflour

FOR THE GARNISH

3 tablespoons finely shredded spring onions

Cut the chicken into 5-cm (2-in) chunks. Mix the soy sauces, Shaoxing rice wine or dry sherry, salt, pepper and sesame oil and pour it over the chicken. Then mix in the cornflour until all the chicken pieces are thoroughly coated. Leave the chicken to marinate for about 30 minutes. Drain the chicken and discard the marinade.

Heat a wok or large frying-pan over a high heat until it is hot. Add the groundnut and sesame oils and, when they are very hot and slightly smoking, add the ginger and pan-fry for about 1 minute until it is crispy. Then add the chicken and stir-fry for 5 minutes or until the chicken begins to brown. Add the soy sauce, sugar, salt, pepper and stock or water and continue to stir-fry for 1 minute. Reduce the heat, cover the wok or pan and simmer for 8 minutes. Remove the cover and boil over a high heat to reduce the sauce. When only a few tablespoons of the sauce remains, add the Shaoxing rice wine or dry sherry and continue to stir-fry for about 2 minutes until the chicken is cooked. Garnish with the spring onions and serve.

GINGER-FLAVOURED PROVENÇAL CHICKEN

The *Provençal style of French cookery is justly famous and is among my very favourite cuisines. Its bright, clean, aromatic character is reminiscent of the Cantonese cooking of my childhood. Earthy spices, garlic and herbs are given wings in imaginative combinations that delight the eye as well as the palate.*

I often create 'East-West' dishes and even entire menus by blending my Chinese cuisine with representative Western foods and styles. Both cultures share a commitment to good food, simply made, but a delight to see and to eat. Here I use chicken thighs, as the Chinese prefer to do, and I combine spices and seasonings from the two cuisines.

Unless they are in season and vine-ripened, you are better off using tinned tomatoes. The dish re-heats well, so it can be prepared in advance. It can also be increased, without any decline in quality, to accommodate a larger group of people.

SERVES 4

750 g (1¾ lb) boneless, skinless chicken
   thighs
3 tablespoons olive oil
6 garlic cloves, crushed
2 tablespoons finely chopped fresh root
   ginger
1 onion, coarsely chopped
1 teaspoon salt
½ teaspoon freshly ground black pepper
750 g (1¾ lb) tinned tomatoes, with liquid
50 g (2 oz) black Nice olives, stoned
300 ml (10 fl oz) *Chicken Stock (see p. 56)*
20 basil leaves
2 teaspoons sugar
2 teaspoons salt
½ teaspoon finely ground black pepper

FOR THE MARINADE

1 tablespoon light soy sauce
2 teaspoons dark soy sauce
1 tablespoon Shaoxing rice wine or dry
   sherry
1 teaspoon salt
½ teaspoon freshly ground black pepper

Cut the chicken into 5-cm (2-in) pieces. In a large bowl, combine the chicken with the soy sauces, Shaoxing rice wine or dry sherry, salt and pepper and mix well. Leave to marinate in the fridge for 30 minutes. Drain the chicken and discard any excess marinade.

Heat a wok or large frying-pan over a high heat until it is hot. Add the oil and, when it is very hot, add the chicken and brown on both sides. Turn the heat down to medium and continue to brown for 5 minutes until it is golden brown. Remove the chicken from the wok and drain in a colander. Pour off all but 2 tablespoons of the oil and fat.

Re-heat the wok, add the garlic, ginger, onion, salt and pepper and stir-fry for 1 minute. Reduce the heat and continue to cook for 3 minutes or until the onion is soft and transparent. Then add the tomatoes, olives and stock. Bring the mixture to a simmer, return the chicken to the wok, reduce the heat, cover and simmer for 15 minutes or until the chicken is cooked. Add the basil leaves, sugar, salt and pepper and cook for another 2 minutes. Turn on to a warm platter and serve at once.

SOOTHING CHICKEN PORRIDGE

*T*his is a common 'comfort food' throughout Asia: nutritious, soothing, satisfying, simple to make and always available. People eat it for breakfast, lunch or dinner, and as a snack. What makes this dish so special are the seasonings and the garnishes, which elevate the porridge to the level of a special treat. Of course, you can determine what those flavours are according to your own whims and preferences. That is what makes it a comfort. Here I use South-east Asian touches because I like them and because they add up to a light but very satisfying dish at any time of the day.

The porridge and chicken can be made in advance. In this case, re-heat them slowly and simply add some more water if the porridge is too thick.

You can buy the Tiensien preserved vegetables in Asian grocery shops and some delicatessens.

SERVES 4

1.5 kg (3 lb) chicken

2.25 litres (4 pints) water

2 teaspoons salt

½ teaspoon freshly ground white pepper

Enough short-grain or long-grain rice to fill a measuring jug to the 150-ml (5-fl oz) level, unwashed

2 tablespoons groundnut oil

3 tablespoons thinly sliced garlic

3 tablespoons thinly sliced shallots

4 eggs

2 red chillies

2 tablespoons finely shredded fresh root ginger

2 tablespoons light soy sauce

2 teaspoons salt

1 teaspoon freshly ground white pepper

3 tablespoons finely chopped Tiensien preserved vegetables

3 tablespoons finely chopped spring onions

Fresh sprigs of coriander

Put the chicken and water together in a large pan and bring to the boil. Lower the heat and simmer uncovered for 20 minutes, skimming occasionally. Add the salt and pepper, cover and simmer for another 15 minutes. Remove the chicken and allow it to cool thoroughly.

Bring the liquid back to the boil and add the rice. Let the mixture come back to the boil and give it several good stirs. Turn the heat down to medium and cover the pan. Let the mixture simmer for about 1 hour, stirring occasionally. The rice grains should break down into a smooth porridge.

Heat a wok or large frying-pan over a high heat until it is hot. Add the oil and, when it is very hot and slightly smoking, reduce the heat, add the garlic and shallots and stir-fry them for 1 minute or until they are brown. Remove them from the wok and drain thoroughly on kitchen paper.

In a small pan, boil the eggs in hot water for 10 minutes. Drain and refresh with cold running water. Crack them lightly and shell them. Continue to run them under cold running water until they are cool enough to handle easily. Cut the hard-boiled eggs into quarters and put them in a bowl. Seed and finely slice the chillies and put them into a small dish. Place the ginger in a small dish. Do the same with the soy sauce, salt and pepper.

Rinse the preserved vegetables under cold running water, squeeze them dry and chop them. Put them into a small dish. Do the same with the spring onions and fresh coriander.

When the chicken is cool enough to handle, remove the meat with your hands and pull it apart into shreds with a fork. Put the chicken in a bowl.

Now uncover the rice and simmer for a further 5 minutes. Ladle the porridge into individual bowls, adding some of the chicken, egg and each of the garnishes to each serving. Serve at once.

QUICK AND HEALTHY STEAMED CHICKEN

Steaming is not only a healthy way to cook food, it also brings out the subtle flavours. By keeping food moist and cooking it slowly in warm vapours, good chicken comes out even better. Chinese cooks tend to steam the entire chicken, but, when I am in a hurry, I simply steam chicken breasts. The result is a quick but healthy meal that takes little time to prepare. The juices from the steamed chicken taste delicious over rice.

SERVES 4

450 g (1 lb) skinless, boneless chicken
  breasts
1 teaspoon coarse sea salt or plain salt
1 tablespoon light soy sauce
1 tablespoon Shaoxing rice wine or dry
  sherry
½ teaspoon freshly ground white pepper
1 egg white
2 teaspoons cornflour
1 teaspoon sesame oil
1½ tablespoons finely shredded fresh root
  ginger

FOR THE GARNISH

3 tablespoons finely shredded spring onions
1 tablespoon groundnut oil
2 teaspoons sesame oil

Combine the chicken with the salt, soy sauce, Shaoxing rice wine or dry sherry, pepper, egg white, cornflour and sesame oil. Leave to marinate for at least 20 minutes.

Next set up a steamer or put a rack into a wok or deep pan and fill it with 5-cm (2-in) of water. Bring the water to the boil over a high heat. Put the chicken in one layer on a heatproof plate and scatter the ginger evenly over the top. Put the plate of chicken into the steamer or on to the rack. Cover the pan tightly and gently steam the chicken until it is just white and firm. It will take about 8-10 minutes to cook, depending on the thickness of the chicken.

Remove the plate of cooked chicken and sprinkle on the spring onions. Heat the two oils together in a small pan. When they are hot, pour the oil mixture over the top of the chicken. Serve at once.

THAI-STYLE CHICKEN

I greatly enjoy the Thai way with chicken. The combinations of exotic lemon grass, garlic and fresh chillies always have my mouth watering. The Thais also use a type of wok and they stir-fry many of their dishes. In this particular Thai-inspired dish, I have taken some elements of Thai flavourings and have created my own tasty chicken dish. It works brilliantly with rice.

SERVES 4

450 g (1 lb) skinless, boneless chicken thighs or 900 g (2 lb) chicken thighs with bone in
1 stalk fresh lemon grass
1 tablespoon groundnut oil
1 onion, thinly sliced
2 tablespoons coarsely chopped garlic
2 teaspoons salt
2 teaspoons finely chopped lime zest
3 fresh red or green chillies, seeded and finely shredded
2 teaspoons sugar
Large handful of fresh basil leaves

FOR THE MARINADE

2 teaspoons light soy sauce
2 teaspoons Shaoxing rice wine or dry sherry
1 teaspoon sesame oil
2 teaspoons cornflour

If you are using unboned thighs, remove the skin and bones from the chicken thighs or have your butcher do it for you. Cut the chicken into 2.5-cm (1-in) chunks and combine it in a bowl with the soy sauce, Shaoxing rice wine or dry sherry, sesame oil and cornflour. Leave to marinate for 20 minutes.

Peel the lemon grass stalk to reveal the tender, whitish centre and cut into 5-cm (2-in) pieces. Smash them with the flat of a knife or cleaver.

Heat a wok or large frying-pan until it is very hot. Add the oil, then the chicken and stir-fry for 5 minutes until the chicken is brown. Remove the chicken and drain off the oil. Return the drained chicken to the wok and add the rest of the ingredients, except the basil leaves. Continue to cook for another 8-10 minutes, stirring from time to time, until the chicken is cooked. Add the basil leaves and give the mixture a good stir. Pour on to a warm platter and serve at once.

BRAISED CHICKEN WITH FRESH WATER CHESTNUTS

Chicken is best when its mild flavour and soft texture are combined with other distinctive tastes and contrasting textures. Sweet, fresh, crispy water chestnuts are thus an admirable partner in any chicken dish.

The clarity of the flavours here, with plain rice, make it a perfect dish for a cool autumn evening. With vegetables, it makes a very satisfying complete meal: nutritious and tasty, but not heavy. Because it re-heats so well, it can be prepared in advance and stored in the fridge.

I do not recommend the use of tinned water chestnuts as they are so watery and soft. If fresh water chestnuts are unavailable, substitute firm, fresh, peeled Asian pear apples or firm, crispy apples. Added at the last moment of cooking, they retain their sweet crunchiness.

SERVES 4

450 g (1 lb) boneless, skinless chicken thighs or 900 g (2 lb) chicken thighs with bone in

2 tablespoons groundnut oil

3 garlic cloves, thinly sliced

1½ tablespoons finely shredded fresh root ginger

225 g (8 oz) fresh water chestnuts, peeled and sliced

3 tablespoons *Chicken Stock (see p.56)* or water

2 tablespoons oyster sauce

1 tablespoon Shaoxing rice wine or dry sherry

1 teaspoon dark soy sauce

1 teaspoon light soy sauce

1 teaspoon sugar

FOR THE MARINADE

2 teaspoons light soy sauce

2 teaspoons Shaoxing rice wine or dry sherry

1 teaspoon sesame oil

2 teaspoons cornflour

If you are using unboned thighs, remove the skin and bones from the chicken thighs or have your butcher do it for you. Cut the chicken into 2.5-cm (1-in) chunks and combine it in a bowl with the light soy sauce, Shaoxing rice wine or dry sherry, sesame oil and cornflour. Leave to marinate for at least 30 minutes in the fridge.

Heat a wok or large frying-pan over a high heat until it is hot. Add the oil and, when it is very hot and slightly smoking, add the chicken and stir-fry for 5 minutes. Remove and drain the chicken. Now drain off all but 2 teaspoons of the oil from the wok.

Re-heat the wok, add the garlic and ginger and stir-fry for 30 seconds. Then add the drained chicken to the wok with the water chestnuts and the remaining ingredients. Reduce the heat to low, cover and cook for 10 minutes, stirring from time to time, until the chicken is cooked. Give the mixture a good stir, pour on to a warm platter and serve at once.

FRAGRANT ROAST AUBERGINE WITH CHICKEN

I *often spend at least two weeks of my summer holiday with my good friends the Pébeyres, who have a country home outside Souillac in south-west France. One of the great pleasures is plucking fresh produce from their gardens to create Asian-inspired dishes. They frequently have fresh aubergines, so one evening I combined them with chicken in a spicy sauce with mint that also happened to be handy. The result was a popular and tasty dish that I have subsequently cooked often for other friends.*

To cut down the fat, I first roast the aubergines in the oven, instead of frying them in the traditional Chinese way. This way, they don't absorb any oil. This step can be done hours in advance and the rest is a quick and easy stir-fry.

SERVES 4

450 g (1 lb) Chinese or ordinary aubergines

450 g (1 lb) skinless, boneless chicken thighs or 900 g (2 lb) chicken thighs with bone in

1½ tablespoons groundnut oil

2 tablespoons thinly sliced garlic

1 tablespoon finely chopped fresh root ginger

3 tablespoons finely chopped spring onions

1 tablespoon chilli bean sauce

1 tablespoon hoisin sauce

2 teaspoons oyster sauce

2 teaspoons Shaoxing rice wine or dry sherry

1 teaspoon light soy sauce

1 teaspoon dark soy sauce

1 teaspoon sugar

Small handful of mint leaves

FOR THE MARINADE

2 teaspoons light soy sauce

2 teaspoons Shaoxing rice wine or dry sherry

1 teaspoon sesame oil

2 teaspoons cornflour

Pre-heat oven to 200°C/400°F/gas 6.

If you are using Chinese aubergines, roast them for 20 minutes and if you are using the large aubergines, roast them for about 30-40 minutes or until they are soft and cooked through. Allow them to cool. Peel them and if using larger aubergines cut them into chunks, then put them in a colander and let them drain for at least 30 minutes. This procedure can be done hours in advance.

If you are using unboned thighs, remove the skin and bones from the chicken thighs or have your butcher do it for you. Cut the chicken into 2.5-cm (1-in) chunks and combine it in a bowl with the light soy sauce, Shaoxing rice wine or dry sherry, sesame oil and cornflour.

Heat a wok or large frying-pan until it is very hot, add the oil, then the chicken and stir-fry for 5 minutes. Remove the chicken from the wok and drain off all but 2 teaspoons of the oil or fat. Return the drained chicken to the wok with the garlic, ginger and spring onions and stir-fry for 5 minutes. Then add the aubergines and all the remaining ingredients, except the mint leaves. Continue to cook for another 3 minutes, stirring from time to time, until the chicken is cooked. Add the mint leaves and give the mixture a good stir. Pour on to a warm platter and serve at once.

BRAISED GARLIC CHICKEN

The wok is a perfect cooking utensil for any type of cookery, not just Chinese or Asian. Its versatility is what makes it so universally popular. This recipe was inspired by a friend's mother from the south of France. Madame Taurines often braised veal with whole garlic. I have substituted chicken and added my own Chinese touches, which work just as well. Braised in this way, the whole garlic becomes mild and sweet. Most of the resulting sauce cooks off, leaving a tender, aromatic chicken dish, and the bonus is that it is quick to make. Serve this dish with potatoes or plain rice and another vegetable dish.

SERVES 4

900 g (2 lb) chicken thighs with bone in
2 teaspoons salt
1 teaspoon freshly ground black pepper
2 tablespoons plain flour
3 tablespoons groundnut oil
15 whole garlic cloves, unpeeled
2 tablespoons Shaoxing rice wine or dry sherry
1 tablespoon light soy sauce
3 tablespoons *Chicken Stock (see p.56)* or water

FOR THE GARNISH

2 tablespoons finely snipped fresh chives

Blot the chicken thighs dry with kitchen paper. Sprinkle them evenly with the salt and pepper, then sprinkle with the flour, shaking off any excess.

Heat a wok or large frying-pan over a high heat until it is hot. Add the oil and, when it is very hot and slightly smoking, turn the heat to low. Add the chicken skin-side down and slowly brown on both sides for about 10 minutes. Drain off all the excess fat, add the garlic and stir-fry for 2 minutes. Then add the Shaoxing rice wine or dry sherry, soy sauce and stock or water. Turn the heat to as low as possible, cover and braise for 20 minutes until the chicken is tender.

When the chicken and garlic are cooked, remove them from the wok with a slotted spoon and place them on a warm platter. Sprinkle with the chives and serve at once.

LETTUCE-WRAPPED CHICKEN

This is my version of a popular Hong Kong dish that uses squab or young pigeon, which is expensive and not always as easily available as chicken.

A simple, savoury dish that goes well with the refreshing crunch of the lettuce and the fried beanthread (transparent) noodles, it is a fun dish to eat and makes a wonderful starter for any meal. Each guest puts a helping of each ingredient into a hollow lettuce leaf (rather like stuffing a pancake) and eats the filled leaf with his or her fingers.

SERVES 4-6

450 g (1 lb) skinless, boneless chicken
 thighs, coarsely minced
225 g (8 oz) red or green pepper (about
 1 large or 2 small)
15 g (½ oz) Chinese dried mushrooms
175 g (6 oz) fresh or tinned (drained weight)
 water chestnuts
225 g (8 oz) iceberg lettuce
300 ml (10 fl oz) plus 1 tablespoon
 groundnut oil
50 g (2 oz) beanthread (transparent)
 noodles
1 tablespoon finely chopped garlic
1 tablespoon finely chopped shallots
3 tablespoons finely chopped spring onions
2 teaspoons dark soy sauce
2 teaspoons Shaoxing rice wine or dry
 sherry
3 tablespoons oyster sauce
½ teaspoon salt
½ teaspoon freshly ground black pepper

FOR THE MARINADE

1 tablespoon Shaoxing rice wine or dry
 sherry
1 tablespoon light soy sauce
2 teaspoons sesame oil
2 teaspoons cornflour

TO SERVE

4 tablespoons hoisin sauce

The chicken can be cut by hand or pulsed in a food processor. Put the minced chicken into a bowl with the Shaoxing rice wine or dry sherry, soy sauce, sesame oil and cornflour, mix well and leave to marinate for about 20 minutes.

Meanwhile cut the pepper into small dice. Soak the dried mushrooms in warm water for 20 minutes, drain them and squeeze out any excess liquid. Trim off the stems and coarsely chop the caps. If you are using fresh water chestnuts, peel and coarsely chop them. If you are using tinned ones, rinse them in cold water and coarsely chop them. Separate and wash the lettuce leaves, wiping off any excess water, and set them aside.

In a large wok or deep-fat fryer, heat the 300 ml (10 fl oz) of oil until it is slightly smoking. Deep-fry the noodles until they are crisp and puffed up. Drain them on kitchen paper. (Drain off and reserve the oil, letting it cool; it can be saved for future use.)

Re-heat the wok until it is very hot, then add 1 tablespoon of the oil in which you fried the noodles. When the oil begins to smoke, add the chicken and stir-fry for about 5 minutes. Remove the chicken and drain.

Wipe the wok or pan clean. Re-heat the wok or pan over a high heat and, when it is hot, add the 1 tablespoon of fresh oil. When it is smoking slightly, add the garlic, shallots and spring onions and stir-fry for 10 seconds. Then add the peppers and stir-fry for another minute. Now add the mushrooms, water chestnuts, dark soy sauce, Shaoxing rice wine or dry sherry, oyster sauce, salt and pepper.

Stir-fry the mixture for 3 minutes and then return the chicken to the mixture and continue to stir-fry for 1 minute, mixing well. Turn on to a warm platter. Arrange the lettuce and noodles on separate platters, put the hoisin sauce into a small bowl, and serve at once.

HONEYED CHICKEN WINGS

often think that chicken wings are a neglected and unglamorous food. Yet I find them one of the most delectable parts of the chicken. They are extremely versatile and quite economical. The Chinese especially love eating them because of their special taste. In this easy-to-make recipe, they are simply braised in a honey-soy mixture. Cooked in a large quantity, they can make an unusual party dish. Served at room temperature, they make wonderful picnic food.

SERVES 4

2 tablespoons groundnut oil

750 g (1¾ lb) chicken wings

3 garlic cloves, crushed

2.5-cm (1-in) thick piece fresh root ginger, unpeeled and crushed

50 ml (2 fl oz) dark soy sauce

2 tablespoons light soy sauce

2 tablespoons Shaoxing rice wine or dry sherry

2 tablespoons honey

Heat a wok or large frying-pan over a high heat until it is hot. Add the oil and, when it is very hot and slightly smoking, add the chicken wings and stir-fry for 5 minutes or until they are brown. Remove them from the wok with a slotted spoon and drain on kitchen paper.

Drain off all the oil and fat and wipe the wok clean. Add the garlic, ginger, soy sauces, Shaoxing rice wine or dry sherry and honey and bring the mixture to a simmer. Return the chicken to this mixture. Reduce the heat to very low, cover and simmer for 30-35 minutes or until the chicken is cooked. Serve at once.

SPICY CHICKEN WITH MINT

The wok is ideal for making quick but tasty dishes. Here is a lovely, spicy chicken dish with fresh mint as a counterbalance. If you grow your own mint, it is likely to be even more delicate and subtle than the shop-bought variety. Mint is probably the most widely used of all the aromatic herbs and the one most readily accessible. A touch of curry is used with the chilli bean sauce to give this dish a real kick. The chicken is velveted to preserve its juiciness and flavour. You can use the traditional oil method or, for a less fattening version, substitute water instead. The peppers provide the dish with a crunchy texture that makes a wonderful complement to the soft, tender chicken. Serve this with plain steamed rice and a salad for a quick, delicious meal.

SERVES 4

450 g (1 lb) skinless, boneless chicken
   breasts
225 g (8 oz) red or green peppers
300 ml (10 fl oz) groundnut oil or water
1 tablespoon groundnut oil
1 tablespoon thinly sliced garlic
150 ml (5 fl oz) *Chicken Stock (see p.56)*
1½ tablespoons Madras curry paste
2 teaspoons chilli bean sauce
2 teaspoons sugar
1½ tablespoons Shaoxing rice wine or dry
   sherry
1 tablespoon light soy sauce
1 teaspoon cornflour blended with 1
   tablespoon water
8 mint leaves

FOR THE MARINADE

1 egg white
1 teaspoon salt
2 teaspoons cornflour

Cut the chicken breasts into 2.5-cm (1-in) cubes. Combine them with the egg white, salt and 2 teaspoons of cornflour in a small bowl. Put the mixture into the fridge for 20 minutes.

Wash and seed the peppers and cut them into 2.5-cm (1-in) cubes.

Heat a wok or frying-pan over a high heat until it is hot, then add the oil. When the oil is very hot, remove the wok from the heat and immediately add the chicken pieces, stirring vigorously to keep them from sticking. When the chicken pieces turn white (about 2 minutes), quickly drain the chicken.

If you choose to use water instead of oil, bring the water to the boil in a pan. Remove the pan from the heat and immediately add the chicken pieces, stirring vigorously to keep them from sticking. When the chicken pieces turn white (about 2 minutes), quickly drain the chicken.

Wipe the wok or pan clean and re-heat until it is very hot. Then add 1 tablespoon of oil. When it is very hot, add the peppers and garlic and stir-fry for 2 minutes. Then add the rest of the ingredients, except the cornflour mixture and mint leaves, and cook for another 2 minutes. Add the cornflour mixture and cook for 20 seconds, stirring, then add the drained chicken to the wok and stir-fry for another 2 minutes, coating the chicken thoroughly with the sauce. Finally add the mint leaves and stir to mix well for 1 minute. Turn on to a warm platter and serve at once.

INDONESIAN-STYLE COCONUT CHICKEN

One of the great pleasures of visiting Indonesia is eating its rich and exotic foods. As in Chinese cuisine, the wok is widely used, but Indonesians also use spices and combinations distinctly un-Chinese. Like many nations in South-east Asia, Indonesia has Chinese influences, but their unique culture makes their food different from that of China.

Here is a delicious recipe that I have adapted from my many visits to Jakarta. This dish re-heats well and, served with rice, can easily make a hearty meal.

SERVES 4

900 g (2 lb) chicken thighs with bone in

2 teaspoons salt

1 teaspoon freshly ground black pepper

2 tablespoons plain flour

3 tablespoons groundnut oil

175 g (6 oz) onions, thinly sliced

5 garlic cloves, crushed

1 tablespoon finely chopped fresh root
   ginger

1 teaspoon ground cumin

2 teaspoons ground coriander

2 tablespoons grated lemon zest

1 tablespoon light soy sauce

3 tablespoons water

2 teaspoons salt

400 ml (15 fl oz) tinned coconut milk

Blot the chicken dry with kitchen paper. Sprinkle evenly with the salt and pepper, then sprinkle with the flour, shaking off any excess.

Heat a wok or large frying-pan over a high heat until it is hot. Add the oil and, when it is very hot and slightly smoking, turn the heat to low. Add the chicken skin-side down and slowly brown on both sides. Remove the chicken and drain on kitchen paper.

Drain off all but 1 tablespoon of the oil and fat. Then add the onions, garlic and ginger and stir-fry for 3 minutes. Then add the cumin, coriander, lemon zest, soy sauce, water, salt and coconut milk. Return the chicken to the sauce, turn the heat to as low as possible, cover and braise for 20 minutes until the chicken is cooked. Transfer to a warm platter and serve at once.

BURMESE-STYLE CHICKEN

A*lthough I have never been to Burma, I have visited a number of Burmese restaurants that have opened in California. The food seems to be a cross between Chinese-Vietnamese and Thai. It is an aromatic and fragrant style of cooking that uses spices to coax flavours from foods.*

Here I have adapted a favourite Burmese chicken dish I have enjoyed. It is a dry-braised dish that is slowly cooked in spices and its own juices. It is again easy to make and delicious to eat. Serve it with plain rice and another vegetable dish for a wholesome meal.

SERVES 4

900 g (2 lb) chicken thighs with bone in
2 teaspoons salt
1 teaspoon freshly ground black pepper
2 stalks fresh lemon grass
3 tablespoons groundnut oil
175 g (6 oz) onions, thinly sliced
6 garlic cloves, crushed
1 tablespoon finely chopped fresh root
   ginger
1 teaspoon ground turmeric
1 teaspoon chilli powder
1 tablespoon light soy sauce
3 tablespoons water

Blot the chicken dry with kitchen paper. Sprinkle evenly with the salt and pepper.

Peel the lemon grass to reveal the tender, whitish centre, crush the stalk and cut into 7.5-cm (3-in) pieces.

Heat a wok or large frying-pan over a high heat until it is hot. Add the oil and, when it is very hot and slightly smoking, turn the heat to low. Add the chicken skin-side down and slowly brown on both sides. Remove the chicken and drain on kitchen paper.

Drain off all but 1 tablespoon of the oil and fat. Then add the onions, garlic, ginger and lemon grass and stir-fry for 3 minutes. Then add the turmeric, chilli powder, soy sauce and water. Return the chicken to the wok and stir-fry to coat with this mixture. Turn the heat to as low as possible, cover and braise for 20 minutes until the chicken is cooked. Transfer to a warm platter and serve at once.

BALINESE-STYLE CHICKEN

*B*ali is not only known for its exotic culture but also for its earthy foods. I remember on my first visit many years ago how impressed I was at the diversity of Balinese cooking. Many of their dishes are simmered or roasted. Here is one of my favourites. It is simple to make and re-heats easily. Serve it with plain rice and vegetables for a complete meal.

SERVES 4

900 g (2 lb) chicken thighs with bone in
2 teaspoons salt
1 teaspoon freshly ground black pepper
2 tablespoons plain flour
3 tablespoons groundnut oil
225 g (8 oz) onions, coarsely chopped
5 garlic cloves, crushed
1 tablespoon finely chopped fresh root
   ginger
3 fresh red or green chillies, seeded and
   chopped
2 teaspoons sugar
1 tablespoon lemon juice
2 tablespoons orange juice
1 tablespoon dark soy sauce
400 ml (15 fl oz) tinned coconut milk

Blot the chicken dry with kitchen paper. Sprinkle evenly with the salt and pepper. Then sprinkle with the flour, shaking off any excess.

Heat a wok or large frying-pan over a high heat until it is hot. Add the oil and, when it is very hot and slightly smoking, turn the heat to low. Add the chicken skin-side down and slowly brown on both sides. Remove the chicken and drain on kitchen paper.

Drain off all but 1 tablespoon of the oil and fat. Then add the onions, garlic, ginger and chillies and stir-fry for 3 minutes. Then add the sugar, lemon juice, orange juice, soy sauce and coconut milk. Return the chicken to the sauce, turn the heat as low as possible, cover and braise for 20 minutes until the chicken is cooked. Transfer to a warm platter and serve at once.

DELECTABLE BROCCOLI CHICKEN

*C*hicken and broccoli are a wonderful combination. In this Vietnamese-inspired recipe, the chicken is first marinated, then fried. Then it is paired with crunchy green broccoli. In Vietnam, Chinese broccoli, which is slightly more woody and bitter, would be used. But here I use the variety found in the West, which is sweeter with a distinctive, mild flavour. Chicken thighs are used because of their robust taste which holds up well to the frying. Serve this dish with rice and another vegetable dish for a wholesome meal.

SERVES 4

450 g (1 lb) fresh broccoli

450 g (1 lb) boneless, skinless chicken thighs

400 ml (14 fl oz) plus 1 tablespoon
   groundnut oil

3 tablespoons coarsely chopped garlic

1 small onion, quartered

2 tablespoons Shaoxing rice wine or dry
   sherry

3 tablespoons water or *Chicken Stock (see
   p.56)*

225 g (8 oz) tomatoes, quartered

3 tablespoons oyster sauce

2 tablespoons Thai fish sauce

1 teaspoon sugar

1 teaspoon salt

½ teaspoon freshly ground black pepper

2 teaspoons sesame oil

FOR THE MARINADE

½ teaspoon freshly ground black pepper

1 tablespoon Thai fish sauce

1 teaspoon light soy sauce

Cornflour, for dusting

Separate the broccoli heads into small florets and peel and slice the stems. Blanch the broccoli pieces in a large pan of boiling salted water for several minutes, then immerse them in cold water. Drain thoroughly.

Cut the chicken into 2.5-cm (1-in) pieces and combine them with the pepper, fish sauce and light soy sauce. Mix well and allow to marinate for 30 minutes. Dust the chicken pieces with cornflour, shaking off any excess.

Heat a wok or large frying-pan over a high heat until it is hot. Add the 400 ml (14 fl oz) of oil and, when it is very hot and slightly smoking, deep-fry the chicken pieces for 8 minutes or until they are golden brown. Remove them with a slotted spoon and drain on kitchen paper. You may have to do this in two or more batches.

Drain off all the oil. Re-heat the wok and add the 1 tablespoon of oil. When it is hot, add the garlic and onion and stir-fry for 1 minute. Then add the blanched broccoli and continue to stir-fry for 1 minute. Add the Shaoxing rice wine or dry sherry and water or stock and continue to stir-fry at a moderate to a high heat for 4 minutes until the broccoli is thoroughly heated through. Add the tomatoes, oyster sauce, fish sauce, sugar, salt, pepper and sesame oil and continue to stir-fry for 30 seconds, then add the drained chicken and stir-fry for 2 minutes or until the chicken is thoroughly heated through. Transfer to a warm platter and serve at once.

VIETNAMESE-STYLE LEMON GRASS CHICKEN

*L*emon grass is a tropical grass (Cymbopogon citratus) *native to southern India and Sri Lanka, yielding an aromatic oil used as flavouring and in perfumery and medicine. It appears often in Vietnamese dishes, giving them a wonderful citrus aroma.*

I especially like its use with chicken, and here is a Vietnamese-inspired recipe that is redolent with lemon grass. It is a tasty dish that is relatively easy to make. Instead of using a whole chicken, I use chicken thighs, which I feel are tastier and easier to handle.

SERVES 4

450 g (1 lb) boneless, skinless chicken thighs
  or 900 g (2 lb) chicken thighs with bone in
1 tablespoon groundnut oil
175 g (6 oz) onions, thinly sliced
6 garlic cloves, crushed
1 tablespoon finely chopped fresh root
  ginger
2 red or green chillies, seeded and coarsely
  chopped
2 teaspoon sugar
100 g (4 oz) roasted peanuts, coarsely
  chopped
1 tablespoon Thai fish sauce

FOR THE MARINADE

5 stalks fresh lemon grass
1 teaspoon salt
½ teaspoon freshly ground black pepper
3 tablespoons finely chopped spring onions

Blot the chicken dry with kitchen paper. If you are using unboned thighs, remove the skin and bones from the chicken thighs or have your butcher do it for you. Cut the chicken into 2.5-cm (1-in) pieces.

Peel the lemon grass to reveal the tender, whitish centre, crush the stalk and cut it into 7.5-cm (3-in) pieces.

In a large bowl, combine the chicken with the lemon grass, salt, pepper and spring onions and allow to marinate at room temperature for 45 minutes.

Heat a wok or large frying-pan over a high heat until it is hot. Add the oil and, when it is very hot and slightly smoking, turn the heat to low. Add the chicken together with the marinade ingredients and stir-fry for 5 minutes. Then add the onions, garlic, ginger and chillies and continue to stir-fry for 10 minutes. Add the sugar and peanuts and continue to stir-fry for 2 minutes. Finally, add the fish sauce and continue to stir-fry for 2 minutes, mixing all the ingredients well. Transfer the contents of the wok to a warm platter and serve at once.

PINEAPPLE CHICKEN

This might be called 'nouvelle Hong Kong' or 'South-east Asia meets Hong Kong'. It is an exotic and unlikely combination. I have eaten this dish several times in Hong Kong and found it delicious every time. The acidic sweetness and texture of the pineapple works extremely well with the delicate taste of the chicken. The pineapple is cooked very quickly, just enough to warm it through.

SERVES 4

450 g (1 lb) boneless, skinless chicken
  breasts, cut into 2.5-cm (1-in) pieces
600 ml (1 pint) groundnut oil or water
2 teaspoons groundnut oil
1 tablespoon finely chopped fresh root
  ginger
1 tablespoon thinly sliced garlic
1½ tablespoons Shaoxing rice wine or dry
  sherry
1 teaspoon salt
1 teaspoon sesame oil
350 g (12 oz) small pineapple, peeled and
  cut into 2.5-cm (1-in) pieces

FOR THE MARINADE

1 egg white
1 teaspoon sesame oil
2 teaspoons cornflour
1 teaspoon salt
½ teaspoon freshly ground white pepper

FOR THE GARNISH

1 tablespoon finely chopped fresh
  coriander

Combine the chicken with the egg white, sesame oil, cornflour, salt and pepper in a bowl. Mix well and chill for about 20 minutes.

Heat a wok until it is very hot and then add the oil. When the oil is very hot, remove the wok from the heat and immediately add the chicken pieces, stirring vigorously to keep them from sticking. When the chicken pieces turn white (after about 2 minutes), quickly drain the chicken.

If you choose to use water instead of oil, bring it to a boil in a pan. Remove the pan from the heat and immediately add the chicken pieces, stirring vigorously to keep them from sticking. When the chicken pieces turn white (about 2 minutes), quickly drain the chicken.

Add the 2 teaspoons of oil to the wok and re-heat. Add the ginger and garlic and stir-fry for 30 seconds. Then add the Shaoxing rice wine or dry sherry, salt, sesame oil and pineapple cubes. Gently stir-fry for 2 minutes or until the pineapple is heated through. Add the drained chicken and stir gently to mix well. Turn on to a warm platter, garnish with the coriander and serve at once.

VIETNAMESE-STYLE CHICKEN CURRY

L *ike other cuisines of South-east Asia, Vietnamese cooking is highly perfumed with herbs such as lemon grass and purple basil. Hot chillies and aromatic ginger are also some of the essentials shared. Curry powder, as well as rich coconut milk, is also used. However, the light influence of China is also evident, Vietnamese curry dishes are slightly lighter and more delicate than Indian dishes.*

In this fragrant dish, the chicken is marinated in a curry paste, then stir-fried with vegetables. It is delicious and goes perfectly with plain rice.

SERVES 4

450 g (1 lb) boneless, skinless chicken thighs
2 tablespoons groundnut oil
2 onions, cut into eighths
300 ml (10 fl oz) *Chicken Stock (see p.56)*
400-ml (14-fl oz) tin coconut milk
4 fresh tomatoes, cut into quarters

FOR THE MARINADE

2 stalks fresh lemon grass
4 whole garlic cloves
2 red or green chillies, seeded and chopped
2 teaspoons sugar
1 tablespoon Madras curry paste
2 tablespoons Madras curry powder
1 teaspoon salt
½ teaspoon freshly ground black pepper
3 tablespoons Thai fish sauce
1 tablespoon water

FOR THE GARNISH

Handful of fresh sprigs of coriander

Cut the chicken into about 5-cm (2-in) chunks.

Peel the lemon grass stalk to reveal the tender, whitish centre and crush it with the flat of a knife. Then cut it into small chunks. In a food processor, combine the garlic, chillies, sugar, curry paste, curry powder, salt, pepper, fish sauce and water and blend to a paste. Mix this with the lemon grass and chicken pieces, and stir until all the pieces are thoroughly coated. Leave the chicken to marinate for about 1 hour at room temperature.

Heat a wok or large frying-pan over a high heat until it is hot. Add the oil and, when it is very hot and slightly smoking, turn the heat to moderate, add the chicken and stir-fry for 5 minutes or until the chicken begins to brown. Add the onions and stir-fry for 3 minutes. Add the stock and coconut milk. Bring the mixture to a simmer, reduce the heat and simmer uncovered for 10 minutes. Then add the tomatoes, stir well and continue to cook for another 2 minutes. Transfer the contents to a bowl. Garnish with coriander and serve.

LEMON GRASS CHICKEN WITH CHILLI

*T*he use of lemon grass with chilli can transform any ordinary chicken into a special treat. The aromatic oils from the lemon grass when used as a marinade and later cooked, give the dish a wonderful citrus scent as well as a subtle taste. Here it is paired with chilli powder or flakes for an explosive combination you are sure to enjoy. This dish re-heats well and goes with plain rice.

SERVES 4

450 g (1 lb) boneless, skinless chicken thighs
1 tablespoon groundnut oil
2 teaspoons Thai fish sauce
1 teaspoon sugar
1 teaspoon dried chilli powder or flakes

FOR THE MARINADE

2 stalks fresh lemon grass
2 tablespoons coarsely chopped garlic
½ teaspoon freshly ground black pepper
2 tablespoons Thai fish sauce
2 teaspoons sugar

Cut the chicken into 2.5-cm (1-in) pieces.

Peel the lemon grass stalk to reveal the tender, whitish centre and crush it with the flat of a knife. Then cut it into 7.5-cm (3-in) pieces.

In a large bowl, combine the chicken with the lemon grass, garlic, pepper, fish sauce and sugar. Allow it to marinate at room temperature for 40 minutes.

Heat a wok or large frying-pan over a high heat until it is hot. Add the oil and, when it is very hot and slightly smoking, add the chicken pieces and the marinade ingredients and stir-fry for 5 minutes or until the chicken is golden brown. Remove the chicken from the wok with a slotted spoon and drain.

Drain off all the oil and fat and re-heat the wok, without wiping. When it is hot, return the chicken to the wok, add the fish sauce, sugar and chilli powder or flakes. Continue to stir-fry for 3 minutes. Serve at once.

THAI-STYLE GINGER CHICKEN

This Thai-inspired recipe is an extremely close relative of a Chinese recipe. Contrary to what most people think, not all Thai dishes have chillies and are spicy. Many of the Thais who have Chinese ancestry come from southern China and their cooking reflects their roots. That is, subtle cooking with nuances, rather than the strong, assertive flavours of chillies that characterize much of Thai cooking. This dish is delicious with plain rice.

SERVES 4

450 g (1 lb) boneless, skinless chicken thighs

12 g (½ oz) Chinese dried wood ears

1 tablespoon groundnut oil

1 small onion, cut into 8 wedges

2 tablespoons coarsely chopped garlic

4 tablespoons finely shredded fresh root
   ginger

1 tablespoon yellow bean sauce

2 teaspoons sugar

1 teaspoon salt

2 tablespoons Shaoxing rice wine or dry
   sherry

FOR THE MARINADE

2 teaspoons light soy sauce

1 teaspoon dark soy sauce

1 tablespoon Shaoxing rice wine or dry
   sherry

½ teaspoon salt

½ teaspoon freshly ground black pepper

1 teaspoon sesame oil

2 teaspoons cornflour

FOR THE GARNISH

3 tablespoons finely shredded spring onions

Cut the chicken into 5-cm (2-in) chunks. Mix the soy sauces, Shaoxing rice wine or dry sherry, salt, pepper and sesame oil and pour it over the chicken. Then mix in the cornflour until all the chicken pieces are thoroughly coated. Leave the chicken to marinate for about 30 minutes, then drain the chicken and discard the marinade.

Soak the dried wood ears for about 20 minutes until soft. Rinse the wood ears in cold water, cut off any hard bits and finely shred them.

Heat a wok or large frying-pan over a high heat until it is hot. Add the oil and, when it is very hot and slightly smoking, add the chicken and stir-fry for 5 minutes or until the chicken begins to brown. Remove the chicken and drain. Pour off all but 1 table-spoon of oil from the wok. Add the onion, garlic, ginger and wood ears and stir-fry for 1 minute. Then add the bean sauce, sugar and salt and continue to stir-fry for 30 seconds. Return the chicken to the wok and continue to stir-fry for 4 minutes. Finally, add the Shaoxing rice wine or dry sherry and con-tinue to stir-fry for 2 minutes or until the chicken is cooked. Garnish with spring onions and serve.

BRAISED DUCK WITH CHESTNUTS

*C*hestnuts have been discovered in tombs dating back to the earliest part of China's recorded history, and are still used fresh and dried in China, as well as in Japan. In China, they are mainly used with braised dishes. Dried chestnuts can be found already peeled in Chinese grocers or supermarkets. They are delicious and actually easier to use than the fresh ones. Soak them overnight, then simmer them for an hour before using them.

   This classic duck recipe re-heats very well. It makes a wonderful, hearty meal especially in cool weather. Serve it with rice and another vegetable dish.

SERVES 4-6

175 g (6 oz) dried or fresh chestnuts
1.6-1.8 kg (3½-4 lb) duck, fresh or frozen
   (preferably a white Pekin duck)
1.2 litres (2 pints) groundnut oil

FOR THE SAUCE

1.75 litres (3 pints) *Chicken Stock (see p.56)* or
   water
600 ml (1 pint) dark soy sauce
300 ml (10 fl oz) light soy sauce
400 ml (14 fl oz) Shaoxing rice wine or
   200 ml (7 fl oz) dry sherry mixed with
   200 ml (7 fl oz) *Chicken Stock (see p.56)*
100 g (4 oz) rock sugar
5 whole star anise
3 pieces Chinese cinnamon bark or
   cinnamon sticks
6 spring onions
3 slices fresh root ginger
5 garlic cloves, crushed

FOR THE GARNISH

A few fresh sprigs of coriander

If you are using dried chestnuts, soak them in warm water overnight. Cook the soaked chestnuts in hot water for 1 hour. If you are using fresh chestnuts, peel them.

   Cut the duck in half lengthways. Dry the halves thoroughly with kitchen paper. Heat the oil in a wok or large frying-pan until it is almost smoking, then deep-fry the 2 halves of the duck, skin-side down. Turn the heat to medium and continue to fry slowly until the skin is browned. This should take about 15-20 minutes. Do not turn the pieces over but baste the duck as it fries. Drain the lightly browned duck on kitchen paper.

   Combine all the sauce ingredients together in a large pan and bring the mixture to a boil. Add the duck halves and chestnuts and turn the heat down to a simmer. Cover the pan and slowly braise the duck for 1 hour or until it is tender.

   Skim off the large amount of surface fat which will be left when the duck is cooked. This procedure will prevent the duck from becoming greasy. Now remove the duck pieces with a slotted spoon. Let them cool and then chop them into smaller pieces. Arrange on a warm platter, garnish with the fresh coriander and serve at once.

   Alternatively you can let the duck cool thoroughly and serve it at room temperature. Once the sauce has cooled, remove any lingering surface fat. Now the sauce can be frozen and re-used to braise duck or chicken.

Braised Duck with Chestnuts

AROMATIC FRIED CHICKEN

*O*ne *of the best fried chicken I have ever eaten was in a Vietnamese restaurant. The chicken had been marinated in an exotic mixture of fish sauce, lime juice, garlic, chilli and sugar. It was then simply tossed in flour and slowly fried. It was absolutely delicious and, with simple steamed rice as a accompaniment, made a memorable meal. A salad or vegetable dish would also complement it nicely.*

SERVES 4

900 g (2 lb) chicken thighs with bone in
3 tablespoons groundnut oil

FOR THE MARINADE

2 teaspoons salt
1 teaspoon freshly ground black pepper
6 garlic cloves, peeled
75 ml (3 fl oz) Thai fish sauce
75 ml (3 fl oz) white Shaoxing rice wine vinegar or cider vinegar
2 fresh red or green chillies, seeded and chopped
1 tablespoon sugar
2 tablespoons lime juice
3 tablespoons chopped shallots
1 tablespoon light soy sauce
1 tablespoon Shoaxing rice wine or dry sherry
Plain flour, for dusting

Blot the chicken dry with kitchen paper.

In a blender, mix the salt, pepper, garlic, fish sauce, vinegar, chillies, sugar, lime juice, shallots, soy sauce and Shaoxing rice wine or dry sherry. Rub this mixture evenly over the thighs and allow to marinate for 1 hour at room temperature. Drain off any excess marinade.

Dust the chicken with flour and shake off any excess. Heat a wok or large frying-pan over a high heat until it is hot. Add the oil and, when it is very hot and slightly smoking, turn the heat to low. Add the chicken skin-side down and slowly brown over a moderately low heat for 10 minutes on each side or until the chicken is cooked. Remove the chicken from the wok, drain on kitchen paper, then transfer to a warm platter and serve at once.

STRANGE-TASTE STIR-FRIED EGGS

The term 'strange-taste' is one I have often wondered about. It is of Szechuan origin and is regularly applied to fragrant Szechuan fish recipes. Given the rather warm climate and lack of refrigeration in the area, I wonder if something other than the cook's imaginative use of seasonings may have generated the strange taste!

Be that as it may, the food is delicious and I am willing to accept the traditional explanation that it is popularly known as 'strange-taste' because it incorporates so many flavours, being hot, spicy, sour, sweet and salty all at the same time. Here the ingredients are used to enliven pork and combined with eggs to make a simple but delicious dish that goes superbly with rice.

SERVES 3-4

225 g (8 oz) minced pork
2 teaspoons light soy sauce
2 teaspoons Shaoxing rice wine or dry
   sherry
2 teaspoons sesame oil
1 teaspoon cornflour
6 eggs, beaten
½ teaspoon salt
2 tablespoons groundnut oil

FOR THE SAUCE

2 teaspoons dark soy sauce
2 teaspoons Chinese black rice vinegar or
   cider vinegar
2 teaspoons chilli bean sauce
2 teaspoons sesame oil
2 teaspoons sugar
1 tablespoon Shaoxing rice wine or dry
   sherry
1 teaspoon roasted Szechuan peppercorns
   (see p.24)
1½ tablespoons finely chopped spring
   onions

FOR THE GARNISH

1 tablespoon finely chopped spring onion
   tops

Combine the pork with the light soy sauce, Shaoxing rice wine or dry sherry, 1 teaspoon of sesame oil and the cornflour in a small bowl. In another small bowl, combine the eggs with the salt and remaining sesame oil.

Heat a wok until it is very hot and then add 1 tablespoon of the groundnut oil. When the oil is very hot and slightly smoking, add the pork and stir-fry for 1 minute. Add the sauce ingredients and cook with the pork for 3 minutes. Remove the pork and sauce and set it aside.

Wipe the wok clean and re-heat it and, when it is hot, add the remaining oil. Immediately, add the eggs and stir-fry until they are barely set. Then return the pork and sauce to the eggs and mix well. Continue to stir-fry for 2 minutes. Transfer to a warm platter and serve at once, sprinkling the spring onion tops over to garnish.

CANTONESE-STYLE CHICKEN WINGS WITH OYSTERS

A thrifty, economical dish my mother use to make which I still love today is this one of chicken wings simmered in a rich oyster sauce. It is extremely easy to make and re-heats quite well. In fact, the chicken wings are also tasty served cold and terrific for picnics.

SERVES 4

675 g (1½ lb) chicken wings
900 ml (1½ pints) groundnut oil

FOR THE MARINADE

1 tablespoon light soy sauce
1 tablespoon Shaoxing rice wine or dry sherry
2 teaspoons sesame oil
½ teaspoon salt
¼ teaspoon freshly ground black pepper
2 teaspoons cornflour

FOR THE SAUCE

1 tablespoon groundnut oil
3 garlic cloves, crushed
2.5-cm (1-in) thick piece fresh root ginger, unpeeled and crushed
3 tablespoons oyster sauce
1 tablespoon light soy sauce
2 tablespoons Shaoxing rice wine or dry sherry
600 ml (1 pint) *Chicken Stock (see p.56)* or *Vegetable Stock (see p.60)*

In a large bowl, combine the wings with the marinade ingredients and mix well. Leave to sit in the marinade for at least 30 minutes.

Heat a wok or large frying-pan over a high heat until it is hot. Add the oil and, when it is very hot and slightly smoking, add the chicken wings and fry them for 5 minutes or until they are golden brown. Remove them from the wok with a slotted spoon and drain on kitchen paper. You may have to do this in several batches.

Drain off all the oil and fat and wipe the wok clean, then make the sauce. Re-heat the wok until it is very hot, then add 1 tablespoon of oil. Add the garlic and ginger and stir-fry for 30 seconds. Then add the oyster sauce, soy sauce, Shaoxing rice wine or dry sherry and stock and bring the mixture to a simmer. Return the chicken to the wok. Reduce the heat to very low, cover and simmer for 30-35 minutes or until the chicken is very tender. Remove the wings with a slotted spoon to a warm platter. Turn up the heat and boil to reduce the sauce until it is slightly thick. Pour this over the chicken and serve at once.

VEGETABLES

———

Perhaps no other food is more associated with the wok than vegetables. In fact, stir-fried vegetables are almost synonymous with the wok.

———

The idea of stir-frying vegetables is what generated the initial popularity of the wok in the West more than 20 years ago. In those early days of over-cooked, boiled, soggy, bland vegetables, the idea of stir-fried vegetables full of colour, flavour and crunchiness came as a revelation. The wok took home kitchens by storm and many adults and children discovered how wonderful fresh vegetables could taste for the first time.

———

Today, stir-frying vegetables in the wok is almost as normal as sautéing a piece of steak. This chapter utilizes the wok in every way possible to cook vegetables. Though it is not all strictly vegetarian, there are many wok recipes here to satisfy the vegetarian.

———

Most of the vegetable recipes are meant to accompany other dishes, but you will find a few main-course vegetable dishes, like the Savoury Stuffed Tomatoes *or* Rainbow Vegetables with Curry.

———

These vegetable recipes are, in the main, simple and extremely easy to make in the wok.

———

EAST-WEST CHIPS

The wok is perfect for making potato chips, or fries as they are known in other parts of the world. Its round, concave shape makes it ideal for deep-frying without wasting any oil.

The secret to making good chips lies in the cooking technique. First, chill the cut potatoes for several hours. This allows the natural starch to set so that when the chips hit the hot oil, they do not act like sponges and become greasy. They must then be dried thoroughly so they are without a trace of moisture. Then use the double-frying technique. The first quick-fry cooks them, then, after letting the chips drain and allowing the oil in the wok to regain the frying point, put the chips in for the second quick-fry. They cook to a crisp and golden perfection.

I then toss the chips in a tasty mix of salt, cayenne, five-spice powder and crushed Szechuan peppercorns. These chips are marvellous with grilled foods and as a snack they are unbeatable. They are a perfect vegetarian dish.

SERVES 4

750 g (1¼ lb) potatoes
900 ml (1½ pints) groundnut oil

FOR THE SEASONING MIXTURE

2 teaspoons salt
½ teaspoon cayenne pepper
½ teaspoon five-spice powder
½ teaspoon whole Szechuan peppercorns, roasted *(see p. 24)* and finely ground
½ teaspoon freshly ground black pepper

Peel and cut the potatoes into strips about 7.5 cm x 5 mm (3 in x ½ in). Put the strips into a large bowl, cover with cold water and chill for 2 hours or overnight.

Combine the ingredients for the seasoning mixture in a small bowl and set aside. Drain the potatoes in a colander, then spin them dry in a salad spinner or pat them dry with kitchen paper. The potatoes should be as dry as possible for the best results.

Heat a wok or large frying-pan over a high heat until it is hot. Add the oil and, when it is very hot and slightly smoking, fry half of the potatoes for 8 minutes. Remove the potatoes with a slotted spoon and drain in a colander; then fry the second batch.

When you are ready to serve them, re-heat the oil until it is very hot. Fry half of the potatoes until they are crispy and golden brown. Remove and drain well on kitchen paper. Re-heat the oil until it is very hot, fry the other half and drain. Transfer the potatoes to a warm platter, toss with the seasoning mix and serve at once.

QUICK AND EASY NOODLE AND BEAN SPROUT SALAD

Northern Chinese love to have small side dishes accompanying their more elaborate meals. Such dishes serve as refreshing interludes between the main courses. They are easily prepared in advance and most often served at room temperature.

But many of these side dishes are excellent when served as components of simpler meals. Here is a basic beansprout salad that I first enjoyed a few years ago at a friend's home in Beijing. It is a wonderful dish to serve with grilled meats on a warm summer evening.

SERVES 4

25 g (1 oz) beanthread (transparent) noodles

450 g (1 lb) fresh bean sprouts

3 tablespoons white rice vinegar

1 teaspoon salt

1 teaspoon sugar

2 teaspoons sesame oil

1 spring onion, finely shredded on the diagonal

Soak the noodles in a large bowl of warm water for 15 minutes. When soft, drain and discard the water. Cut them into 7.5-cm (3-in) lengths using scissors or a knife. Pick over the bean sprouts, discarding any brown ones. Blanch them for 1 minute in a wok filled with boiling water. Drain well and place in a bowl.

In a small bowl, combine the vinegar, salt, sugar and sesame oil. Toss the bean sprouts with this mixture while they are still warm. Mix in the beanthread noodles and spring onion. Chill for at least 30 minutes before serving.

SIMPLE BEIJING-STYLE MARINATED CUCUMBER SALAD

My good friend, Lillian Robyn, is originally from Beijing. Now married to an American and living in America, she still cooks in the Beijing style. A meal in her home is always a special treat for me. I have enjoyed this refreshing salad at her home many times. It can be prepared hours ahead and is thus perfect for multicourse meals or simply by itself with hot rice.

SERVES 4

750 g (1¼ lb) cucumbers

2 teaspoons salt

1 tablespoon chilli bean sauce

1 teaspoon light soy sauce

1 teaspoon sugar

½ teaspoon chilli oil

2 teaspoons sesame oil

Cut the unpeeled cucumbers into 2.5-cm (1-in) slices, sprinkle with salt and put them into a colander to drain for 20 minutes. Squeeze the cucumber slices in a linen tea towel to remove any moisture. Blot them dry with kitchen paper.

In a small bowl, mix the chilli bean sauce, soy sauce, sugar, chilli oil and sesame oil. Toss the cucumber slices in this sauce and let them sit in the fridge overnight. Drain off any excess moisture before serving.

RAINBOW VEGETABLES WITH CURRY

M ild curry dishes with vegetables are popular in Hong Kong. The particular spices in curry add an exotic taste that is quite a change from the usual garlic and/or ginger seasonings most commonly used in Chinese cookery. This assortment of differently coloured vegetables (hence the name) is usually served at banquets. But there is no need to wait for a special occasion to enjoy such a vegetarian taste treat.

SERVES 4

225 g (8 oz) Chinese leaves (Peking cabbage)
225 g (8 oz) Chinese greens, such as Chinese
    flowering cabbage or bok choy
225 g (8 oz) carrots
225 g (8 oz) asparagus

FOR THE SAUCE

1 tablespoon groundnut oil
2 tablespoons finely chopped shallots
1½ tablespoons Madras curry paste
300 ml (10 fl oz) tinned coconut milk
2 teaspoons sugar
2 teaspoons salt
1 tablespoon Shaoxing rice wine or dry
    sherry
2 teaspoons sesame oil

Cut the Chinese leaves into 4-cm (1½-in) strips. Then cut the Chinese greens into 4-cm (1½-in) pieces. Peel and cut the carrots into 4-cm (1½-in) x 5-mm (½-in) segments. Cut the asparagus into 4-cm (1½-in) pieces.

In a large pan of boiling salted water, blanch the leaves for about 5 minutes. Remove them with a slotted spoon and drain thoroughly. Then blanch the Chinese greens for 3 minutes in the same water. Remove and drain. Now blanch the carrots for 5 minutes and the asparagus for 3 minutes. Remove and drain thoroughly. Arrange the blanched vegetables on a warm serving platter.

Heat a wok or large frying-pan over a high heat until it is hot. Add the oil and, when it is very hot and slightly smoking, add the shallots and stir-fry for 1 minute. Then add the curry paste and coconut milk. Bring the mixture to a boil and add the sugar, salt and Shaoxing rice wine or dry sherry. Stir to mix well. Finally, add the sesame oil. Pour the sauce over the platter of vegetables and serve at once.

STIR-FRIED LETTUCE WITH SAVOURY BACON

Stir-fried lettuce always sounds a bit strange to Western ears, but once you realize that there are few things that cannot be cooked in the wok, you understand everything. The intense heat of the wok stir-frying technique means quick cooking. This preserves the nutritional content as well as the taste and texture of almost any vegetable. Indeed, as in this recipe, contact with the wok imparts a gentle smoky flavour to the food. Thus, we turn inexpensive and prosaic iceberg lettuce into a surprisingly tasty dish. The savoury bacon gives the lettuce an added flavour, but omit the bacon and you have a fine vegetarian dish.

SERVES 4 AS A SIDE DISH

175 g (6 oz) bacon
750 g (1¾ lb) iceberg lettuce
2 tablespoons groundnut oil
1 teaspoon light soy sauce
1 teaspoon dark soy sauce
½ teaspoon sugar
½ teaspoon salt
½ teaspoon freshly ground black pepper
2 teaspoons Shaoxing rice wine or dry sherry
2 teaspoons sesame oil

Cut the bacon into thin shreds widthways. Heat a wok or large frying-pan over a high heat until it is hot. Turn the heat to low, add the bacon and cook until it is brown and crispy. Remove with a slotted spoon and drain well on kitchen paper.

Separate the lettuce leaves and tear all the large leaves in half.

Heat a wok or large frying-pan over a high heat until it is hot. Add the oil and, when it is very hot and slightly smoking, add the lettuce leaves and stir-fry for 1 minute. Then add the rest of the ingredients except the sesame oil and continue to stir-fry for 1 minute. Finally, stir in the sesame oil. Remove the lettuce leaves with a slotted spoon with some of the sauce and arrange on a warm serving dish. Garnish with the bacon and serve at once.

BROCCOLI IN FRAGRANT WINE SAUCE

Broccoli is a vegetable of sturdy character. It has a rich colour and a distinctive taste and texture that allows it to be paired with strong seasonings and flavours — for example, the ginger and Shaoxing rice wine of this dish. The recipe is of Shanghai origin. The justly famous yellow Shaoxing wine is produced in that region of China and quite understandably it has attained a prominent place in Shanghai cuisine. This is a quick, easy and fragrant wok dish that can serve as a perfect side dish or as a main vegetarian treat.

Segundo##

SERVES 4

450 g (1 lb) fresh broccoli
1½ tablespoons groundnut oil
2 tablespoons finely shredded fresh root ginger
1 teaspoon salt
½ teaspoon sugar
½ teaspoon freshly ground black pepper
5 tablespoons Shaoxing rice wine or dry sherry
2 teaspoons sesame oil

Separate the broccoli heads into small florets, then peel and slice the stems. Blanch the broccoli pieces in a large pan of boiling salted water for 3 minutes and then immerse them in cold water. Drain thoroughly.

Heat a wok or large frying-pan over a high heat until it is hot. Add the oil and, when it is very hot and slightly smoking, add the ginger shreds, salt, sugar and pepper and stir-fry for a few seconds. Add the blanched broccoli. Add the Shaoxing rice wine or dry sherry and continue to stir-fry over a moderate to a high heat for 4 minutes until the broccoli is thoroughly heated through. Add the sesame oil and continue to stir-fry for 30 seconds. Transfer to a warm plate and serve at once.

BRAISED CHINESE RADISH WITH CHILLI

*C*hinese white radish, sometimes called mooli, deserves a greater role in cookery than it usually receives. Its central virtue is its ability to absorb the flavours of other ingredients. This results in a very satisfying and tasty vegetable dish that stands on its own and is also an excellent companion to other dishes. It is easy to make – again, the wok does its magic – and re-heats nicely. If you use water instead of stock, the result is an ideal vegetarian dish.

SERVES 2-4

750 g (1¾ lb) Chinese white radish (mooli)
1 tablespoon groundnut oil
2 dried red chillies
3 tablespoons finely chopped spring onions
1 teaspoon salt
1 tablespoon yellow bean paste
1 teaspoon chilli bean sauce
2 teaspoons sugar
2 teaspoons dark soy sauce
150 ml (5 fl oz) Shaoxing rice wine or dry sherry
150 ml (5 fl oz) water or *Chicken Stock (see p.56)*
2 teaspoons sesame oil

Peel the radish and cut it at a slight diagonal into 2.5-cm (1-in) thick slices.

Heat a wok or large frying-pan over a high heat until it is hot. Add the oil and, when it is very hot and slightly smoking, add the chillies and stir-fry for 30 seconds. Add the spring onions and radish and continue to stir-fry for 1 minute. Then add the rest of the ingredients, except the sesame oil. Bring the mixture to a boil, lower the heat, cover and simmer for 30 minutes or until the radish is soft and tender.

Add the sesame oil, turn the heat up to high and rapidly reduce the liquid until most of it has evaporated. Transfer to a warm platter and serve at once.

HONG KONG-STYLE BROCCOLI AND BABY CORN

Creative innovation is a virtue in Hong Kong cuisine and chefs there are quick to adopt non traditional vegetables into their repertoire. In this case, we find broccoli, flown in fresh daily from California, and baby corn, flown in from Thailand. Put them together with traditional Chinese seasonings and flavourings and you have a colourful and nutritious blending of East and West, and so easy to prepare in your wok and serve as a side dish. If you use the dark soy sauce instead of the oyster sauce, it would make this dish a perfect one for vegetarians.

SERVES 4

450 g (1 lb) fresh broccoli
225 g (8 oz) fresh baby corn
50 g (2 oz) Chinese black mushrooms
1½ tablespoons groundnut oil
1 teaspoon salt
½ teaspoon freshly ground black pepper
1 teaspoon sugar
1 tablespoon Shaoxing rice wine or dry
    sherry
1 tablespoon light soy sauce
3 tablespoons oyster sauce or dark soy sauce
2 teaspoons sesame oil

Separate the broccoli heads into small florets, then peel and slice the stems. Blanch the broccoli pieces and baby corn in a large pan of boiling salted water for 3 minutes and then immerse them in cold water. Drain thoroughly.

Soak the mushrooms in warm water for 20 minutes. Drain them and squeeze out the excess liquid. Remove and discard the stems and finely shred the caps into thin strips.

Heat a wok or large frying-pan over a high heat until it is hot. Add the oil and, when it is very hot and slightly smoking, add the broccoli, corn and mushrooms and stir-fry for 3 minutes. Add the salt, pepper, sugar, Shaoxing rice wine or dry sherry, soy sauce and oyster sauce or dark soy sauce and continue to stir-fry at a moderate to a high heat for 2 minutes until the vegetables are thoroughly heated through. Add the sesame oil and continue to stir-fry for 30 seconds. Transfer to a warm platter and serve at once.

BRAISED CHINESE MUSHROOM BEANCURD CASSEROLE

first tasted this vegetarian dish while visiting a Daoist temple in China. The rich and flavour-ful mushrooms impart their smoky tang to the deep-fried beancurd, while the various spices and sauces add delightful dimensions. It is a typically vegetarian way to experience simple but memorable pleasures — and so easy to prepare. The 'wok master' in the temple handled his wok in a way that was poetry in action, but we can all prepare this dish. If you use water instead of stock, the dish is quite suitable for vegetarians.

SERVES 4

50 g (2 oz) Chinese black mushrooms
100 g (4 oz) button mushrooms
225 g (8 oz) firm fresh beancurd
450 ml (15 fl oz) groundnut oil
3 tablespoons finely chopped spring onions
1 tablespoon coarsely chopped garlic
1 tablespoon light soy sauce
2 teaspoons dark soy sauce
1 tablespoon Shaoxing rice wine or dry sherry
2 teaspoons sugar
1 teaspoon chilli bean sauce
½ teaspoon freshly ground black pepper
50 ml (2 fl oz) *Chicken Stock (see p.56)* or water

Soak the mushrooms in warm water for 20 minutes. Drain them and squeeze out the excess liquid. Remove and discard the stems and finely shred the caps into thin strips.

Wash and slice the button mushrooms.

Cut the beancurd into 2.5-cm (1-in) cubes. Drain on kitchen paper for 10 minutes.

Heat a wok or large frying-pan over a high heat until it is hot. Add the oil and, when it is very hot and slightly smoking, deep-fry the beancurd cubes in batches. Drain each batch on kitchen paper. Drain off all but 1½ table-spoons of the oil. When the beancurd is cool enough, slice each cube in half.

Re-heat the wok or large frying-pan with the reserved oil over a high heat until it is hot. When it is very hot and slightly smoking, add the spring onions and garlic and stir-fry for 30 seconds. Add all the mushrooms and stir-fry for 2 minutes, mixing them well. Then add the soy sauces, Shaoxing rice wine or dry sherry, sugar, chilli bean sauce, pepper and stock or water. Turn the heat down and cook for 5 minutes, stirring continuously, until the fresh mushrooms are thoroughly cooked. Add the beancurd and continue to cook for 2 min-utes. Turn the heat back to high and continue to cook until most of the liquid has been evaporated. Transfer to a warm platter and serve at once.

BRAISED PEKING CABBAGE WITH BEAN SPROUTS

Chinese cuisine is justifiably famous for its vegetable cookery and for its vegetarian sub-cuisines. In its long history, Chinese cuisine has always given vegetables pride of place. This means, of course, that vegetables are treated with care and discernment. Only the most appropriate cooking techniques are employed and only the most congenial flavourings are added. Here is a traditional and very economical recipe using Chinese leaves (Peking cabbage) and nutritious crunchy bean sprouts. Delicious, and it is so easily prepared and cooked.

SERVES 4

750 g (1¾ lb) Chinese leaves (Peking cabbage)
225 g (8 oz) fresh bean sprouts
1½ tablespoons groundnut oil
2 tablespoons finely shredded fresh root ginger
2 tablespoons dark soy sauce
1 tablespoon light soy sauce
2 teaspoons sugar
½ teaspoon salt
½ teaspoon freshly ground black pepper
150 ml (5 fl oz) *Vegetable Stock (see p.60)*
2 teaspoons sesame oil

Cut the Chinese leaves into 5-cm (2-in) wide strips. Trim and discard any brown ends from the bean sprouts.

Heat a wok or large frying-pan over a high heat until it is hot. Add the oil and, when it is very hot and slightly smoking, add the ginger and stir-fry for 10 seconds. Add the Chinese leaves and stir-fry for 30 seconds. Add the soy sauces, sugar, salt and pepper and continue to stir-fry for 1 minute. Add the stock and cook for 10 minutes. Finally, add the bean sprouts and stir-fry for 2 minutes. Stir in the sesame oil, transfer to a warm platter and serve at once.

EASY MANGETOUT AND SWEET WATER CHESTNUTS

*M*angetout is the apt French name for these delicious, small, crisp, sweet early peas which can indeed be completely consumed as they are, right out of the garden. I recommend only that you trim their ends and delicate strings. Paired with the sweet crunchiness of the fresh water chestnuts, and with the Chinese black mushrooms adding a contrasting texture and distinct flavour, the mangetout makes a refreshing change to ordinary peas, carrots, onions and whatever. With your wok, it takes but minutes to cook and, as a side dish, it nicely complements any meat or chicken.

SERVES 4

225 g (8 oz) fresh or tinned (drained weight)
   water chestnuts
50 g (2 oz) Chinese black mushrooms
1 tablespoon groundnut oil
3 tablespoons finely chopped spring onions
225 g (8 oz) mangetout, trimmed
1 tablespoon light soy sauce
1 tablespoon Shaoxing rice wine or dry
   sherry
2 tablespoons dark soy sauce
1 teaspoon salt
½ teaspoon freshly ground black pepper
1 teaspoon sugar
3 tablespoons water
2 teaspoons sesame oil

If you are using fresh water chestnuts, peel them. If you are using tinned water chestnuts, drain them well and rinse in cold water. Thinly slice the water chestnuts. Soak the mushrooms in warm water for 20 minutes. Drain them and squeeze out the excess liquid. Remove and discard the stems and finely shred the caps into thin strips.

Heat a wok or large frying-pan over a high heat until it is hot. Add the oil and, when it is very hot and slightly smoking, add the spring onions and stir-fry for 10 seconds. Add the mangetout, mushrooms and fresh water chestnuts if you are using them and stir-fry for 1 minute. Make sure you coat them thoroughly with the oil. Add the rest of the ingredients, except the sesame oil, and continue to stir-fry for another 3 minutes. If you are using tinned water chestnuts, add these now and cook for a final 2 minutes or until the vegetables are cooked. Stir in the sesame oil, transfer to a warm platter and serve at once.

STIR-FRIED CELERY IN TWO-BEAN SAUCE

*C*elery *is a much-neglected vegetable in my opinion. It is used in stocks, chopped and added to salads or simply used as a filler. I love its distinctive taste and flavour and often use it as a main vegetable by itself, simply stir-fried. It should be still be crunchy, which is part of its attraction. This is an easy dish to make and is a wonderful accompaniment to any meal.*

SERVES 4

750 g (1¾ lb) celery (about 1 head)
1 tablespoon groundnut oil
1 teaspoon sesame oil
2 tablespoons thinly sliced garlic
3 tablespoons Shaoxing rice wine or dry
  sherry
2 teaspoons yellow bean sauce
2 teaspoons chilli bean sauce
3 tablespoons water

Remove the stalks of the celery and rinse thoroughly under cold running water. String the tough outer stalks of celery with a paring knife. Chop the celery stalks and leaves across into 2.5-cm (1-in) pieces.

Heat a wok or large frying-pan over a high heat until it is hot. Add the oils, and when they are very hot and slightly smoking, add the garlic and celery and stir-fry for 2 minutes. Then add the Shaoxing rice wine or dry sherry, bean sauces and water and continue to stir-fry for 5 minutes or until the celery is thoroughly cooked. Transfer to a warm dish and serve at once.

SPINACH WITH FRIED GARLIC

*T*his recipe, inspired by one of the best Chinese restaurants in London, Fung Shing, is a delicious but simple method for cooking spinach. The garlic is slowly fried, removed and then the spinach is cooked in the same oil. The garlic is then added just as a crispy aromatic garnish. It is very simple to prepare and may be served hot or cold.*

SERVES 4

750 g (1¾ lb) fresh spinach
1½ tablespoons groundnut oil
1 teaspoon salt
2 tablespoons thinly sliced garlic
1 teaspoon sugar

Wash the spinach thoroughly. Remove all the stems, leaving just the leaves.

Heat a wok or large frying-pan over a high heat until it is hot. Add the oil and reduce the heat to moderate. Add the salt and garlic and slowly stir-fry for 2 minutes or until the garlic is golden brown and crisp. Remove the garlic with a slotted spoon and drain on kitchen paper. Then add the spinach. Stir-fry for about 2 minutes to coat the spinach leaves thoroughly with the oil and salt. When the spinach has wilted to about one-third of its original size, add the sugar and continue to stir-fry for another 4 minutes. Transfer the spinach to a warm plate and pour off any excess liquid. Sprinkle with the fried garlic. Serve either hot or cold.

STIR-FRIED COURGETTES WITH FRESH CHILLI

Courgettes are economical and abundantly available. A quick stir in the wok and this easy side vegetable dish can be prepared in minutes, or it can be a delicious vegetarian treat. Here I add fresh chillies to give them a lift. These vegetables can be watery depending on size; I recommend the smaller ones.

SERVES 4

750 g (1¾ lb) courgettes
1 tablespoon groundnut oil
2 tablespoons thinly sliced garlic
1 tablespoon finely chopped fresh root
  ginger
2 tablespoons finely chopped spring onions
4 fresh red or green chillies, seeded and
  finely shredded
1 teaspoon salt
½ teaspoon freshly ground black pepper
2 teaspoons sugar
3 tablespoons water
2 teaspoons sesame oil

Diagonally slice the courgettes into 5-mm (¼-in) rounds.

Heat a wok or large frying-pan over a high heat until it is hot. Add the oil and, when it is very hot and slightly smoking, add the garlic, ginger, spring onions and chillies and stir-fry for about 30 seconds. Then add the courgettes, salt, pepper and sugar and stir for another 30 seconds until they are well coated with the spices and flavourings. Add the water and continue to stir-fry over a high heat for 5 minutes until most of the water has evaporated and the courgettes are cooked. At this point, add the sesame oil, transfer to a warm dish and serve immediately.

RICH AUBERGINE WITH TOMATO AND BASIL

*T*his savoury treat combines two of my favourite vegetables, aubergines and tomatoes. The smaller, long, thin Chinese aubergines are preferable to the thicker European variety because of their slightly sweeter and milder taste. However, you may use the European type. Leave the skins of the aubergines on as they enhance the texture of the dish.

Ordinarily, such a dish is oven-baked but because many Chinese homes lack modern cookers, the wok is used instead. It is, in practice, the perfect utensil for preparing this Italian-inspired dish. It can be served hot or at room temperature, and is delicious as a vegetarian plate or as a wonderful accompaniment to grilled meats.

SERVES 4

450 g (1 lb) Chinese aubergines or ordinary aubergines
225 g (8 oz) fresh or tinned tomatoes
75 ml (3 fl oz) extra-virgin olive oil
5 garlic cloves, peeled and crushed
2 teaspoons salt
½ teaspoon freshly ground black pepper
2 teaspoons sugar
3 tablespoons finely chopped basil leaves
1 tablespoon lemon juice

Trim the aubergines and cut them on the diagonal into 5 x 1-cm (2 x ½-in) slices.

If you are using fresh tomatoes, plunge them into a large pan of boiling water for a few seconds, removing them with a slotted spoon. Then peel, seed and cut them into 2.5-cm (1-in) chunks. If you are using tinned tomatoes, chop them into small chunks.

Heat a wok or large frying-pan over a high heat until it is hot. Add the oil and, when it is moderately hot, add the garlic and stir-fry for 30 seconds. Then add the aubergine slices, salt and pepper and continue to stir-fry for 2 minutes.

Add the tomatoes and sugar to the aubergine and continue to cook for 5 minutes. Turn the heat to low, cover and cook slowly for 15 minutes until the aubergine is quite tender. Stir in the basil leaves and lemon juice and give the mixture several good stirs. Transfer to a warm platter and serve at once or allow to cool and serve at room temperature.

STIR-FRIED SPICY BROCCOLI

I think we need to look again at ways in which to cook this nutritious and delectable vegetable. All too often it is simply boiled to death, which is so unappealing. Stir-frying it with spices transforms it into a special treat. Served warm or at room temperature, it makes a lovely side dish or part of a vegetarian feast.

SERVES 4

450 g (1 lb) fresh broccoli
1½ tablespoons groundnut oil
2 tablespoons garlic, coarsely chopped
1 teaspoon salt
½ teaspoon freshly ground black pepper
2 tablespoons Shaoxing rice wine or dry
   sherry
1 tablespoon chilli bean sauce
1 teaspoon sugar
4–5 tablespoons water
2 teaspoons sesame oil

Separate the broccoli heads into small florets and peel and slice the stems. Blanch the broccoli pieces in a large pan of boiling salted water for several minutes, then immerse them in cold water. Drain thoroughly.

Heat a wok or large frying-pan over a high heat until it is hot. Add the oil and, when it is very hot and slightly smoking, add the garlic, salt, pepper, Shaoxing rice wine or dry sherry, chilli bean sauce and sugar. Stir-fry for a few seconds and then add the blanched broccoli. Add a few tablespoons of water. Stir-fry at a moderate to a high heat for 4 minutes until the broccoli is thoroughly heated through. Add the sesame oil and continue to stir-fry for 30 seconds. The broccoli is now ready to serve.

SESAME BEANCURD

Beancurd is not only nutritious but can be delicious if it is cooked properly. The Japanese are skilled at turning this seemingly bland food into a tasty dish. This Japanese-inspired recipe is simple to make and fun to eat. The beancurd is fried and then served with a dipping sauce. It makes a terrific vegetarian dish.

SERVES 4

450 g (1 lb) soft beancurd
5 tablespoons plain flour
2 eggs, beaten
5 tablespoons roasted sesame seeds
6 tablespoons groundnut oil

Drain the beancurd thoroughly, then place it on kitchen paper and continue to drain for 15 minutes.

Gently cut the beancurd into 2.5-cm (1-in) pieces. Sprinkle the beancurd evenly with the flour, then dip it in the beaten egg and sprinkle with the sesame seeds.

Heat the oil in a wok until it is moderately hot, then gently add the beancurd and allow it

FOR THE SAUCE

4 tablespoons Japanese mirin rice wine

4 tablespoons Japanese rice vinegar

50 ml (2 fl oz) light soy sauce

½ teaspoon freshly ground black pepper

2 teaspoons sugar

to brown slowly without burning. Turn over and cook the other side. Drain well on kitchen paper. You may have to do this in several batches.

Mix the sauce ingredients together. When the beancurd is cooked, arrange on a warm platter with the sauce and serve at once.

CRISPY BEANCURD WITH TOMATOES

Beancurd is a protein-rich food coagulated from an extract of soya beans and when it is not properly prepared, it can be quite bland and boring. However, it is simple to turn this food into something special and delicious. This is an easy dish to make, especially when tomatoes are in season. If you use water instead of the chicken stock, you can turn this into a delectable vegetarian dish.

SERVES 2-4

450 g (1 lb) firm fresh beancurd

450 g (1 lb) fresh or tinned tomatoes

400 ml (15 fl oz) groundnut oil

2 tablespoons coarsely chopped garlic

3 tablespoons thinly sliced shallots

1 tablespoon light soy sauce

1 teaspoon salt

½ teaspoon freshly ground black pepper

2 teaspoons sugar

150 ml (5 fl oz) *Chicken Stock (see p.56)* or
   water

FOR THE GARNISH

Handful of fresh sprigs of coriander

Drain the beancurd thoroughly, then set it on kitchen paper and continue to drain for 15 minutes. Gently cut the beancurd into 2.5-cm (1-in) pieces.

If you are using fresh tomatoes, plunge them in boiling water for 10 seconds, drain them, peel, seed and cut them into 2.5-cm (1-in) cubes. If you are using tinned tomatoes, chop them into small chunks.

Heat the oil in a wok until it is hot and deep-fry the beancurd in batches. When each batch is lightly browned, remove and drain well on kitchen paper.

Drain off all but 1 tablespoon of oil, re-heat and when it is hot, add the garlic and shallots and stir-fry for 30 seconds. Then add the tomatoes, soy sauce, salt, pepper and sugar and stir-fry for 1 minute. Now add the stock or water, reduce the heat and simmer for 5 minutes. Return the beancurd to the wok and heat through. Transfer to a warm platter, garnish with coriander and serve at once.

SAVOURY STUFFED TOMATOES

*W*hen visiting family friends in the south of France, I always look forward to eating stuffed tomatoes. Mme Taurines seasons her dish with abundant garlic and Provençal herbs. It is so aromatic that you can smell it down the street. It is served with plain rice and a simple salad. A bonus is that it can be made in advance and re-heated with no noticeable deterioration in the quality of the dish. Here is my East-West version of her delectable dish.

SERVES 4-6

6 large tomatoes
25 g (1 oz) Chinese black mushrooms
2 tablespoons groundnut oil
3 tablespoons coarsely chopped garlic
3 tablespoons finely chopped shallots
3 tablespoons finely chopped spring onions
2 teaspoons finely chopped fresh root
  ginger
350 g (12 oz) minced pork
2 teaspoons salt
½ teaspoon freshly ground black pepper
1 teaspoon sugar
1 tablespoon light soy sauce
1 tablespoon Shaoxing rice wine or dry
  sherry
1 teaspoon sesame oil
1 egg white, beaten
150 ml (5 fl oz) *Chicken Stock (see p.56)* or
  water
3 tablespoons oyster sauce
2 teaspoons sugar

Cut a small slice off the top of each tomato, with the dimple in the centre. Using a spoon, gently scoop out the pulp of the tomato. Strain the pulp and reserve the liquid, which will be used to moisten the filling. Blot the insides of the tomatoes with kitchen paper.

Soak the mushrooms in warm water for 20 minutes. Then drain them and squeeze out the excess liquid. Remove and discard the stems and finely chop the caps.

Heat a wok or large frying-pan over a high heat until it is hot. Add 1 tablespoon of the oil, and, when it is very hot and slightly smoking, add the garlic, shallots, spring onions and ginger and stir-fry for 1 minute. Remove and allow the mixture to cool thoroughly. In a large bowl, combine the pork with the mushrooms, salt, pepper, sugar, soy sauce, Shaoxing rice wine or dry sherry, sesame oil and egg white. Mix well and add the stir-fried garlic mixture. Stuff the mixture into the tomatoes.

Wipe the wok clean and re-heat over a high heat. When it is hot, add the remaining 1 tablespoon of oil and turn the heat down to moderate. Brown the tomatoes, filling side down. This should take about 5 minutes. Then gently turn the tomatoes and cook for another 3 minutes. Add the stock or water, oyster sauce, sugar and the reserved tomato juice from the pulp. Bring the mixture to a simmer, turn the heat to low, cover and cook for 15-20 minutes or until the stuffing in the tomatoes is cooked thoroughly. Gently transfer to a warm platter and serve at once.

BRAISED AUBERGINE CASSEROLE WITH PRAWNS

Aubergines with their vivid colour, subtly rich taste, and soft texture are such a delight to eye and palate. Their mild flavours can be nicely matched with practically any other food or seasoning. Here, in an unlikely combination, I have paired them with prawns. Their distinctive flavours at once contrast with and enhance the taste of the aubergines. This is a very traditional recipe, where the aubergine skins are left on, as we Chinese also enjoy their texture.

SERVES 4

450 g (1 lb) Chinese or ordinary aubergines

2 teaspoons salt

175 g (6 oz) raw prawns

1½ tablespoons groundnut oil

2 tablespoons coarsely chopped garlic

1½ tablespoons finely chopped fresh root ginger

3 tablespoons finely chopped spring onions, white part only

1 tablespoon dark soy sauce

1 tablespoon light soy sauce

1 tablespoon chilli bean sauce

1 tablespoon whole yellow bean sauce

1 tablespoon Shaoxing rice wine or dry sherry

1 tablespoon sugar

1 tablespoon Chinese black vinegar or cider vinegar

2 teaspoons Szechuan peppercorns, roasted and ground

300 ml (10 fl oz) *Chicken Stock (see p.56)* or water

FOR THE GARNISH

2 teaspoons sesame oil

2 tablespoons chopped green spring onion tops

Roll-cut the Chinese aubergines by cutting them at a slight diagonal slant, rolling them half-way round and then cut again. If you are using the large variety, trim and cut them into 2.5-cm (1-in) cubes, sprinkle them with salt (only if you are using ordinary aubergines – you do not need to salt Chinese aubergines) and leave them in a sieve to drain for 20 minutes. Then rinse them under cold running water and pat them dry with kitchen paper.

Peel the prawns and discard the shells. Using a small sharp knife, remove the fine digestive cord. Wash the prawns and pat them dry with kitchen paper. Coarsely chop them and set them aside.

Heat a wok or large frying-pan over a high heat until it is hot. Add the oil and, when it is very hot and slightly smoking, add the garlic, ginger and spring onions and stir-fry them for 30 seconds, then add the aubergines and continue to stir-fry for 1 minute. Add the rest of the ingredients, except the prawns. Turn the heat down and cook uncovered for 10-15 minutes until the aubergine is tender, stirring occasionally.

Return the heat to high and continue to stir until the liquid has been reduced and has thickened slightly. Add the prawns and cook for another 2 minutes. Turn the mixture on to a warm serving dish and drizzle in the sesame oil, garnish with the chopped spring onion tops and serve at once.

STIR-FRIED CABBAGE WITH CARROTS

*C*abbage, in all its splendid varieties, has long been a part of the Chinese diet. It saddens me to read that today in China the younger generation regard this sturdy vegetable as 'poor man's food', and therefore unworthy of gracing their tables.

This recipe is a traditional one, a simple but tasty recipe using carrots to brighten the cabbage. Use salted water to soften the cabbage in both taste and texture. This is an easy dish to make and is a fine accompaniment for any meat or fish dish.

SERVES 2-4

750 g (1½ lb) green cabbage
1 tablespoon plus 1 teaspoon salt
100 g (4 oz) carrots
1½ tablespoons groundnut oil
¼ teaspoon freshly ground black pepper
1 teaspoon sugar
2 teaspoons Shaoxing rice wine or dry
   sherry
2 teaspoons sesame oil

Trim the cabbage by removing any tough outer leaves. Core and discard the centre stem. Finely shred the cabbage leaves. In a large bowl, toss the cabbage shreds with a tablespoon of salt, then cover with cold water and leave to sit for 1 hour. Rinse well in fresh cold water and drain. Peel and slice the carrots, then finely shred them.

Heat a wok or large frying-pan over a high heat until it is hot. Add the oil and, when it is very hot and slightly smoking, add the remaining salt, pepper, sugar and carrots and stir-fry for 1 minute. Then add the cabbage and Shaoxing rice wine or dry sherry and continue to stir-fry over a high heat for 3 minutes. Add the sesame oil and give the mixture a few good stirs. Transfer to a warm serving dish and serve at once.

SWEET AND SOUR ONIONS

*T*he wok is ideal for preparing this delicious vegetable recipe. These sweet and sour onions are a simple food that can proudly complement any main course. The onions are stir-fried in the wok, then allowed to cool in the sauce. The result is a delicious relish for any meats or fish. Or it can be served as part of a tasty vegetarian meal. Try to get the red onions which are sometimes a bit sweeter.

SERVES 4-6

450 g (1 lb) red or yellow onions
1 tablespoon groundnut oil
2 tablespoons coarsely chopped garlic
½ teaspoon salt
1 tablespoon dark soy sauce
2 tablespoons black or red rice vinegar
2 tablespoons sugar

Cut the onions into 2.5-cm (1-in) thick slices.

Heat a wok or large frying-pan over a high heat until it is hot. Add the oil and, when it is very hot and slightly smoking, add the garlic and stir-fry for 20 seconds, then add the salt and onions. Continue to stir-fry for 1 minute. Now add the soy sauce, vinegar and sugar and continue to cook for 3 minutes, until it is well mixed. Turn the mixture on to a platter, allow it to cool and then chill for at least 1 hour so that it is well chilled before serving.

SIMPLE STIR-FRIED MUSHROOMS

*T*he wok is perfect for making quick and easy dishes that are also very tasty and satisfying. Here is one of my favourites, always reliable fare when I am in a hurry but want an enjoyable treat. It is quick, easy and economical. Stir-frying them in the wok leaves the mushrooms slightly firm with a wonderful texture: nothing mushy about them. I like to leave them whole which makes their preparation even easier.

SERVES 2-4

1 tablespoon groundnut oil
450 g (1 lb) fresh button mushrooms
1 teaspoon salt
2 teaspoons Shaoxing rice wine or dry
  sherry
2 teaspoons light soy sauce
1 teaspoon sugar
150 ml (5 fl oz) water
2 teaspoons sesame oil

Heat a wok or large frying-pan over a high heat until it is hot. Add the oil and, when it is very hot and slightly smoking, add the mushrooms and salt and stir-fry them for 1 minute. Then add the Shaoxing rice wine or dry sherry, soy sauce, sugar and water and continue stir-frying for 5 minutes or until the mushroom liquid has been reabsorbed by the mushrooms or evaporates. Finally, add the sesame oil, give the mushrooms a few stirs and serve at once.

RED-COOKED SMOKY BRAISED MUSHROOMS

All mushrooms are not equal in taste or texture. Chinese dried mushrooms have a rich, smoky flavour and they most readily absorb all the seasonings and flavours of the juices in which they have been braised.

Here is a luscious vegetarian dish which is easy to make and unlocks the special taste and deep aromas of these mushrooms. The sugar in this recipe adds a nice dimension and gives the mushrooms a wonderful sheen. This dish is easy to make and re-heats well, which makes it ideal for multicourse entertaining. It also pairs well with other vegetable dishes. Chinese dried mushrooms can be bought at Chinese grocers and some supermarkets but if you can't get them, this recipe is almost as delicious made entirely with fresh ones.

SERVES 2-4

50 g (2 oz) Chinese dried mushrooms
Boiling water
1 tablespoon groundnut oil
1½ tablespoons Shaoxing rice wine or dry
  sherry
2 tablespoons dark soy sauce
1 tablespoon rock sugar or ordinary sugar

Pick through the mushrooms and choose the largest and best-looking ones. Soak the Chinese dried mushrooms in just enough boiling water to cover them for 30 minutes and then drain them well through a fine sieve. Keep the mushroom soaking liquid. Let it settle and pour off most of the liquid, leaving any sand at the bottom. Save 300 ml (10 fl oz) of the liquid and set it aside. Squeeze out any excess liquid from the mushrooms through the sieve and add to the rest of the mushroom liquid. Remove the tough stems and leave the caps whole.

Heat a wok or large frying-pan over a high heat until it is hot. Add the oil and, when it is very hot and slightly smoking, add the mushrooms and stir-fry for 15 seconds. Now add the Shaoxing rice wine or dry sherry, soy sauce, sugar and reserved mushroom soaking liquid. Reduce the heat to a simmer and cook for 10 minutes until most of the liquid has been reduced. Serve at once or allow it to cool and re-heat when ready to serve.

STEAMED AUBERGINES WITH RED PEPPERCORNS

Chinese cooks rarely steam vegetables, preferring to either blanch them quickly in hot, lightly salted water or to stir-fry them quickly in the wok. However, aubergines do lend themselves to steaming. They are rarely baked, as most Chinese homes lack ovens, but steaming them whole and then covering them with a tasty sauce is not only easy but also a very nutritious way of enjoying aubergines. Steaming brings out the subtle taste and texture of the aubergines, which have enough robustness to stand up to an assertive sauce. Try to get the Chinese variety if you can; you will find them slightly sweeter. This is a most enjoyable vegetarian recipe.

SERVES 4

450 g (1 lb) Chinese or ordinary aubergines

1½ tablespoons groundnut oil

3 tablespoons coarsely chopped garlic

1½ tablespoons finely chopped fresh root ginger

3 tablespoons finely chopped spring onions, white part only

2 tablespoons light soy sauce

1 tablespoon sugar

1 tablespoon Chinese black vinegar or cider vinegar

2 teaspoons Szechuan peppercorns, roasted and ground

1 tablespoon sesame oil

FOR THE GARNISH

2 tablespoons chopped green spring onion tops

If you are using the Chinese aubergines, leave them whole. If you are using the ordinary large variety, trim and cut them in half and score them on the skin side by cutting diagonal crossways indentations.

Next, set up a steamer or put a rack into a wok or deep pan and fill it with 5-cm (2-in) of water. Bring the water to the boil over a high heat. Put the aubergines on to a heat-proof plate and carefully lower it into the steamer or on to the rack. Turn the heat to low and cover the wok or pan tightly. Steam gently for 30-40 minutes or until the aubergines are very soft to the touch. Remove from the wok and keep in a warm place. Clean out the wok and wipe it dry.

Heat a wok or large frying-pan over a high heat until it is hot. Add the oil and, when it is very hot and slightly smoking, add the garlic and stir-fry for 30 seconds, then add the ginger and spring onions and continue to stir-fry for 1 minute. Add the rest of the ingredients. Turn the heat down and cook uncovered for 2 minutes and pour the sauce over the aubergines. Garnish with the chopped spring onion tops and serve at once.

STIR-FRIED CARROTS AND PARSNIPS

*T*he wok adapts itself to the needs of all vegetables: soft, hard, dry, leafy, moist, sliced or diced. Carrots and parsnips have a natural sweetness that the wok preserves and that makes them enjoyable by themselves and wonderful company for meat or poultry.

SERVES 4

450 g (1 lb) carrots

450 g (1 lb) parsnips

1½ tablespoons groundnut oil

2 garlic cloves, crushed

2 teaspoons finely chopped fresh root
    ginger

1 teaspoon salt

½ teaspoon freshly ground black pepper

1 tablespoon light soy sauce

1 tablespoon sugar

150 ml (5 fl oz) water

FOR THE GARNISH

2 tablespoons finely chopped fresh
    coriander

Peel and roll-cut the carrots and parsnips by cutting a diagonal slice at one end then rolling it half-way before making the next diagonal slice.

Heat a wok or large frying-pan over a high heat until it is hot. Add the oil and, when it is very hot and slightly smoking, add the garlic and ginger and stir-fry for 10 seconds. Add the carrots and parsnips and stir-fry for 1 minute. Then add the salt, pepper, soy sauce, sugar and water. Cover and cook over a high heat for 8 minutes or until all the vegetables are tender. There should be very little sauce left. Turn on to a warm platter, garnish with the coriander and serve at once.

ZESTY ONION AND PEAS

*G*reen peas can be extraordinarily full of taste when picked fresh from the garden. However, with today's busy lifestyle, frozen small peas can be a great alternative. With modern freezing techniques and the wok, you can easily whip up a lovely vegetarian side dish for your table in a matter of minutes. Just don't overcook this or any other vegetable.

SERVES 2-4

225 g (8 oz) red onions, peeled

1 tablespoon groundnut oil

225 g (8 oz) frozen petit pois

1 teaspoon salt

½ teaspoon freshly ground black pepper

3 tablespoons water

2 teaspoons sesame oil

Cut the onions in half, then into 2.5-cm (1-in) slices.

Heat a wok or large frying-pan over a high heat until it is hot. Add the oil and, when it is very hot and slightly smoking, add the onions and stir-fry for 2 minutes until they become slightly soft. Then add the peas, salt, pepper and water and continue to stir-fry for 2 minutes. Finally stir in the sesame oil and give the mixture several good turns. Transfer to a serving dish and serve at once.

COCONUT VEGETABLE STEW

This is an adaptation of a popular Thai standard. I learned it from my good friend, Chalie Amatyakul, who founded the Thai Cooking School at The Oriental in Bangkok. It is a simple dish that can easily be done in the wok. There is a secret, however: do not add all the vegetables at once. As in the technique of stir-frying, with stewing, different vegetables require different cooking times. When the cooking times are carefully observed, the whole dish comes out perfectly done.

SERVES 4

2 x 400 ml (14 fl oz) tins coconut milk

2 teaspoons salt

½ teaspoon freshly ground black pepper

1 tablespoon Thai fish sauce

100 g (4 oz) fresh baby corn

175 g (6 oz) Chinese leaves (Peking cabbage), shredded

175 g (6 oz) haricot verts or runner beans, trimmed

100 g (4 oz) bamboo shoots, shredded

175 g (6 oz) spinach leaves, washed

Bring the coconut milk to a simmer in the wok. Add the salt, pepper and fish sauce. Add the corn and Chinese leaves, cover and simmer for 3 minutes. Then add the beans, cover and simmer for another 3 minutes. Finally, add the bamboo shoots and spinach leaves and cook for another 2 minutes, uncovered. Transfer to a warm dish and serve immediately.

MUSHROOM BEANCURD

This is a superb vegetarian dish that is simple to make and delicious to eat. Chinese mushrooms, with their intriguing smoky flavours, are braised with beancurd, which readily absorbs the seasonings and the essence of the mushrooms. An unusual and very nutritious treat. This dish also re-heats well which makes it ideal for entertaining.

SERVES 4

100 g (4 oz) Chinese dried mushrooms

600 ml (1 pint) boiling water

450 g (1 lb) firm fresh beancurd

1½ tablespoons groundnut oil

3 tablespoons finely shredded spring onions

1½ tablespoons finely shredded fresh root ginger

1½ tablespoons Shaoxing rice wine or dry sherry

2 tablespoons dark soy sauce

Soak the Chinese dried mushrooms in the boiling water for 30 minutes, then drain well through a fine sieve. Keep the mushroom soaking liquid. Let it settle and pour off most of the liquid, leaving any sand at the bottom. Squeeze out any excess liquid from the mushrooms through the sieve and add to the reserved mushroom liquid. Remove the tough stems and finely shred the caps.

Cut the beancurd into 2.5-cm (1-in) cubes.

Heat a wok or large frying-pan over a high heat until it is hot. Add the oil and, when it is

1 teaspoon salt

½ teaspoon freshly ground black pepper

1 teaspoon sugar

1 tablespoon sesame oil

very hot and slightly smoking, add the spring onions and ginger and stir-fry for 15 seconds. Add the Shaoxing rice wine or dry sherry, soy sauce, salt, pepper and sugar. Then add the mushroom caps, beancurd cubes and the reserved mushroom soaking liquid. Reduce the heat to a simmer, cover and cook for 15 minutes. Add more liquid if needed. Return the heat to high and continue to cook until most of the liquid has been reduced. Add the sesame oil and turn the mixture gently several times to mix well. Transfer to a serving dish and serve at once or allow it to cool and re-heat when ready to serve.

THAI-STYLE CAULIFLOWER

This is a Thai-inspired way to cook cauliflower. The flavours are assertive, which is fine as the cauliflower is a sturdy vegetable. This dish is tasty enough to serve as a main course by itself.

SERVES 4

750 g (1½ lb) cauliflower

1 tablespoon groundnut oil

4 garlic cloves, crushed

2 tablespoons seeded and finely shredded fresh red chilli

3 tablespoons finely shredded spring onions

2 tablespoons finely chopped fresh coriander

1 tablespoon light soy sauce

1 teaspoon dark soy sauce

1 teaspoon salt

1 teaspoon sugar

½ teaspoon turmeric

450 ml (15 fl oz) water

2 teaspoons sesame oil

Cut the cauliflower into small florets.

Heat a wok or large frying-pan over a high heat until it is hot. Add the oil and, when it is very hot and slightly smoking, add the garlic, chilli and spring onions. Stir-fry for about 20 seconds to flavour the oil. Quickly add the cauliflower florets and stir-fry them for 1 minute. Next add the fresh coriander, soy sauces, salt, sugar, turmeric and water. Turn the heat down, cover and simmer for 10 minutes or until the cauliflower is tender. Stir in the sesame oil and turn on to a warm serving platter and serve at once.

HEALTHY BEANCURD WITH BROCCOLI

Although beancurd is a very nutritious food, on its own it is naturally quite bland in taste. But, most emphatically, it does not have to remain bland. Here it is paired with some assertive spices and robustly flavoured broccoli for a colourful vegetable dish that is anything but bland. It may serve as a main course or an alternative vegetable side dish.

SERVES 4

450 g (1 lb) fresh broccoli
450 g (1 lb) firm fresh beancurd
400 ml (14 fl oz) groundnut oil
1 teaspoon salt
½ teaspoon freshly ground black pepper
2 tablespoons coarsely chopped garlic
3 tablespoons thinly sliced shallots
1 tablespoon Shaoxing rice wine or dry sherry
1 tablespoon light soy sauce
2 tablespoons dark soy sauce
2 teaspoons sugar
3 tablespoons water
1 tablespoon sesame oil

Separate the broccoli heads into small florets; then peel and slice the stems. Blanch the broccoli pieces in a large pan of boiling salted water for 3 minutes and then immerse them in cold water. Drain thoroughly. Drain the beancurd thoroughly, then set it on kitchen paper and continue to drain for 15 minutes. Gently cut the beancurd into 2.5-cm (1-in) pieces.

Heat the oil in a wok until it is hot and deep-fry the beancurd in two batches. When each batch is lightly browned, remove and drain it well on kitchen paper.

Drain off all but 1 tablespoon of the oil from the wok. Re-heat the wok and, when it is hot, add the salt, pepper, garlic and shallots and stir-fry for 30 seconds. Then add the broccoli, Shaoxing rice wine or dry sherry, soy sauces, and sugar and stir-fry for 1 minute. Now add the water, cover, reduce the heat and simmer for 5 minutes. Return the beancurd to the wok and heat through. Add the sesame oil, transfer to a warm serving dish and serve at once.

THAI-STYLE SWEET AND SOUR VEGETABLES

This is a straightforward vegetarian dish, quick and easy to make. It takes but a few minutes of cooking time in the wok. The sweet and sour flavouring gives depth and zest to this colourful mixture of vegetables. Serve this as a side dish or a main vegetarian course.

SERVES 4

450 g (1 lb) firm fresh beancurd

4 spring onions

225 g (8 oz) cucumber

275 g (10 oz) pineapple

400 ml (14 fl oz) groundnut oil

3 garlic cloves, crushed

1 medium onion, sliced

1 green pepper, seeded and sliced

3 tablespoons light soy sauce

2 teaspoons salt

2 teaspoons sugar

2 teaspoons Chinese white rice vinegar or
  cider vinegar

1 teaspoon chilli bean sauce

2 tablespoons water

Cut the beancurd into 2.5-cm (1-in) cubes. Trim the spring onions and cut them into 2.5-cm (1-in) segments.

Peel the cucumber, slice it in half lengthways and, using a teaspoon, remove the seeds. Then cut the cucumber into 2.5-cm (1-in) pieces. Peel, core and cut the pineapple into 2.5-cm (1-in) pieces.

Heat the oil in a deep-fat fryer or large wok until it almost smokes, then deep-fry the beancurd cubes in two batches. When each batch of beancurd cubes is lightly browned, remove and drain well on kitchen paper.

Drain most of the oil from the wok, leaving 1 tablespoon. Re-heat the wok until it is hot, add the garlic and stir-fry for 30 seconds. Then add the onion and pepper and continue to stir-fry for 2 minutes. Add the beancurd and cucumber and continue to stir-fry for 4 minutes. Finally add the pineapple, soy sauce, salt, sugar, vinegar, chilli bean sauce and water and continue to stir-fry for 2 minutes. Transfer to a warm dish and serve at once.

FRIED SWEET POTATO STICKS

*T*he wok is perfect for making these sweet potato sticks. Its round, concave shape makes it ideal for deep-frying without wasting any oil. Sweet potatoes are easier to handle than white potatoes and they can be used in more and different ways. Their distinctive taste and texture make them ideal to eat as snacks or as an accompaniment to any main course.

SERVES 4

750 g (1½ lb) sweet pototoes
900 ml (1½ pints) groundnut oil
1 tablespoon salt
½ teaspoon freshly ground black pepper
1 teaspoon sugar

Peel and cut the sweet potatoes into strips about 7.5 cm x 5 mm (3 x ¼ in). Put the sweet potatoes into a large bowl and cover with cold water. Chill for 2 hours or overnight.

Drain the sweet potatoes in a colander, then spin them dry in a salad spinner or pat them dry with kitchen paper, making sure they are as dry as possible.

Heat a wok or large frying-pan over a high heat until it is hot. Add the oil and, when it is very hot and slightly smoking, fry half the sweet potatoes for 8 minutes. Remove the sweet potatoes with a slotted spoon and drain in a colander; then fry the second batch.

When you are ready to serve them, re-heat the oil until it is very hot again. Fry half the potatoes until they are crispy and golden brown. Remove and drain well on kitchen paper. Re-heat the oil until it is very hot, fry the other half and drain. Transfer the potatoes to a warm platter, toss with the salt, pepper and sugar and serve at once.

RICE, NOODLES AND PASTA

Probably the question I am most frequently asked about the wok is how to use it to make fried rice. This is a question that seems to intrigue many cooks. I am not surprised because properly stir-fried rice will result in a smoky and delicious flavour that is quite addictive.

Using the wok to stir-fry rice or noodles, or even to make pasta or porridge, again shows the versatility of the wok. It has so many uses in rice and pasta cookery — such as to brown noodles or to stir-fry a large amount of pasta — that it is unbeatable. In fact, once you discover how easy it is to stir-fry a large batch of noodles, you will never use your frying-pan again!

EGG FRIED RICE

The Chinese hate to waste anything. To throw away food is unconscionable. This is a lesson my mother taught me very well and, to this day, even in affluent and, I must say, wasteful America, I cannot bring myself simply to discard left-over food.

Fortunately, the wok is most useful when it comes to making the best of left-overs. The trick is to create tasty, nutritious meals by means of the wok stir-fry technique. Here I take bits of left-over cucumber and corn and blend them with spicy embellishments. You will enjoy a tasty treat and feel virtuous as well. Remember that your cooked rice should be very cold before you put it into the wok. If you want a vegan version, simply leave out the eggs.

SERVES 2-4

Enough long-grain white rice to fill a measuring jug to the 400-ml (14-fl oz) level

2 eggs, beaten

2 teaspoons sesame oil

½ teaspoon salt

2 tablespoons groundnut oil

225 g (8 oz) onions, coarsely chopped

2 teaspoons salt

½ teaspoon freshly ground black pepper

175 g (6 oz) cucumber, peeled, seeded and diced

100 g (4 oz) fresh or frozen corn kernels

1 teaspoon chilli oil

Cook the rice according to the *Steamed Rice* recipe *(see p.210)* at least 2 hours in advance or the night before. Allow it to cool thoroughly and then put it in the fridge.

Combine the eggs with the sesame oil and salt.

Heat a wok or large frying-pan over a high heat until it is hot. Add the oil and, when it is very hot and slightly smoking, add the onions, salt and pepper and stir-fry for 2 minutes. Then add the beaten eggs and stir-fry for 1 minute. Add the rice and continue to stir-fry for 3 minutes. Finally, add the cucumber, corn and chilli oil and continue to stir-fry for 5 minutes. Turn on to a warm platter and serve hot or cold as a rice salad.

SPICY MALAY-STYLE LAKSA

*T*his is another well-travelled dish. Laksa means a one-dish meal of rice noodles, with either seafood or chicken. Although it originated in far-off Malaysia, I first encountered it in London thanks to my friend Jenny Lo. Being of Chinese-Malaysian descent herself, she is fortunate in that the fine Malaysian restaurant, the Singapore Garden, is located near her home.

The authentic version of the recipe calls for some rather exotic and difficult-to-find ingredients. Moreover, it demands a great deal of preparation time. I have therefore modified it to make it more accessible for home cooking. I believe I have retained the spirit of the dish in the process. It certainly looks and tastes as good as the original! Once the chicken has been prepared, the wok infuses smoky flavours to the aromatic ingredients, which makes it all rather easy to cook and enjoy.

SERVES 4

1.5 kg (3 lb) whole chicken
2.25 litres (4 pints) water
2 teaspoons salt
½ teaspoon freshly ground white pepper
450 g (1 lb) raw prawns
2 fresh red chillies
2 tablespoons groundnut oil
2 tablespoons finely chopped garlic
2 tablespoons finely chopped fresh root ginger
100 g (4 oz) shallots or onions, thinly sliced
1 teaspoon ground coriander
½ teaspoon turmeric
225 g (8 oz) rice noodles, rice vermicelli or rice sticks
400 ml (14 fl oz) tinned coconut milk
2 teaspoons Madras curry paste
1½ tablespoons salt
½ teaspoon freshly ground black pepper
1 teaspoon sugar

FOR THE GARNISH

3 tablespoons thinly sliced spring onions
200 g (8 oz) bean sprouts, blanched
Fresh sprigs of coriander

Put the chicken and water together in a large pan and bring it to a boil. Lower the heat and simmer uncovered for 20 minutes, skimming all the time. Add the salt and pepper, cover and simmer for another 25 minutes. Remove the chicken and allow it to cool thoroughly. Reserve the liquid.

Peel the prawns and remove the fine digestive cord. Wash the prawns and pat them dry with kitchen paper. Cut the chillies in half and finely shred them, removing the seeds.

Heat a wok or frying-pan over a high heat until it is hot. Add the oil and, when it is very hot and slightly smoking, reduce the heat, add the garlic, ginger, chillies and shallots or onions and stir-fry for 2 minutes. Add the coriander, turmeric and the liquid from the chicken. Turn the heat to low, cover and simmer for 20 minutes.

When the chicken is cool enough to handle, remove the meat with your hands and pull it apart into shreds with a fork. Set aside. Soak the rice noodles, vermicelli or sticks in a bowl of warm water for 25 minutes. Drain them in a colander or sieve.

Add the coconut milk, prawns and rice noodles, vermicelli or sticks to the simmering liquid. Season with curry paste, salt, pepper and sugar and continue to cook for 2 minutes. Add the chicken and cook for 2 minutes. Ladle the mixture into a large soup tureen and serve with the garnishes on the side.

HAINANESE CHICKEN RICE

*H*ainan is a large island off the south China coast. It is not noted for its cuisine, but this chicken rice dish is famous as a most popular and satisfying 'comfort food'. The best versions of it are to be found in Singapore and Malaysia and it is a standard item in street food stalls, restaurants, hotel room services and home kitchens there. I always enjoy this dish when I visit that part of the world.

Note, though, that this is not the original recipe. In Hainan the whole chicken is traditionally used, including the head and feet. The version here uses an normal Western chicken and is still delectable, but do use the best and freshest chicken available. It may be served at room temperature and, as it re-heats nicely, it can be prepared in advance.

SERVES 4

1-1.5 kg (2¼-3 lb) free-range or corn fed chicken
1 tablespoon salt
1.75 litres (3 pints) or more *Chicken Stock (see p.56)*
6 slices fresh root ginger
6 spring onions
½ teaspoon freshly ground black pepper
1 tablespoon groundnut oil
2 tablespoons finely chopped garlic
1 teaspoon salt
Enough long-grain white rice to fill a measuring jug to the 400 ml (14 fl oz) level

FOR THE GARNISH

450 g (1 lb) cucumber (about 1)
225 g (8 oz) tomatoes
2 spring onions

FOR THE GINGER AND SPRING ONION SAUCE

4 tablespoons finely chopped spring onions, white part only
2 teaspoons finely chopped fresh root ginger
1 teaspoon salt
2 tablespoons groundnut oil

Rub the chicken evenly with salt. Place it in a large pan and cover with the stock. Add more stock if necessary to cover and bring to a boil. Add the ginger, spring onions and pepper. Cover tightly, reduce the heat and simmer gently for 30 minutes. Turn off the heat and leave covered tightly for 1 hour. Remove the chicken from the pan and allow it to cool. Skim off any surface fat from the stock. Measure 900 ml (1½ pints) of stock and set it aside. (This will be used to cook the rice.)

Heat a wok or large frying-pan over a high heat until it is hot. Add the oil and, when it is very hot and slightly smoking, add the garlic and salt and stir-fry for 1 minute. Then add the rice and continue to stir-fry for 2 minutes. Now add the reserved stock to the rice, bring the mixture to a boil and continue boiling until most of the liquid has evaporated. Turn the heat to very low and cover tightly. Let the rice cook undisturbed for 15 minutes. Remove the wok from the heat and let the rice rest for 5 minutes before serving it.

Now prepare the garnishes. Peel the cucumber, slice it in half lengthways and, using a teaspoon, remove the seeds. Then slice the cucumber. Thinly slice the tomatoes. Slice the spring onions on the diagonal. Arrange the slices on a platter and set aside.

To make the ginger and spring onion sauce, mix the spring onions, ginger and salt together in a heatproof bowl. Heat the wok

2 fresh red chillies, seeded and finely
    chopped
2 teaspoons sesame oil
1 teaspoon sugar
½ teaspoon salt

until it is very hot, add the oil and, when it is very hot and slightly smoking, pour it on the ginger-spring onion mixture and mix well.

To make the chilli-sesame sauce, add the red chillies to the sesame oil, sugar and salt and mix well in a small bowl.

Transfer the chicken to a chopping board, cut it into bite-sized pieces and arrange it on a warm platter. Re-heat the remaining stock and serve it in a soup tureen. Serve the rice in bowls with the garnishes and the sauces.

GUO BU LI'S BEEF NOODLE SOUP

Versatility is what the wok is all about, and here it is used to make a soup that is hearty, savoury and satisfying, using braised beef and beanthread noodles. I discovered the dish at a modest Chinese restaurant in Berkeley, California.

SERVES 4

1 kg (2¼ lb) beef brisket (with some fat and
    tendon), cut into 4-cm (1½-in) cubes
3 tablespoons Shaoxing rice wine or dry
    sherry
2 tablespoons dark soy sauce
1 tablespoon light soy sauce
3 whole star anise
½ teaspoon freshly ground black pepper
Salt to taste
1.75 litres (3 pints) *Chicken Stock (see p.56)*
100 g (4 oz) beanthread (transparent)
    noodles
450 g (1 lb) spinach

FOR THE GARNISH

5 tablespoons chopped spring onions

Bring a large pan of salted water to a boil. Put the meat in the water and blanch for 10 minutes. Skim the surface constantly; this removes all the scum and impurities. Drain the meat and discard the water.

Add the beef to a wok, then add the Shaoxing rice wine or dry sherry, soy sauces, star anise, pepper, salt and stock. Bring the mixture to a simmer, reduce the heat, cover and simmer slowly over a low heat for 2 hours or until the meat is tender.

While the meat is cooking, soak the noodles in a large bowl of warm water for 15 minutes. When soft, drain and discard the water. Wash the spinach thoroughly. Remove all the stems, leaving just the leaves.

When the meat is cooked, skim off any surface fat, add the noodles and simmer for another 10 minutes. Then add the spinach leaves and cook for another 2 minutes. Ladle the soup into a large tureen or individual bowls, garnish with spring onions and serve immediately.

PIQUANT HOKKIEN-STYLE PRAWN AND NOODLE SOUP

In Malaysia there are many Chinese. Understandably, therefore, Malaysian cuisine has many Chinese characteristics. This dish is Malaysian, but 'Hokkien' refers to that region of southern China from whence many Chinese migrated centuries ago, bringing with them, of course, their regional style of cooking. By all accounts, the Malaysian influence greatly improved the Hokkien approach to food.

In China, Hokkien is not regarded as a gourmet's paradise. However, this dish is certainly a fine blending of Malay and Chinese influences. I first enjoyed it as a speciality offering at one of the many street food stalls one finds in every city throughout Asia. The wok, together with a fierce and fiery heat, is the implement of choice in such places. These food stalls and the open air food markets are marvellous spectacles to behold. Most impressive are the stir-fried dishes, the quick fried noodles, and the simple soups one can see being made and enjoy, produced as if on assembly line. I have simplified this recipe, adapting it to rely upon what ingredients can be readily found locally. Even with this modification, it remains a delicious treat.

SERVES 4-6

225 g (8 oz) fresh Chinese egg noodles

1 tablespoon sesame oil

225 g (8 oz) rice noodles, rice vermicelli or
  rice sticks

450 g (1 lb) raw prawns

4 tablespoons groundnut oil

175 g (6 oz) shallots, thinly sliced

5 tablespoons coarsely chopped garlic

1 tablespoon chilli bean sauce

1 tablespoon Madras curry paste

1.75 litres (3 pints) *Chicken Stock (see p.56)*

2 teaspoons salt

FOR THE GARNISH

225 g (8 oz) bean sprouts, blanched

3 tablespoons spring onions, thinly cut on
  the diagonal

Cook the egg noodles for 3-5 minutes in a pan of boiling water. Drain and plunge them into cold water. Drain thoroughly and toss them in the sesame oil. (Tightly covered with cling film, they can be kept in this state for up to 2 hours in the fridge.) Soak the rice noodles, vermicelli or sticks in a bowl of warm water for 25 minutes. Drain them in a colander or sieve. Peel the prawns and discard the shells. Using a small sharp knife, remove the fine digestive cord. Wash the prawns and pat them dry with kitchen paper.

Heat a wok or large frying-pan over a high heat until it is hot. Add 3 tablespoons of the oil and, when it is very hot and slightly smoking, turn the heat to low, add the shallots and fry until they are lightly brown and crispy. Remove them with a slotted spoon and drain well on kitchen paper. Re-heat the wok and add the remaining oil. When it is hot, add the garlic and stir-fry for 1 minute. Add the chilli bean sauce and curry paste and stir-fry for 2 minutes. Pour this into a bowl and set aside.

Bring the stock to a simmer in a large pan, add the salt, then add the prawns and cook gently over low heat for 2 minutes. Now add the garlic-chilli-curry mixture and continue to simmer for 1 minute. Add the egg and rice noodles, vermicelli or sticks and continue to cook for 3 minutes. Turn the contents of the wok into a large soup tureen, garnish with the bean sprouts, spring onions and fried shallots and serve at once.

FRIED RICE WITH CHINESE SAUSAGE

The wok offers the best means of transforming left-over rice into something a bit special. In this recipe, the Chinese sausages and dried smoky mushrooms combine with the rice to make an elegant and substantial one-dish meal.

If you have no left-over rice, simply prepare some from scratch using chicken stock instead of plain water. This will enrich the flavour of the rice. The dried Chinese sausages with their aromatic slightly sweet taste will enhance the flavour of any dish. They may be found at Chinese grocers and are well worth the search. They freeze successfully if well wrapped.

SERVES 4

Enough long-grain white rice to fill a
   measuring jug to the 400-ml (14-oz) level
50 g (2 oz) Chinese dried mushrooms
225 g (8 oz) Chinese sausages
2 eggs, beaten
1 teaspoon sesame oil
1 teaspoon salt
½ teaspoon freshly ground black pepper
2 tablespoons groundnut oil
3 tablespoons finely chopped spring onions
2 teaspoons sesame oil

Cook the rice according to the *Steamed Rice* recipe *(see p.210)* using stock instead of water at least 2 hours in advance or the night before. Allow it to cool thoroughly and then put it in the fridge.

Soak the mushrooms in warm water for 20 minutes. Then drain them and squeeze out the excess liquid. Remove and discard the stems, then finely shred the caps into thin strips. Cut the sausages into small dice. In a bowl, combine the eggs with the sesame oil, salt and pepper.

Heat a wok or large frying-pan over a high heat until it is hot. Add the oil and, when it is very hot and slightly smoking, add the sausage and stir-fry for 2 minutes. Then add the mushrooms and eggs and continue to stir-fry for 2 minutes. Add the rice, mix well and continue to stir-fry for another 5 minutes until the rice is heated through and well mixed. Add the spring onions and sesame oil and continue to stir-fry for 2 minutes. Transfer to a warm platter and serve at once.

QUICK PRAWN FRIED RICE

*H*ere we have an example of how the wok is ideal for preparing quick, nutritious, tasty meals. *This popular Cantonese prawn and rice dish takes but a few minutes to put on the table once the major ingredients have been assembled.*

SERVES 4

Enough long-grain white rice to fill a
   measuring jug to the 400-ml (14-fl oz)
   level
225 g (8 oz) raw prawns
100 g (4 oz) fresh or frozen peas
2 tablespoons groundnut oil
1 tablespoon finely chopped garlic
2 teaspoons salt
½ teaspoon freshly ground black pepper
3 tablespoons finely chopped spring onions,
   white part only

FOR THE GARNISH

2 tablespoons finely chopped spring onions

Cook the rice according to the *Steamed Rice* recipe *(see p.210)* at least 2 hours in advance or the night before. Allow it to cool thoroughly and then put it in the fridge.

Peel the prawns and, if you are using large uncooked ones, cut them to remove the fine digestive cord. Wash them and pat them dry with kitchen paper. Blanch the prawns in a pan of boiling water for 2 minutes. Remove with a slotted spoon and discard the water. When the prawns are cool enough to handle, cut them into 2.5-cm (1-in) pieces.

Blanch the peas in a pan of boiling water for about 5 minutes if they are fresh; if they are frozen, simply thaw them. Drain them in a colander.

Heat a wok or large frying-pan over a high heat until it is hot. Add the oil and, when it is very hot and slightly smoking, add the garlic and stir-fry for 30 seconds. Add the cooked rice and stir-fry for 3 minutes. Then add the peas, salt and pepper. Continue to stir-fry the mixture for 5 minutes over a high heat. Then add the spring onions and prawns and continue to stir-fry for 2 minutes. Turn the mixture on to a warm platter and garnish with the spring onions. Serve at once, or let it cool and serve as a cold rice salad.

REFRESHING CUCUMBER WITH NOODLES

Cucumbers are too often ignored or taken for granted. But they have their virtues and this recipe displays them nicely. Prepared this way, the cucumbers retain their distinctive taste and a bit of their crunchiness. This noodle dish takes minutes to cook in the wok and is a sparkling alternative to potatoes or rice. It is a perfect vegetarian dish.

SERVES 4

225 g (8 oz) fresh or dried thin egg noodles

2 teaspoons sesame oil

750 g (1¾ lb) cucumbers (about 1½)

2 teaspoons salt

2 tablespoons groundnut oil

1½ tablespoons finely chopped garlic

3 tablespoons finely chopped spring onions

2 teaspoons chilli bean sauce

1 teaspoon salt

½ teaspoon freshly ground black pepper

2 teaspoons sugar

2 teaspoons sesame oil

If you are using fresh noodles, blanch them first by boiling them for 3-5 minutes in a pot of boiling water. If you are using dried noodles, cook them in boiling water for 4-5 minutes. Plunge the noodles in cold water, drain them thoroughly, toss them in sesame oil and put them aside until you are ready to use them. They can be kept in this state, if tightly covered with cling film, for up to 2 hours in the fridge.

Peel the cucumbers, slice them in half lengthways and, using a teaspoon, remove the seeds. Then cut the cucumber halves into 7.5-cm x 3 mm (3 x ⅛-in) shreds. Sprinkle them with the salt and mix well. Put the mixture in a colander and let it sit for 20 minutes to drain. This rids the cucumber of any excess liquid. When the cucumber shreds have drained, rinse them in water and then squeeze any excess moisture from them in a linen tea towel. Set aside.

Heat a wok or large frying-pan over a high heat until it is hot. Add the oil and, when it is very hot and slightly smoking, add the garlic, spring onions and cucumbers and stir-fry for about 30 seconds. Then add the noodles, chilli bean sauce, salt, pepper and sugar and stir for another 30 seconds until they are well coated with the spices and flavourings. Continue to stir-fry over a high heat for 3-4 minutes until most of the water has evaporated and the cucumbers are cooked. At this point, add the sesame oil, transfer to a warm platter and serve immediately.

STIR-FRIED PASTA WITH ORANGE AND CURRY

O*ne of the quickest and easiest ways to prepare Italian pasta is in the wok. I love using whatever left-overs I have in the fridge and quickly stir-frying cooked pasta with some curry paste. With a bit of imagination, the wok turns a simple pasta dish into an ambrosial delight.*

This recipe makes a fine starter for a multicourse meal or can easily be a main course with salad. In warm weather, serve it at room temperature.

SERVES 4

450 g (1 lb) dried Italian pasta, such as fusilli
   or farfalle
3 tablespoons olive oil
3 tablespoons coarsely chopped garlic
1 tablespoon finely chopped fresh root
   ginger
1 small onion, chopped
2 tablespoons finely chopped orange zest
6 bacon rashers, rinded and chopped
225 g (8 oz) red pepper, cut into 1-cm (½-in)
   dice
225 g (8 oz) yellow pepper, cut into 1-cm
   (½-in) dice
2 teaspoons sugar
300 ml (10 fl oz) *Chicken Stock (see p.56)*
400-g (14-oz) tin chopped tomatoes
3 tablespoons Madras curry paste
2 tablespoons tomato purée
1 teaspoon salt
½ teaspoon freshly ground black pepper

FOR THE GARNISH

Handful of fresh basil, chopped
Handful of fresh chives, snipped

Cook the pasta in a large pan of salted water, according to the instructions on the packet. Drain well and set aside.

Heat a wok or large frying-pan over a high heat until it is hot. Add the olive oil and, when it is very hot and slightly smoking, add the garlic, ginger, onion and orange zest and stir-fry for 2 minutes. Then add the bacon and continue to stir-fry for 3-4 minutes or until the bacon is browned. Next add the peppers, sugar, stock, tomatoes, curry paste, tomato purée, salt and pepper. Turn the heat down, cover and simmer for 30 minutes.

Add the drained pasta and mix well in the wok. Turn the mixture out onto a large warm platter, garnish abundantly with plenty of basil and chives and serve at once.

Stir-fried Pasta with Orange and Curry

THAI-STYLE NOODLES WITH CHICKEN

During my frequent visits to Bangkok, I always savour this modest noodle dish. It is a typical Thai creation and a very popular item at the city's street stalls, where it is cooked in a wok while the customer waits. The aromas rising from the hot wok as the noodles are being prepared make it impossible to pass by without sampling the dish. I suspect in origin it is a south Chinese recipe, but distinctive spices and flavourings make it an authentic Thai treat. It is equally good cold or at room temperature and it may be served during warm months as part of a simple grill.

SERVES 4

225 g (8 oz) flat rice noodles, rice vermicelli
  or rice sticks
450 g (1 lb) boneless, skinless chicken
  breasts
1 egg white
½ teaspoon salt
2 teaspoons cornflour
300 ml (10 fl oz) groundnut oil or water
1 tablespoon groundnut oil
2 eggs, beaten
1 teaspoon sesame oil
½ teaspoon salt

FOR THE SAUCE

2 tablespoons Thai fish sauce
2 teaspoons Chinese black rice vinegar or
  cider vinegar
2 teaspoons chilli bean sauce
2 teaspoons sesame oil
2 teaspoons sugar
1 tablespoon Shaoxing rice wine or dry
  sherry

FOR THE GARNISH

50 g (2 oz) roasted peanuts, crushed
3 tablespoons finely chopped spring onions
Fresh sprigs of coriander

Soak the rice noodles, vermicelli or sticks in a bowl of warm water for 25 minutes. Drain them in a colander or sieve. Cut the chicken breasts into strips about 7.5 cm (3 in) long. Combine them with the egg white, salt and cornflour in a small bowl; place it in the fridge for about 20 minutes.

Heat a wok until it is very hot and then add the oil. When the oil is very hot, remove the wok from the heat and immediately add the chicken pieces, stirring vigorously to keep them from sticking. When the chicken pieces turn white (about 2 minutes), quickly drain the chicken. Drain off all but 2 tablespoons of the oil from the wok.

If you choose to use water instead of oil, bring it to a boil in a pan. Remove the pan from the heat and immediately add the chicken pieces, stirring vigorously to keep them from sticking. When the chicken pieces turn white (about 2 minutes), quickly drain the chicken and all the water from the wok.

Wipe the wok clean. Heat it until it is hot, then add the 1 tablespoon of oil. Mix the eggs with the sesame oil and salt. Immediately, add the egg mixture and stir-fry for 2 minutes or until the eggs have set. Remove and drain on kitchen paper, cut the eggs into strips and set aside.

Re-heat the wok and add the 2 tablespoons of reserved oil (2 tablespoons of fresh oil if you used water before). Add the rice noodles, vermicelli or sticks and stir-fry for 2 minutes, then add the sauce ingredients and bring to the boil. Return the cooked chicken to the pan and stir-fry the mixture for another 2 minutes, coating the pieces thoroughly with the sauce. Turn on to a large warm platter, sprinkle the garnishes over and serve at once, or let it cool and serve at room temperature.

FAMILY-STYLE MUSHROOM RICE WITH BEANCURD

My mother was an expert at preparing economical and nutritious meals – and quickly. With her wok and a supply of beancurd, she had the essentials of such meals. In this recipe, mushrooms add their smoky flavour and unique texture to the beancurd and rice. Such a dish indicates how delicious pure vegetarianism can be. It may also be paired with another vegetable platter to make a fully-rounded dinner.

SERVES 4

Enough long-grain white rice to fill a
   measuring jug to 400-ml (14-fl oz) level
600 ml (1 pint) water
50 g (2 oz) Chinese dried mushrooms
400 ml (14 fl oz) plus 2 tablespoons
   groundnut oil
225 g (8 oz) firm fresh beancurd
2 tablespoons thinly sliced fresh root ginger
225 g (8 oz) fresh button mushrooms, thinly
   sliced
2 teaspoons chilli bean sauce
1 teaspoon salt
½ teaspoon freshly ground black pepper
3 tablespoons finely chopped spring onions

Cook the rice according to the *Steamed Rice* recipe *(see p.210)* at least 2 hours in advance or the night before. Allow it to cool thoroughly and then put it in the fridge.

Soak the dried mushrooms in warm water for 20 minutes. Then drain them and squeeze out the excess liquid. Remove and discard the stems and finely shred the caps into thin strips. Cut the beancurd into 2.5-cm (1-in) cubes.

Heat the 400 ml (14 fl oz) of oil in a deep-fat fryer or large wok until it almost smokes, then deep-fry the beancurd cubes in batches. When each batch of beancurd cubes is lightly browned, remove and drain well on kitchen paper. Let the cooking oil cool and then discard it.

Heat a wok or large frying-pan over a high heat until it is hot. Add the 2 tablespoons of oil and, when it is very hot and slightly smoking, add the ginger and stir-fry for 30 seconds. Then add the button mushrooms and dried mushrooms and stir-fry for 5 minutes. Now add the cool rice and continue stir-frying for 5 minutes. Then add the chilli bean sauce, salt, pepper, beancurd and spring onions. Mix well, turn on to a warm platter and serve at once.

CURRY RICE NOODLES WITH VEGETABLES

*T*his is a vegetarian version of that popular Hong Kong dish called Singapore noodles. These light and subtle rice noodles are an ideal foil for the spicy sauce. A bonus is that it is easy to make. As this is a vegetarian meal, I use a lot of coconut milk to make it really tasty. This recipe is equally delicious served with a fish or meat dish. It is also wonderful cold and makes a lovely and unusual picnic offering.

SERVES 4-6

225 g (8 oz) thin rice noodles

50 g (2 oz) Chinese dried mushrooms

225 g (8 oz) frozen petit pois

225 g (8 oz) Chinese leaves (Peking cabbage)

3 tablespoons groundnut oil

3 tablespoons thinly sliced garlic

1 tablespoon finely chopped fresh root ginger

6 fresh red or green chillies, seeded and finely shredded

1 teaspoon salt

½ teaspoon freshly ground white pepper

6 fresh or tinned water chestnuts, sliced

3 spring onions, finely shredded

FOR THE CURRY SAUCE

2 tablespoons light soy sauce

3 tablespoons Madras curry powder

2 tablespoons Shaoxing rice wine or dry sherry

1 tablespoon sugar

1 teaspoon salt

1 teaspoon freshly ground black pepper

400 ml (14 fl oz) tinned coconut milk

FOR THE GARNISH

Fresh coriander leaves

Soak the rice noodles in a bowl of warm water for 25 minutes. Then drain them in a colander or sieve.

Soak the mushrooms in warm water for 20 minutes. Then drain them and squeeze out the excess liquid. Remove and discard the stems and finely shred the caps into thin strips.

Put the peas in a small bowl and let them thaw. Finely shred the Chinese leaves.

Heat a wok or large frying-pan over a high heat until it is hot. Add the oil and, when it is very hot and slightly smoking, add the garlic, ginger and chillies and stir-fry the mixture for 30 seconds. Then add the salt, pepper, water chestnuts, mushrooms, Chinese leaves and spring onions and stir-fry for 1 minute. Then add the rice noodles and peas and continue to stir-fry for 2 minutes. Now add all the sauce ingredients and continue to cook over a high heat for another 5 minutes or until most of the liquid has evaporated. Turn the noodles on to a large warm platter, garnish with the coriander leaves and serve at once.

VEGETARIAN HOT BEANTHREAD NOODLES

*B*eanthread, or Cellophane, noodles are delightfully light. They make a great vegetarian noodle dish with other vegetables. They are also quite easy to prepare and go well with almost any kind of vegetables. The noodles provide a wonderful satiny texture to the entire dish. The spicy seasonings in this recipe give the noodles body and character, and I think it makes an excellent dish for lunch or a light supper.

SERVES 4

175 g (6 oz) beanthread (transparent) noodles

100 g (4 oz) carrots

100 g (4 oz) firm fresh beancurd

225 g (8 oz) Chinese flowering cabbage or bok choy

1 tablespoon groundnut oil

2 tablespoons black beans, coarsely chopped

3 tablespoons finely chopped spring onions

2 tablespoons coarsely chopped garlic

1 tablespoon finely chopped fresh root ginger

300 ml (10 fl oz) water

2 tablespoons Shoaxing rice wine or dry sherry

1½ tablespoons chilli bean sauce

1 tablespoon whole yellow bean sauce

2 tablespoons light soy sauce

2 teaspoons dark soy sauce

½ teaspoon salt

½ teaspoon freshly ground black pepper

2 teaspoons sesame oil

FOR THE GARNISH

2 teaspoons finely chopped spring onions

Soak the noodles in a large bowl of warm water for 15 minutes. When they are soft, drain them and discard the water. Cut them into 7.5-cm (3-in) lengths using scissors or a knife.

Peel and finely shred the carrots. Drain the beancurd on kitchen paper and carefully shred it. Finely shred the Chinese cabbage or bok choy.

Heat a wok or large frying-pan over a high heat until it is hot. Add the oil and, when it is very hot and slightly smoking, add the black beans, spring onions, garlic and ginger and stir-fry quickly for 15 seconds. Add the carrots and stir-fry for 2 minutes, then add the beancurd and vegetables. Carefully mix together without breaking up the beancurd. Then add all the rest of ingredients, except the sesame oil and cook the mixture over a gentle heat for about 2 minutes. Now add the drained noodles and sesame oil and cook the mixture for a further 3 minutes. Ladle some noodles into individual bowls or into one large serving bowl, garnish with the spring onions and serve at once.

MALAYSIAN-STYLE RICE NOODLES

One of the most exciting aspects of visiting Malaysia is eating at all the food hawkers' stalls. Here you can find all manner of food that is skilfully prepared and extremely savoury and tasty. The strong aromas of garlic, ginger and chillies permeate, it is a food lovers' paradise. A favourite of mine is made with rice noodles. The Chinese influence can easily be detected in the use of the Chinese sausages, which are rich and sweet. This recipe is substantial enough for a one-dish lunch or makes a delightful addition to other dishes.

SERVES 2-4

225 g (8 oz) broad flat dried rice noodles
225 g (8 oz) raw prawns
175 g (6 oz) Chinese sausages or ham
4 spring onions
2 eggs, beaten
2 teaspoons sesame oil
A pinch of salt
½ teaspoon freshly ground black pepper
3 tablespoons groundnut oil
2 tablespoons coarsely chopped garlic
3 fresh red or green chillies, seeded and finely chopped
2 small onions, thinly sliced
3 tablespoons light soy sauce
3 tablespoons oyster sauce
2 tablespoons Shaoxing rice wine or dry sherry
2 teaspoons chilli bean sauce
100 ml (3½ fl oz) *Chicken Stock (see p.56)*
175 g (6 oz) fresh bean sprouts
Handful of fresh coriander leaves

Soak the rice noodles in a bowl of warm water for 25 minutes. Then drain them in a colander or sieve. Peel the prawns and discard the shells. Using a small sharp knife, remove the fine digestive cord. Wash the prawns and pat them dry with kitchen paper. Slice the sausages on a slight diagonal to about 2.5-cm (1-in) thick, and do the same with the spring onions.

Combine the eggs with the sesame oil, salt and half the pepper and set aside.

Heat a wok or large frying-pan over a high heat until it is hot. Add 1 tablespoon of the oil and, when it is very hot and slightly smoking, add the egg mixture and stir-fry for 2 minutes or until the egg has set. Remove it and place it on a platter. When it is cool enough to handle, chop it lengthways and set aside.

Re-heat the wok over a high heat and, when it is very hot, add the remaining oil. Then add the shredded spring onions, garlic, chillies and onions and stir-fry for 2 minutes. Add the prawns and sausages and stir-fry for 1 minute. Then add the rice noodles, soy sauce, the rest of the black pepper, the oyster sauce, Shaoxing rice wine or dry sherry, chilli bean sauce and stock and continue to stir-fry for 2 minutes. Finally, add the bean sprouts and cooked egg and continue to cook for 2 minutes. Stir in the fresh coriander leaves for 30 seconds. Transfer to a warm platter and serve at once.

INDONESIAN-STYLE FRIED RICE

This is my version of the famous nasi goreng — a one-meal rice dish inspired by the imaginative chefs of the Grand Hyatt Jakarta. Their opulent version uses much more meat than may be found in the traditional recipe. It is garnished with satay (meat on skewers), fried chicken and prawns, along with a fried egg. The rice dish itself has prawns and additional chicken meat. I have taken some of the best features of the Grand Hyatt's creation and have incorporated them into my version of that delectable rice dish.

SERVES 4-6

Enough long-grain white rice to fill a measuring jug to the 400-ml (14-fl oz) level
2 eggs, beaten
2 teaspoons sesame oil
½ teaspoon salt
225 g (8 oz) boneless, skinless chicken thighs
175 g (6 oz) raw prawns
2 tablespoons groundnut oil
2 tablespoons coarsely chopped garlic
1 small onion, finely chopped
2 teaspoons finely chopped fresh root ginger
1 tablespoon shrimp paste
½ teaspoon salt
½ teaspoon freshly ground black pepper
1 tablespoon chilli bean sauce
1 tablespoon oyster sauce
2 teaspoons dark soy sauce

FOR THE GARNISH

3 tablespoons finely chopped spring onions
Handful of fresh coriander

Cook the rice according to the *Steamed Rice* recipe *(see p.210)* at least 2 hours in advance or the night before. Allow it to cool thoroughly and then put it in the fridge.

Combine the eggs with the sesame oil and salt. Cut the chicken into 1-cm (½-in) dice.

Peel the prawns and remove the fine digestive cord. Cut them into 1-cm (½-in) pieces.

Heat a wok or large frying-pan over a high heat until it is hot. Add the oil and, when it is very hot and slightly smoking, add the garlic, prawns, onion, ginger, shrimp paste, salt and pepper. Stir-fry for 2 minutes. Then add the chicken and stir-fry for 2 minutes. Add the rice and continue to stir-fry for 3 minutes. Finally, add the chilli bean sauce, oyster sauce and dark soy sauce and continue to stir-fry for 2 minutes. Add the egg mixture and continue to stir-fry for another minute. Turn on to a platter, garnish with the spring onions and fresh coriander and serve hot or cold as a rice salad.

THAI-STYLE CURRY RICE

The Thais are geniuses with spices — they can transform everyday recipes into glorious and tasty dishes. One I particularly enjoy eating in Thailand is curry rice. This popular platter is perfect for a quick snack which one can enjoy there from pavement vendors. It is simple to make and surely makes a change from the ordinary plain rice. In fact, it is a meal by itself.

SERVES 4-6

Enough long-grain white rice to fill a
　measuring jug to the 400-ml (14-fl oz)
　level
2 eggs, beaten
2 teaspoons sesame oil
2½ teaspoons salt
225 g (8 oz) chicken breasts
2 tablespoons groundnut oil
2 tablespoons coarsely chopped garlic
1 small onion, finely chopped
1 tablespoon finely chopped fresh root
　ginger
½ teaspoon freshly ground black pepper
175 g (6 oz) red peppers, seeded and diced
100 g (4 oz) fresh or frozen corn kernels
1 teaspoon chilli oil
1 tablespoon Madras curry powder

FOR THE GARNISH

3 tablespoons finely chopped spring onions

Cook the rice according to the *Steamed Rice* recipe *(see p.210)* at least 2 hours in advance or the night before. Allow it to cool thoroughly and then put it in the fridge.

Combine the eggs with the sesame oil and ½ teaspoon of the salt.

Cut the chicken into 1-cm (½-in) dice.

Heat a wok or large frying-pan over a high heat until it is hot. Add the oil and, when it is very hot and slightly smoking, add the garlic, onion, ginger, 2 teaspoons of the salt and the pepper. Stir-fry for 2 minutes. Then add the chicken and stir-fry for 2 minutes. Add the rice and continue to stir-fry for 3 minutes. Finally, add the peppers, corn, chilli oil and curry powder and continue to stir-fry for 2 minutes. Add the egg mixture and continue to stir-fry for another minute. Turn on to a warm platter, garnish with the spring onions and serve hot or cold as a rice salad.

FRAGRANT RICE

R*ice is a cereal grass that is cultivated extensively in Asia and is a staple food throughout the world. It is an adaptable food that blends well with any spices. Here is a tasty Vietnamese-inspired rice dish that is easily made in the wok. The result is a fragrant, tempting rice dish that re-heats well. Serve this rice by itself or as a light and delicious side dish.*

SERVES 2-4

Enough long-grain white rice to fill a
    measuring jug to the 400-ml (14-fl oz)
    level
1 stalk fresh lemon grass
2 tablespoons dried shrimps
2 tablespoons groundnut oil
225 g (8 oz) onions, coarsely chopped
2 tablespoons coarsely chopped garlic
3 tablespoons thinly sliced shallots
3 tablespoons finely chopped spring onions
2 red or green chillies, seeded and finely
    chopped
2 teaspoons sugar
2 teaspoons salt
½ teaspoon freshly ground black pepper

Cook the rice according to the *Steamed Rice* recipe *(see p.210)* at least 2 hours in advance or the night before. Allow it to cool thoroughly and then put it in the fridge.

Peel the lemon grass stalk to reveal the tender, whitish centre and cut into 5-cm (2-in) pieces. Smash them with the flat side of a cleaver or knife. Soak the dried shrimps in warm water for 30 minutes. Drain well. In a food processor, chop the dried shrimp. Remove and set aside.

Heat a wok or large frying-pan over a high heat until it is hot. Add the oil and, when it is very hot and slightly smoking, add the lemon grass and shrimps and stir-fry for 20 seconds. Then add the onions, garlic, shallots, spring onions, chillies, sugar, salt and pepper. Stir-fry for 3 minutes. Then add the rice and continue to stir-fry for 5 minutes. Turn on to a warm platter and serve hot or cold as a rice salad.

TAIWANESE PORK CHOPS WITH NOODLE SOUP

Another user-friendly wok recipe, this is a delicious one-dish meal which I have greatly enjoyed at countless food stalls in Taipei, the capital of Taiwan. Tasty pork chops are marinated, then deep-fried and served with a hearty bowl of soup and noodles. It is the type of basic food that is mouth-watering, sustaining and altogether satisfying.

SERVES 2, AS A WHOLE MEAL

2 x 175-g (6-oz) pork chops with bone in

1.2 litres (2 pints) *Chicken Stock (see p.56)*

225 g (8 oz) wheat or egg noodles, fresh or dried

Cornflour, for dusting

600 ml (1 pint) groundnut oil

FOR THE MARINADE

1 tablespoon light soy sauce

½ teaspoon salt

¼ teaspoon freshly ground black pepper

1 teaspoon five-spice powder

1 teaspoon Shaoxing rice wine or dry sherry

½ teaspoon chilli powder or chilli flakes

1 tablespoon finely chopped garlic

2 teaspoons white rice vinegar

FOR THE GARNISH

Handful of fresh coriander leaves

Combine the pork chops with the soy sauce, salt, pepper, five-spice powder, Shaoxing rice wine or dry sherry, chilli powder or flakes, garlic and vinegar and marinate for 45 minutes.

Bring the stock to a simmer. Then, in a separate pan, cook the noodles for 3-5 minutes in boiling salted water. Drain well, then drop the noodles into the stock. Take the stock and noodles off the heat.

Remove the pork chops from the marinade and dust with cornflour, shaking off any excess. Save any excess marinade and put it into the stock with the noodles.

Heat a wok or large frying-pan over a high heat until it is hot. Add the oil and, when it is very hot and slightly smoking, add the pork chops, reduce the heat to medium and fry the pork chops for 5 minutes. Remove with a slotted spoon and drain well on kitchen paper. Ladle broth and noodles into individual serving bowls or a large bowl, top with the pork chops, garnish with fresh coriander and serve at once.

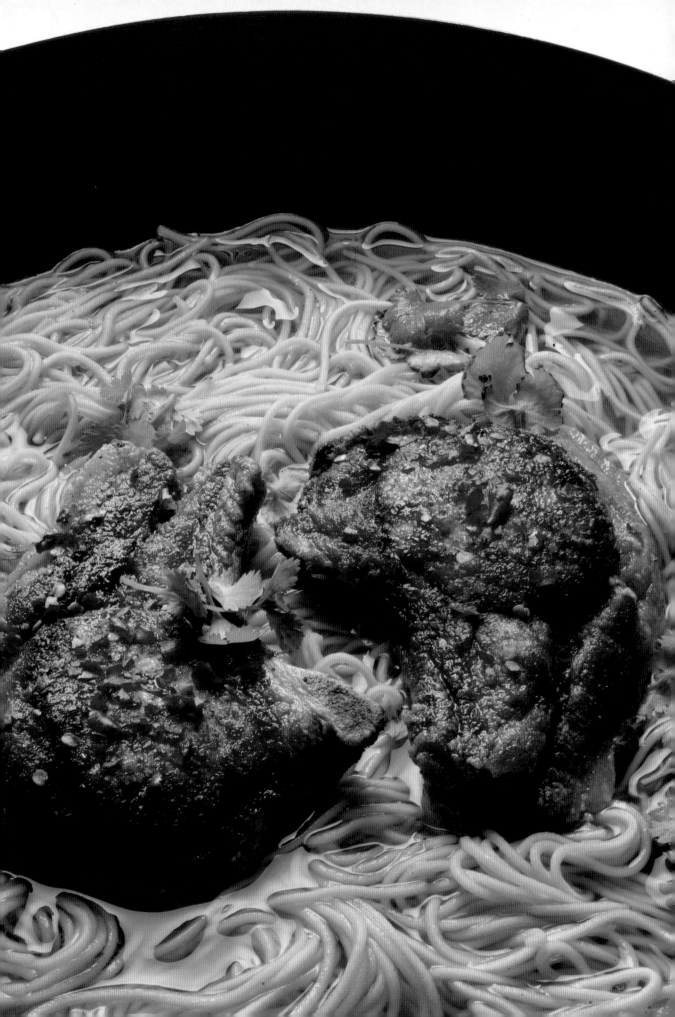

BEANTHREAD NOODLES WITH CRAB

*B*eanthread noodles are light and easy to use. They are a good alternative to noodles made with wheat. The silky texture of the noodles is a nice contrast to the rich crabmeat. Be sure to get the freshest crabmeat available. This dish literally takes about 15 minutes to prepare and even less to stir-fry in the wok. Serve with rice or as an unusual first course.

SERVES 4

100 g (4 oz) dried beanthread (transparent) noodles

1½ tablespoons groundnut oil

2 tablespoons coarsely chopped garlic

2 teaspoons finely chopped fresh root ginger

3 tablespoons thinly sliced shallots

225 g (8 oz) fresh crabmeat

3 tablespoons finely chopped spring onions

300 ml (10 fl oz) *Chicken Stock (see p.56)*

1 tablespoon light soy sauce

2 tablespoons oyster sauce

FOR THE GARNISH

Handful of fresh sprigs of coriander

Soak the noodles in a large bowl of warm water for 15 minutes. When soft, drain and discard the water. Cut the noodles into 7.5-cm (3-in) lengths using scissors or a knife.

Heat a wok or large frying-pan over a high heat until it is hot. Add the oil and, when it is very hot and slightly smoking, add the garlic, ginger and shallots and stir-fry for 1 minute. Then add the crabmeat and spring onions and stir-fry for 30 seconds. Add the beanthread noodles and stir-fry, mixing well. Finally add the stock, soy sauce and oyster sauce and stir-fry until most of the liquid has evaporated. Transfer the contents of the wok to a warm platter, garnish with the fresh coriander and serve at once.

GARLIC FRIED RICE

G arlic is one of my favourite seasonings. This is to be expected because, like ginger and soy sauce, garlic is indispensable in Chinese cookery. Without garlic, Chinese food would be something quite other than it is, and not nearly so good. Simply put, garlic makes the most bland food come alive. Here I have paired it with rice to make a special fried rice that is quickly stir-fried in the wok to give it an additional smoky flavour. A simple but delightfully garlicky treat.

SERVES 4

Enough long-grain white rice to fill a
    measuring jug to the 400-ml (14-fl oz)
    level
2 tablespoons groundnut oil
225 g (8 oz) onions, coarsely chopped
3 tablespoons coarsely chopped garlic
2 teaspoons salt
½ teaspoon freshly ground black pepper
2 tablespoons finely chopped fresh
    coriander

Cook the rice according to the *Steamed Rice* recipe *(see p.210)* at least 2 hours in advance or the night before. Allow it to cool thoroughly and then put it in the fridge.

Heat a wok or large frying-pan over a high heat until it is hot. Add the oil and, when it is very hot and slightly smoking, add the onions, garlic, salt and pepper. Stir-fry for 4 minutes. Then add the rice and continue to stir-fry for 5 minutes or until the rice is heated through. Finally, add the fresh coriander. Give the mixture several good stirs. Turn on to a warm platter and serve at once.

STEAMED RICE

*S*teaming rice the Chinese way is simple, direct and efficient. I prefer to use long-grain white rice, which is drier and fluffier when cooked and gives the most authentic results in wok cooking. There are many varieties but I particularly like basmati or Thai fragrant rice which are widely available. Don't use pre-cooked or 'easy-cook' rice for Chinese cookery as both these types of rice have insufficient flavour and lack the texture and starchy taste fundamental to Chinese rice.

The secret of preparing rice that is not sticky is to cook it first in an uncovered pan at a high heat until most of the water has evaporated. Then the heat should be turned down to very low, the pan covered and the rice cooked slowly in the remaining steam. As a child I was always instructed never to peek into the rice pan during this stage or else precious steam would escape and the rice would not be cooked properly, thus bringing bad luck.

Here is a good trick to remember: if you make sure that you cover the top of the rice with about 2.5 cm (1 in) of water, it should always cook properly without sticking. Many packet recipes for rice specify too much water and the result is a gluey mess. Never uncover the pan once the simmering process has begun; time the process and wait. Follow my method and you will have perfect steamed rice, the easy Chinese way.

Most Chinese eat quite large quantities of rice (about 150 g/5 oz per head, which is more than many Westerners are able to manage). This recipe and that for Fried Rice *allows about 375 g (13 oz) dried weight, of rice for four people. If you want more than that, just increase the quantity of rice, but remember to add enough water so that the level of water is about 2.5 cm (1 in) above the top of the rice.*

SERVES 4

**Enough long-grain white rice to fill a
  measuring jug to the 400-ml (14-fl oz)
  level**
600 ml (1 pint) water

Put the rice into a large bowl and wash it in several changes of water until the water becomes clear. Drain the rice and put it into a heavy pan with the water and bring it to the boil. Continue boiling until most of the surface liquid has evaporated. This should take about 15 minutes. The surface of the rice should then have small indentations like pitted craters. At this point, cover the pot with a very tight-fitting lid, turn the heat down to as low as possible and let the rice cook undisturbed for 15 minutes. There is no need to 'fluff' the rice. Let it rest for 5 minutes before serving.

DESSERTS

Desserts are not the forte of wok cookery; indeed, desserts are the one weak element in all of Chinese cookery. Hence, with these recipes, I have introduced quick and easy Western themes, but with an East-West or South-east Asian accent manifest in the emphasis on fruit. These desserts are all extremely easy to prepare and deliciously refreshing. Fruits are versatile, and cleanse the palate nicely after the more complex Asian flavourings and seasonings of earlier courses.

There are a few steamed dessert recipes too, such as the Fluffy Steamed Cantonese Cake, *or* Thai-style Steamed Pumpkin Custard, *which are easy to make in the wok. You should, however, use a non-reactive wok (such as a good non-stick one) for desserts like* Stewed Pineapple *because the acid in the fruit will react with a carbon steel wok.*

FLUFFY STEAMED CANTONESE CAKE

Our family had a typical Chinese kitchen, that is, one that was small and compact. We did have a small oven in our Chicago flat, but my mother used it for storing extra pots and pans. In the traditional Chinese home, ovens are a rarity because they are too bulky and so expensive to use. Commercial bakers were resorted to when necesssary for a banquet or family celebration.

At home, we relied on the ever-useful wok for all our cooking needs. Instead of baking a cake in the oven, my mother steamed cakes in the wok. The result was a light, fluffy cake that was absolutely delicious, and still remains one of my favourite childhood memories. I recall very clearly waiting by the wok for the cake to be done, always ready for that first slice.

Here, I have added to my mother's recipe my own touches of butter, lemon zest and vanilla essence. This cake is delicious served warm or cold.

SERVES 4-6

2 tablespoons butter
200 g (7 oz) plain flour
2 teaspoons baking powder
½ teaspoon bicarbonate of soda
A pinch of salt
5 eggs, separated
185 g (6½ oz) caster sugar
150 ml (5 fl oz) skimmed or semi-skimmed
    milk
2 teaspoons vanilla essence
1½ tablespoons finely chopped lemon zest
Vanilla ice-cream to serve

Generously butter a 20-cm (8-in) cake tin. Sift the flour, baking powder, bicarbonate of soda and salt together.

In a bowl, beat the egg yolks with the sugar for 5 minutes until they are well incorporated. Add the milk, vanilla essence and lemon zest. Mix well and add the sifted ingredients. Continue mixing well until you have a smooth mixture.

In a separate bowl, beat the egg whites until they are stiff with soft peaks. Fold the egg whites into the cake mixture. Pour the cake mixture into the prepared tin.

Next set up a steamer or put a rack into a wok or deep pan and fill it with 5 cm (2 in) of water. Bring the water to the boil over a high heat. Put the cake on to the steamer or the rack. Turn the heat to low and cover the wok or pan tightly. Steam for 25 minutes or until a cocktail stick inserted into the centre of the cake comes out clean.

Remove the cake from the steamer. The cake should be light and springy to the touch. Unmould the cake on to a platter, slice and serve. It is delicious with plain vanilla ice-cream.

POACHED GINGER PEARS

I n Chinese culture, pears are a traditional symbol of longevity and fidelity. Moreover, their appeal extends beyond the grave, to the dead who cannot forget the pleasure they brought. Thus, I was told as a child never to bring home pears on the fifteenth day of the seventh month, for at that time ghosts were roaming the earth seeking pears, among other things. So, on that day the pears might contain ghosts who would bring bad luck into the house. It was quite believable to me at the time.

Pears also traditionally bring happiness, and this means that they should be eaten whole, never divided. Chinese pears are quite different from Western ones, being round and crisp like apples, rather than the soft and pear-shaped fruit with which we are most familiar.

In Chinese cuisine, the pear is most often cooked and served as part of a soup. In this French-inspired recipe, however, the pears are poached with ginger, resulting in a delicious, refreshing dessert. For a richer dessert, serve it with cream or a compatible ice-cream.

In using a wok to make this dessert, switch to a non-reactive one, that is, a non-stick wok. A basic carbon steel wok will react to the acid from the lemon and may lose its seasoning.

SERVES 4

4 firm pears
1 lemon
6 tablespoons Chinese rock sugar or sugar
600 ml (1 pint) water
1 vanilla pod, split in half
8 slices fresh root ginger

Peel the pears and cut them in half. Remove the core and seeds. Cut the lemon in half, squeeze the juice on the pears and mix well. Combine the sugar, water, vanilla pod and fresh ginger in a non-stick wok and boil the mixture together until the sugar has completely dissolved. Add the pears, cover and simmer over a low heat for 20-25 minutes or until they are tender. The cooking time will depend on the ripeness of the pears.

When the pears are cooked, remove them with a slotted spoon together with the vanilla pod and ginger slices. Over a high heat, reduce the liquid to a syrup by boiling it fast. Discard the ginger slices, but keep the vanilla pod and, when it dries, put it in sugar to keep for future use.

Pour the syrup over the pears and serve at once. Alternatively, you can let the mixture cool, cover it with cling film and chill until you are ready to serve it.

WARM BERRY COMPOTE WITH BASIL

This dessert is inspired by the English summer pudding I have enjoyed many times. It works to perfection only when berries are at their peak of flavour. It is a refreshing and simple dessert to make and is delicious served warm as well as cold. The touch of basil adds a piquant accent which balances the slight acidity of the berries. Any combination of berries in season will work well, and the more variety the better. I love it with cream or vanilla ice-cream. Again, if you use a wok, make sure it is a non-stick one so that the acid of the berries does not react with the carbon steel.

SERVES 4

100 g (4 oz) sugar

150 ml (5 fl oz) water

1 vanilla pod, split in half

175 g (6 oz) strawberries

175 g (6 oz) raspberries

175 g (6 oz) blueberries

2 tablespoons unsalted butter

3 fresh basil leaves, finely shredded

Using a non-stick or coated wok, bring the sugar and water to a boil, add the vanilla pod and simmer for 10 minutes. Remove the vanilla pod and save for future use.

Add the berries and butter and simmer for 2 minutes, just enough to warm and not to cook them. Remove from the heat, add the basil, stir gently, transfer to a warm bowl and serve at once.

THAI-STYLE STEAMED PUMPKIN CUSTARD

In Thailand, I have many times enjoyed this delectable and unusual dessert. It is a custard steamed inside a small pumpkin. The pumpkin is gently cooked in hot vapours which keeps it extremely moist while its rich sweet flavours suffuse the pudding.

I have changed it slightly so that you may serve this in ramekins. This dessert can be served hot or cold which makes it ideal for entertaining. If you are serving the desserts cold, you could serve them with some clotted cream.

SERVES 6

450 g (1 lb) cooked pumpkin or squash
5 eggs, beaten
175 g (6 oz) sugar
½ teaspoon salt
400 ml (14 fl oz) tinned coconut milk

Purée the cooked pumpkin or squash in a food processor or blender. Add the eggs, sugar, salt and coconut milk and continue to purée until it is well mixed. Pour into individual ramekins or small dishes.

Next, set up a steamer or put a rack into a wok or deep pan and fill it with 5 cm (2 in) of water. Bring the water to the boil over a high heat. Carefully place the ramekins or dishes into the steamer or on to the rack. Turn the heat to low and cover the wok or pan tightly. Steam gently for 20 minutes or until the custard has set. Remove and serve or allow them to cool and serve later.

WATERMELON SALAD

The watermelon is the fruit of a vine that originated in Africa. How it made its way to Asia is uncertain but there is no doubt about the popularity of its sweetness, coolness and rich colours. Watermelon is the perfect dessert for Asian meals, which are so often spicy and aromatic.

SERVES 4

150 ml (5 fl oz) water
3 tablespoons sugar
2 tablespoons lime juice
675 g (1½ lb) fresh watermelon cubes

Start by making the syrup. Bring the water and sugar to a boil in a wok over a high heat. When the sugar has melted, add the lime juice. Allow the syrup mixture to cool thoroughly.

Remove the watermelon rind and discard it. Cut the watermelon into 2.5-cm (1-in) pieces. In a large bowl, gently combine the syrup mixture with the watermelon. Let it sit for 10 minutes, then serve at once.

STEWED PINEAPPLE

Pineapples are a New World fruit. Columbus brought some samples back to Europe in 1493, giving Europeans their first taste of the fruit. Despite its long history, the pineapple is still thought of as being an exotic fruit. Used extensively in Asia for savoury specialities as well as simple dishes, its tart taste is always welcome as a refreshing end to any meal.

When pineapples are cooked briefly, their tartness is mellowed and the texture softens. They are transformed into a luscious cooked fruit. For a lighter dessert, omit the ice-cream or clotted cream.

SERVES 4

675 g (1½ lb) fresh pineapple
1 vanilla pod
300 ml (10 fl oz) water
100 g (4 oz) sugar
Vanilla ice-cream or clotted cream, to serve

Peel the pineapple and cut it into thick pieces, discarding the tough core. Split the vanilla pod in half lengthways.

In a large, non-reactive wok, combine the vanilla pod, water and sugar. Simmer for 10 minutes. Then add the pineapple and simmer for 5 minutes. Serve warm with either ice-cream or clotted cream.

PINEAPPLE FRITTERS

This is a delectable way to enjoy pineapple. The crispy coating makes a nice contrast to the soft sweetness of the fruit. Quick and easy, it is always pleasing.

SERVES 4

450 g (1 lb) fresh pineapple
600 ml (1 pint) groundnut oil for deep-
   frying

FOR THE BATTER

50 g (2 oz) potato flour or cornflour
25 g (1 oz) plain flour
1 teaspoon baking powder
1 teaspoon bicarbonate of soda
A pinch of salt
2 teaspoons groundnut oil
150 ml (5 fl oz) water

Peel the pineapple and cut it into thick pieces, discarding the tough core.

Mix the batter by combining the potato flour or cornflour with the plain flour, baking powder, bicarbonate of soda, salt, oil and water. Blend until you have a smooth batter.

Heat a wok or large frying-pan over a high heat until it is hot. Add the oil and, when it is very hot and slightly smoking, turn the heat down to moderate.

Dip the pineapple pieces into the batter mixture using a slotted spoon and drain off any excess batter. Deep-fry them for 2 minutes or until golden brown. Remove with a slotted spoon and drain on kitchen paper. Repeat the process until you have fried all the fruit. Serve at once.

EXOTIC FRUIT SALAD

My favourite dessert is a simple one, consisting of mixed fresh fruits: nutritious, colourful, soothing and fresh-tasting. The combinations are endless, but here is a rather exotic example I often enjoy.

SERVES 4-6

450 g (1 lb) fresh pineapple
450 g (1 lb) papaya
2 bananas
Juice of 1 lime
2 tablespoons sugar

Peel the pineapple and cut it into thick pieces, discarding the tough core. Slice the papaya in half lengthways and remove the seeds. Peel away the skin and cut the flesh into slices. Peel and slice the bananas. Combine all the fruit in a large bowl, add the lime juice and sugar and mix well. Serve at once.

BANANAS IN SWEET COCONUT MILK

*A*sian bananas are of a different variety from the ones found in Europe. They tend to be quite small and are best when very ripe. In Thailand, they are slowly cooked in coconut milk and the result is a sweet, wonderful dessert, resembling a light pudding. This is a simple, unusual and very satisfying dessert that works just as well with Western bananas.

SERVES 4

450 g (1 lb) fresh, ripe bananas
400 ml (15 fl oz) tinned coconut milk
150 ml (5 fl oz) water
3 tablespoons sugar
¼ teaspoon salt

Peel the bananas and cut them into bite-size pieces.

Combine the coconut milk, water, sugar and salt in a non-reactive wok. Bring the mixture to a simmer. Add the banana pieces and simmer for 2 minutes. Remove from the heat and serve at once.

REFRESHING GRAPEFRUIT SALAD

*C*ultural traditions are very difficult to overcome. In the West in general, grapefruit is a 'morning' fruit, a way to begin the day, but in China it is most often served as a refreshing dessert.

Grapefruit works especially well after aromatic and flavourful courses as it pleases as well as cleanses the palate, making the perfect close to a fine meal. I have added strawberries for colour and the candied ginger for a special bite.

SERVES 4

4 grapefruit
2 tablespoons lemon juice
2-4 tablespoons sugar
225 g (8 oz) fresh strawberries, hulled and
  cleaned
2 tablespoons candied ginger, finely
  chopped

Peel and slice the grapefruit into segments. Combine the grapefruit segments and strawberries in a large serving bowl, sprinkle with the lemon juice and sugar and toss in the candied ginger. Wrap the bowl tightly in cling film until you are ready to serve the fruit.

INDEX